George Malcolm Thomson was born in 1899 and educated at school and university in Edinburgh. He became a journalist and in due course migrated to Fleet Street. For many years he was a member of the Beaverbrook organisation, acting, before his retirement in 1970, as senior editorial adviser. For most of World War II he moved in government circles, acting as principal personal secretary to Lord Beaverbrook. He is the author of several books, among them *The Crime of Mary Stuart*, and most recently, the brilliantly successful biography, *Sir Francis Drake*, which has sold, in its various British editions, more than one hundred thousand copies, and is now available as an Omega paperback. Mr Thomson is married with two children and lives in Hampstead.

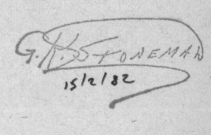

To Alexis

George Malcolm Thomson

The North-West Passage

Futura Publications Limited
A Futura Book

A Futura Book

First published in Great Britain 1975
by Martin Secker & Warburg Limited

First Futura Publications edition 1976

ISBN 0 8600 7419 6
Printed in Great Britain by
Richard Clay (The Chaucer Press) Ltd,
Bungay, Suffolk

Futura Publications Limited
110 Warner Road, Camberwell,
London SE5

Contents

Acknowledgments

For guidance and help at many points I owe a debt of gratitude to many people, above all to the staff of the London Library and of the British Library, both in the Reading Room and in the Map Room; and to the staff at the National Maritime Museum, Greenwich. If my footsteps have strayed at any point in exploring the authorities, the fault will be mine alone. I have also to acknowledge the editorial counsel I received from my friend Mr John Cruesemann. Sybil Rang I must thank once more for prompt and efficient work in typing and re-typing the manuscript as it gradually emerged from crude beginnings. My publishers, Tom Rosenthal, David Farrer and John Blackwell, have been benevolent and encouraging, for which I am deeply in their debt.

George Malcolm Thomson

'After he had explored the expanse of
the Northern Ocean in his ships, there
lay before his eyes at length the darksome
bounds of a falling world.'
        Adam of Bremen, 11th century.

The Cloud Bridge of Illusion

> 'The answer to your enquiry as to what people go to seek in Greenland and why they fare thither through such great perils is to be sought in man's threefold nature. One motive is fame and rivalry. A second motive is curiosity. The third is desire for gain.'
>
> The King's Mirror. (Anon. Norwegian, circa 1240)

It was as wild, as cruel, as sustained as any venture in the whole history of man, but it began soberly enough as a commercial proposition: the search for a navigable channel leading westwards from Europe round the north of the American continent to the Pacific, to the Far East, to Cathay! It persisted out of myth and against probability. As if the magnetism of the North were not confined to the compass needle but exerted its power over the minds of men, ignorant as well as learned, adventurous and stay-at-home alike, helmsmen turned the beaks of their vessels towards the Pole Star and the setting sun. The search was dangerous, a course leading into worsening hardships. But was there not a basic justice in the Creator's ordering of His world which reserved the richest rewards for those who had dared most and suffered worst? It was in some kind of rough congruity with Christian philosophy. One could not say more than that, but it was already enough to incline the minds of the religious, seafaring men of the Atlantic seaboard to believe in something which they could not yet prove and which was not, in fact, true – that the quest for a North-west Passage, navigable and commercially useful, would be realized.

This channel did not exist where men reasoned it must be – or, at least did not exist, in any form which could be of practical use to seamen, in any age down to our own. The whole enterprise was founded on a misapprehension, a geographical fiction, a fairy-tale, springing out of the kind of stories sailors tell to amaze landsmen or delude other sailors, to which were soon added the inferences, speculations and downright inventions that scholars manufacture to amaze themselves. But the channel seemed real enough in the eyes of sixteenth-century merchants and mariners. There its gates were open, somewhere behind the Northern fogs and the barrier of ice which hid secrets untold. There the path lay for the bold and the fortunate, glistening, beckoning, elusive, as strange as the flashing lights in those skies, as full of promise as—

Coming down to the hard question of cash, the sailors and the business-men turned their globes, measured with their compasses, and calculated that if the Passage were found, 2,000 leagues would be cut off the voyage between Europe and the Far East. Two thousand leagues – six thousand miles! It was a prospect of particular interest to the City of London, since it would enable British merchantmen to break the monopoly of the carrying trade to Asia which, ever since Vasco de Gama, had been enjoyed by Portuguese caravels. British goods would undersell Portuguese goods in the China market. Silks, spices, ivory, gold dust and precious stones would be brought to the Thames instead of the Tagus. London would become . . . But there is no need to elaborate the commercial arguments for the Quest as it presented itself to men in Tudor England. What is more remarkable, yet in accord with the quirks of human genius, is that the Quest continued long after the North-west Passage had ceased to serve any economic inter-est whatever. A time came, when the Suez Canal was dug and the Panama Canal was soon to be cut, when Vasco de Gama's route was as obsolete as Magellan's. But the search for the Passage went on. Fuelled first by com-mercial interest, it was kept in motion by a spirit just as ardent and in-finitely purer. Man had been given a challenge; he must answer it in courage, skill and obedience to his intuition. The human mind is a prey to mystic impulses as well as to reason. The search for the North-west Passage provided over the centuries the most prolonged trial of that irrational quality. Certainly, the searchers were put to no ordinary tests.

Seas cold enough to kill a man in minutes. Floating mountains of ice able to crush a ship like a biscuit. Snow that blinded the helmsman and frost that formed on the deck thick enough and fast enough to overturn a vessel. Storms of incredible fury. Sea creatures of monstrous size. It was as if, up there in the North, beyond the rim of civilized – if not of human – life, there was a concentric fortress of disaster hiding at its heart – what? For most men, an occasion of shuddering. For some men, magic . . .

On the western shore of the Ocean, there was a continent – was it Asia as Columbus thought? Or was it the new continent which men were beginning to call America? Or, was it possibly, not a continent at all but a group of islands off the coast of Cathay? Gradually, as the years passed, after the decisive discovery by Columbus, the picture seemed to become clearer – There was a continent to the west of Europe. A land mass of varying width of which one could only say with assurance that it was narrow in the middle. To the south of it, there was a strait where storms of terrifying violence raged. To the north-west, must there not likewise be a strait? Symmetry seemed to demand it; men were ready to draw it on their maps. Other men were ready to look for it.

Once Europe had known more about the Arctic than it remembered at the time Columbus discovered America. Once there had been a bishop at Gardar in Greenland with sixteen parishes under his care. Greenland had paid tithes to the Pope, and taxes to the King of Norway, had even sent money to help finance the Crusades. Its people, descendants of Icelanders, had grown oats and barley and raised cattle and horses on their pastures. They did a modest export business in polar bears and white falcons, regarded as sporting birds particularly suitable to bishops. Twelve Greenland falcons were sent by the Duke of Burgundy to the Ottoman Sultan Bayazid as a ransom for his son. No doubt, the whiteness of the falcon, like that of the bear, was regarded as particularly awe-inspiring and, therefore, suitable to the ice-bound regions from which the bird came. In time, however, the Greenland settlements which the Vikings had founded centuries before dwindled and died – died or were absorbed by intermarriage with the Eskimos. The Black Death struck Greenland more savagely even than Europe. The climate of the region grew colder. The Eskimos became more numerous and aggressive. It is not certain what was the decisive factor in wiping out that first Christian Greenland. All that can be said is that, one year, the ship which came annually from Bergen did not trouble to arrive.

Pope Alexander VI wrote to the Icelandic bishops in 1492, the year of Columbus, pointing out that no ship was known to have visited Greenland for eighty years, although he recalled that his predecessor had appointed a bishop of that territory. He could remember the prelate's name, having picked him himself. His Holiness suggested that the Icelandic bishops should look further into the matter. What was happening in that outpost of Christendom? And, with that final demonstration of fatherly solicitude, Greenland sank for a time from the thought of Europe, although for a few more years ships from Hamburg made an occasional voyage there, and a few scholars, reading Adam of Bremen ('There are other islands in the great ocean, of which Greenland is not the least'), might have it brought to their minds. A few fishermen roaming beyond their normal hunting grounds probably glimpsed it from time to time behind its girdle of ice.

The very name Greenland, which the Vikings had given it, seems to have been forgotten by 1500. Portuguese voyagers who sighted it then named it 'Labrador', while Frobisher, landing there seventy-eight years later, gave it the name 'West England'. But as a result of the voyages of Columbus, Vasco de Gama and Magellan, a new curiosity about the Arctic regions came into life.

John Cabot, an Italian sailor, who may have been born in Genoa but later became a citizen of Venice, had peddled an idea round Spain and Portugal. No success. No takers. He then thought he might interest the English King, Henry VII. It was 1494, just two years after Columbus had returned from the discovery of the West Indies, which he thought was Asia. Cabot's idea was simply this: By sailing westwards in high latitudes he might open up a shorter route to the spices of Asia than his fellow-countryman, Columbus, had found. Henry, a shrewd if penny-pinching monarch, succumbed to Cabot's propaganda. He was, indeed, particularly susceptible to it because he had in 1488 missed an offer sent him by Christopher Columbus through his brother, Bartholomew. As a result of accidents of one kind and another, Bartholomew's proposals, which were accompanied by a persuasive map of the world, arrived in London too late. Bartholomew was captured and robbed by pirates, and by the time he reached the ear of the King, his brother Christopher had left for the Indies in Spanish service. Now John Cabot offered King Henry a second chance to take part in the world-changing adventure beyond the Atlantic. This time the King did not miss it. After all, it need cost him nothing more than a piece of parchment assigning to 'our well-beloved John Cabot' and his four sons the right to govern such unknown lands as they might discover. Trade with these countries was to be a monopoly of the Cabots, subject to a twenty per cent capital gains tax payable to the Crown. The arrangement was equally satisfactory to both parties. Cabot and his family settled in Bristol, a proud and prosperous city which brought in more wine and exported more cloth than any seaport in England outside London. And from Bristol he sailed in May 1497, in a ship of 50 tons named the *Mathew*, with a crew of eighteen. Thirty-five days after leaving port, the *Mathew*, sailing due west from the south-west point of Ireland, reached the Newfoundland coast, probably – for the matter is not certain – at its northernmost cape. It was St John's Day, 24 June.

Cabot spent a month reconnoitring the east coast of Newfoundland. He went ashore once to take possession of the territory in the name of King

Henry. He noted the abundance of cod in the sea and saw that the land was well-clad with forest. Then he sailed back to Bristol, where the *Mathew* arrived on 6 August and her captain made his way to London to report to the King, the thin-lipped Tudor who sat on England's throne, and receive from him a reward of £10 and, later, an annuity of £20. More than that, King Henry gave Cabot powers to commandeer six English ships of two hundred tons or less at the usual rate, so that he could continue his coastal reconnaissance westwards until he reached Cipango, an island off the coast of China where, it was believed, all the spices in the world were grown. In the end, Cabot sailed from Bristol in May 1498 with five ships, one of which was provided by the King. By the end of July it was known in London that one of the ships had reached an Irish port, in distress. The other four ships were never heard of again. So ended in obscure but complete disaster the first attempt to reach the Far East by a northern sea route.

Cabot had the same basic misconceptions about geography that Columbus had. Neither of them believed in the existence of America. Each thought that, the world being round, which as educated men they knew, the Indies lay on the far side of the Atlantic: Greenland was a northward extension of Asia and Newfoundland was an island, if it *was* an island, off the coast of Asia. But very soon, as America was further explored, it became clear that the matter was not so simple as that. The fact of America as a separate new continent was reluctantly acknowledged, although its size will still much under-estimated and its shape was a subject on which the fancy of cartographers was much exercised.

The most persistent belief was that America was pierced by a strait leading to the Pacific. Where did it open and where did it emerge? These were questions which nobody could answer with certainty and which many answered with confidence. John Cabot's son, Sebastian, a distinguished navigator who became Pilot Major of Spain, is reported to have set off in 1509 to find a way by the north round America. He had two ships and, so it is said, a crew of 300, which seems too many. However, he brought back fascinating reports which he told to Peter Martyr, an Italian scholar whom he met in Spain. For example, he described the polar bears' method of catching cod. The bear lies in ambush on the shore near trees whose leaves fall into the water. The cod comes to eat the leaves and is grabbed by the bear. A garbled version of the truth, or a pure invention? Sebastian was reported to have said that he had entered Hudson's Strait (as it was later named) and would have continued on his way to Cathay had he not been forced to turn back by a mutiny of his crew. Whether this is so or not, there seems to be no doubt that Sebastian (reporting his own findings or those of his father) believed he knew where the North-west Passage was to be found.

Not everybody shared this belief. When in 1521 he proposed to sail with five ships to Newfoundland, the Drapers' Company of London, approached for advice and no doubt for capital by Henry VIII, turned the proposal down with something like derision. Sebastian, they pointed out, had never been to Newfoundland himself; and if he was as clever as he said he was, one ship would be enough for his purpose. All this shows a certain scepticism about Sebastian's character, which may have been justified although, if every silver-tongued promoter of voyages of discovery in the sixteenth century were to be regarded as a rogue, the list would be long and some of the names in it would be impressive. It is possible, incidentally, that the Newfoundland which Cabot was planning to reach was not the island we know by that name but another island altogether, somewhere in the Pacific and, it may be, quite imaginary. In the state of knowledge as it prevailed at that time about the extent of the oceans and the relative position of the continents, such a state of confusion is probable.

One day in Valladolid the Venetian ambassador to Spain told Sebastian that news of the projected expedition from England had reached the ears of the Council of Ten. On hearing this, Cabot was thrown into a state verging on panic. 'I earnestly beseech you keep the thing a secret, as it will cost me my life.' And he added the promise that, if the expedition were launched he would make Venice a partner. His alarm, if it was genuine, probably sprang from the fact that he was a Spanish official, the Pilot Major of King Ferdinand, yet he was proposing an enterprise which, if it succeeded, would do grave damage to Spanish interests! It was more than twenty years later, when he was in England, and free to talk, that he made his claim to have rounded the northern cape of America on the voyage to reach Cathay which his mutinous crew had frustrated. Sebastian Cabot died in 1557, a humorous, light-hearted old gentleman, as fond of revelry as his father had once been fond of fine clothes. His great enterprise of discovery remained unfulfilled. However, he had helped to keep active the belief that there was a short cut for ships sailing to Asia. It might join the Gulf of Mexico to the Pacific, but on the whole Cabot thought, that the weight of evidence indicated a strait, opening somewhere between 61° and 69°N, i.e. where Hudson's Strait is to be found.

Cabot was not, however, the only adventurer excited by the thought of a North-west Passage in those early years of the sixteenth century. Robert

Thorne, an Admiralty official in Bristol and later a successful merchant in Seville, urged on Henry VIII the dazzling prospects held out to England by Northern discovery. Pointing out that this was the only direction that remained to be explored, for 'of the four parts of the world, it seemeth three parts are discovered by other princes, so that rest to be discovered the said north parts.' Thorne went on, 'Sailing northwards and passing the Pole, descending to the Equinoctial line, we shall hit these [Spice] islands a shorter way than the Portuguese.' The Portuguese route was 4,300 leagues long, the route by the North shorter by 2,000 leagues. To those who objected that there were strong climatic objections to his proposal, Thorne, writing in the warmth of his study in Spain, had a brusque retort: 'There is no land uninhabitable nor sea unnavigable.'

He died before he had the chance to put his optimistic dictum to the test of experience. But Henry VIII acted at once on Thorne's proposals, sending out two ships, the *Dominus Vobiscum* and the *Mary of Guildford*, which left Plymouth in June 1527. The *Dominus Vobiscum* was lost in a storm but the *Mary* reached Newfoundland or, it may be, Labrador. Her captain, Master Rut, came·upon icebergs and deep water. After a stay of ten days in a wilderness he found nothing but moss and the footprints of 'great beasts'; no inhabitants, no signs of human settlement. Depressed by what he saw, he sailed south to Cape Breton and Nova Scotia, sending men ashore here and there to report on the nature of the country. Bearing further southwards, the *Mary* was next heard of in the Caribbean. A Spanish captain, Gines Navarro, while loading cassava at an island off Hispaniola was hailed by an English ship. The English captain said that he and his friends, in a ship of King Henry's, had set out on an expedition to find a passage leading to 'the land of the Great Khan'. Towards the end of November, this English ship put into the harbour of Santo Domingo asking for water and food. Permission to enter the port was given and a pilot was sent to bring the ship in. Then a gun captain on the fort fired an inhospitable cannon and his shot nearly hit the ship. Without more ado, Rut hurried off eastwards to Puerto Rico, where he had better luck. He was allowed to buy food and to go his way. He arrived back in England early in 1528 having contributed nothing whatever to the quest for the North-west Passage. Master Rut, who was regularly employed on the Bordeaux run bringing back wine for the royal household, does not seem to have had the staying-power that makes the great explorers.

More determined were the attempts to find the mysterious channel made at this time by Giovanni Verrazano, an Italian gentleman in the

French service, who took two ships 'to discover Cathay' in 1523. Backed by a group of Italian bankers in Lyons who were interested in the prospect that a short cut to China would mean cheaper silk, Verrazano saw enough of America to conclude that it was a new continent and not at all a part of Asia. He had, however, no idea of its width. Cruising along the eastern coast of North America, he saw water on the other side of an isthmus a mile wide and 200 miles long. Verrazano concluded that he was seeing the Pacific. It is likely that he was looking at Pamlico Sound which lies within the Outer Banks of North Carolina. But if Verrazano was wrong, he was in good company. As late as 1716 it was thought that the American colonists had only to cross the Blue Ridge mountains of Virginia to find the Pacific stretched out before them.

So far as finding the 'north American strait' was concerned, neither the English nor the French had accomplished anything by these voyages. The same may be said of the attempt made by a Portuguese pilot, Estevan Gomez, who was sent out by the Emperor Charles V two months after Verrazano returned to France. Gomez was not the kind of man whom one at first glance trusts with an important mission. He had sailed as a pilot with Magellan on his great voyage of circumnavigation. In Magellan's Strait, Gomez had mutinied, seized the ship he was in and fled to Spain where, not unnaturally, he was summarily thrown into prison. His defence, if it can be called that, was that as an entrance to the Pacific Magellan's Strait was altogether too far off to be useful. He proposed instead that a way should be sought through North America. His argument was so convincing that the Emperor released him from prison and supplied him with a new caravel of 50 tons, the *Anunciada*, with which to prove his case. The ship sailed from Corunna in September 1524, and sighted the coast of America in the region of Cape Breton in February of the following year.

Gomez awaited the coming of spring in the Gulf of St Lawrence; then he sailed west far enough to convince himself that the St Lawrence was too beset by ice to be a likely way through to the Pacific. Further south, he made a fresh attempt, hopefully entering the Penobscot River in Maine, but very soon came to the conclusion that it was, after all, no more than a river. After a time he concluded that he would be unlikely to find the strait he was seeking on that stretch of the American coast. He turned to trade; again he met disappointment. The only goods he could find were of a kind which could easily be obtained in Europe. No spices. No silk. No drugs. He captured some unwary Indians as slaves and took them back to Corunna. There – final blow – the authorities forced him to free his human cargo. But, as it turned out, all was not completely lost for Gomez. He had kept the confidence of the monarch. In 1533 the Emperor made him a knight for his distinguished services with Magellan's fleet.

Soon after his return to Spain, the quest was taken up in a different quarter. One of the justices of the supreme court of Santo Domingo, the Licenciate Luis Vacquez de Ayllon, had a patent from the Emperor to explore the North American coast and to follow any strait he might find there and establish a colony. Ayllon equipped a substantial fleet, carrying 500 people, bond and free, and 80 horses and landed, probably somewhere on the coast of North Carolina. But the country was malarial and the local Indians suspicious. The colony was a failure. Ayllon lost two ships and arrived back in Santo Domingo with only 150 survivors of his original company. He had added a little information for the cartographers of America. But he had found no strait to Cathay.

'It is to the southward not the icy north,' concluded Peter Martyr, 'that everyone in search of a fortune must turn.' And Spaniards, at least, were ready to agree with him. After all, the south was theirs, the mines of Mexico and Peru. As for the Portuguese, they had under their control the only route to the Far East that was in use, the way round the Cape of Good Hope. They had no interest in opening up another. Two other nations were, however, still interested in the possibilities that lay to the North. The French were unwilling to concede that all America belonged to Spain or to Portugal. And the English, more interested in trade than in conquest, were still haunted by the dream of a northward seaway to Cathay.

French Canada in part owes its existence to a French attempt to find the North-west Passage. The story began when François Premier, during a pilgrimage to Mont-Saint-Michel in 1532, met a mariner of St Malo named Jacques Cartier. If any man was likely to find new lands in the New World for France, it was he; a sailor who had already voyaged to Newfoundland and Brazil. So the King was assured by the Abbot of Mont-Saint-Michel, an exalted dignitary who, among other offices, held that of Grand Almoner of France.

The King had never reconciled himself to a situation in which, by Papal Bull, France was excluded from the colonization of America in favour of Spain and Portugal. As a good son of the Church, he was bound to pay some respect to a Pope's decree, but as a sensible man, a contemporary of Henry VIII of England, he thought that what one Pope had decided another could rescind, or at least amend. And just a year after meeting

9

Jacques Cartier, the King's son, who later became Henri II, married Catherine de' Medici, niece of the current Pope, Clement VII. Their Pope was not only allied by marriage to the French royal family, but, for reasons of his own, was on bad terms with the ruler of Spain, the Emperor Charles V. Accordingly, at Marseilles, the Pope, the King and the Abbot of Mont-Saint-Michel agreed that the Bull of Demarcation applied only to lands already found at the time it was issued and could not possibly be relevant to territories that might be discovered later. It was a sensible view, although it was not likely to be acceptable south of the Pyrenees. It had practical results.

Jacques Cartier, captain and pilot for the King, set sail from Saint Malo on 20 April 1534, in command of two small ships with a total crew of 61. He made a landfall at Newfoundland on 10 May, after an unusually fast crossing, and spent that summer exploring the south coast of Labrador and the west coast of Newfoundland. He then passed on to the shores of the Gulf of St Lawrence, the land which is now the province of New Brunswick. There the soil and the climate were a great improvement on those of Newfoundland.

Cartier was an observant and, for those days, a sensitive man. In his account of how he had cruised off Prince Edward Island, he remarked on the charm of sailing along a wooded coast in early summer listening to the birdsong and smelling the grass. He entered Chaleur Bay, hoping that it might lead him to the channel to China. The trees were tall enough to provide masts for a ship of 300 tons, the soil was rich, the water full of salmon. As for the 'sauvages', Mic-Mac Indians who lived on fish, he made friends with them easily enough. Cartier was a good diplomat as well as a resolute sailor. The Indians, men and women, stripped themselves of the furs which they were wearing in exchange for knives, hatchets, combs and suchlike goods which the French sailors offered. It was all strange and fascinating. But there was one drawback: Cartier had not found the strait leading to China.

On 24 July at the entrance to Gaspé Harbour, Cartier put up a thirty-foot cross bearing the inscription 'Vive le Roy de France' and a carved panel showing the fleur-de-lis. When an Indian chief (a Huron) objected to what he guessed was a declaration of sovereignty, Cartier smoothed him down with presents. On 1 August a council of the leading men on the expedition decided that the time had come to return to France. They reached Saint Malo three weeks later.

Cartier could tell of extraordinary things he had seen. Better still, he had brought with him two Indian youths, sons of Donnaconna, an important Huron chief, as living testimonies to the wonders he described: the great auk, the seas teeming with fish, the pleasant forests and rich soil. More important, he was confident that, in those few weeks on the Gulf of St Lawrence, he had detected the entrance to a great seaway penetrating America and, he could not doubt, eventually leading to Cathay. He hoped to go back to probe the secret further.

He did just that in the following year, 1535. On this occasion he commanded a fleet of three naval vessels with a company of 112 men among whom were the two Indians he had taken away with him in the previous year. His orders, when he sailed from Saint Malo, were to explore the country beyond Newfoundland and, more vaguely, to discover 'certain distant lands'. At Anticosti Island, where he had turned back the year before, he went further on, sailing to the west. This magnificent stream was, the Indian boys told him, the great river of Hochelaga and the highway to Canada. Ahead, somewhere beyond the wooded shores and the distant mountains, was a mysterious land, the Kingdom of Saguenay. Cartier entered the Great River, very deep, very rapid and (at its entrance) very dangerous to navigators without pilots and without experience of its whims. He noted the strange creatures in the sea, white whales, walruses, snapping turtles. At length he reached the point where the Saguenay River flows into the great estuary of the St Lawrence. An island on which wild grapevine was growing freely he named Ile de Bacchus, just as the Vikings, for the same reason, had named their settlement Vinland. There he met once more the Indian chief, Donnaconna, whose two sons he had taken to France and who embraced him gratefully on hearing how well the boys had been treated. Rowing upstream in the ships' boats, Cartier came to an Indian village at the foot of an imposing rock. The strategic value of the place struck him at once. He was looking at the site of what has become Quebec.

At this point, difficulties arise between Cartier and his Indian friend Donnaconna who, it was clear, did not wish the Frenchmen to go any further upstream to Hochelaga. It seemed that the chief of that place claimed to be Donnaconna's superior. With the French ships and guns at his back, Donnaconna would be in a position to reverse that claim. But what if Cartier fell under the spell of the other chief and become *his* ally? It was a risk which Donnaconna was not prepared to take. He tried to bribe his visitor by presenting him with his niece and two boys. Cartier refused to bought off by these gifts. And one of the Indian boys who had made the trip to Europe now volunteered to pilot a pinnace to Hochelaga.

Donnaconna tried a last throw to prevent the enterprise. Three medicine men, with horns and blackened faces, paddled in canoes round Cartier's flagship, making wild cries. This was intended to warn the French that if they went upstream they would certainly die in the snow and ice. Unperturbed, Cartier replied that Jesus had assured him that ahead the weather was good.

He set sail upstream in his smallest vessel, a pinnace of 40 tons, towing two longboats. On 2 October, thirteen days later, he arrived at Hochelaga, an Indian town of fifty large dwellings situated three miles from the river bank and defended by a wooden wall. Where Hochelaga was then, Montreal stands today. But from the top of a hill which Cartier named Mont Royal, he saw something that made his heart sink. Not far above the point where he had left his pinnace were rapids which no vessel larger than a canoe could negotiate. He could sail no further up the river. The Great River, magnificent channel though it might be, was not the Passage to Cathay. A century later, a Frenchman gave the rapids their rueful and appropriate name, Lachine Rapids. Nearer to China Cartier could not reach on this route. Deeply disappointed, he returned to Quebec to spend the winter there.

During those winter months, he was tempted to an act of perfidy by the exciting tales Donnaconna told about the gold and rubies to be found in the hidden kingdom of Saguenay. There was even a white population there. This was the kind of story Cartier had come all the way from France to hear. It was certainly the kind of story that the King in his palace at Fontainebleau wanted to hear. Gold and rubies! To match the wealth that the Spaniards had found in Mexico and Peru. White people and, therefore, civilization. Cartier decided to kidnap the Indian and take him back to France so that he could tell the story in person to François Premier.

This, by a discreditable trick, he duly accomplished, carrying off Donnaconna and nine other Hurons to France, which they reached after an ocean crossing that lasted only three weeks. The Huron chief convinced the King, as he had convinced Cartier, that in the kingdom of Saguenay he would find a prize equal to anything their majesties of Spain and Portugal had won in the Indies. Although Donnaconna's story, repeated on oath before a notary public, did not vary in its main outline, from time to time he added tempting new ingredients. Gold and rubies had been the chief produce of the fabulous kingdom in his first, enticing sketches of it. Now

Donnaconna mentioned cloves, nutmeg and pepper. Oranges and pomegranates grew in the Saguenay orchards. And, lest there should be any flagging of wonder in his audience, he threw in human anecdotes – men with one leg, men without an arm, men with wings instead of arms.

The King was resolved that Cartier's next expedition should be for the purpose of winning Saguenay, the home of these strange beings. It should be on a larger scale than the earlier ventures, and a nobleman should command it, the Sieur de Roberval, who, although a Protestant, was a personage of high distinction. This time there was hardly a pretence of looking for the sea route to Cathay.

News of the expedition alarmed Charles V, who thought it presaged a new attempt to break into Spain's private sea, the Pacific. The King of Portugal, not the liveliest mind of the age, roused himself enough to seek news of the project from a mistress of the French King, to whom he sent a former lover laden with presents. The English ambassador in Paris, who was also on the *qui vive*, reported to Henry VIII that the French king was sending ships to seek the spice trade by a shorter way through 'mare glacearum'. But, as it turned out, Cartier's days as an explorer were nearly over.

He had penetrated six hundred miles into the North American continent. He had discovered a vast stretch of rich, half-empty country where there could be – and soon was – another France. He had been dazzled by an imaginative Indian's tales of a non-existent kingdom, where gold and rubies abounded, as later on Raleigh was dazzled by the myth of El Dorado.

In May 1541 Cartier was ready to sail on his third voyage, having spent the intervening months profitably enough in piracy, the customary diversion of the idle mariner. He and Roberval had ten ships between them and a passenger list which included volunteer colonists and a number of convicts in chains. In the end, Roberval was not ready to sail in time and ordered Cartier to take five of the ships and go ahead of him. This Cartier did without delay, and made the first attempt at a French settlement in Canada on the Great River some miles above the site of Quebec.

Then he set off with a few companions on a long reconnaissance by boat in search of the kingdom of Saguenay. He was looking for the Ottawa River as the most likely route to the kingdom but the rapids above Montreal were too much for him. He turned back and found his new settlement in acute danger of being over-run by Indians. He resolved to sail to France. All he had to show for his voyage were some barrels of 'gold' (pyrites) and 'diamonds' (quartz). At St John's, Newfoundland, he met

Roberval, who had left France a year after Cartier, having been so plagued by shortage of money that he had taken to piracy to stave off his creditors. Now he ordered Cartier to return with him to Canada. But Cartier vanished eastwards. He had had enough.

It may be said that when Cartier turned aside from exploration in northern waters to the search for treasure and a non-existent kingdom in Canada, the French chapter in the quest for the North-west Passage came to an end. It was, at least, interrupted. Cartier had failed in his original task where, in fact, he could not have succeeded. But the failure of this hope held the seeds of a later, dazzling triumph of a different kind. In his vain search for the elusive North-west Passage and his quest for phantom Saguenay, he had laid the foundation of the greatest of French achievements in colonization, New France – Quebec. Thus in his case, as in that of so many other explorers of the North, 'Over the cloud bridge of illusion lies the path of human progress.'*

The Arctic had a magic of its own for the early voyager. It had mystery. It had a magnetism that could not be denied. It was forbidding and alluring at the same time. It appealed to courage, endurance, fortitude and to greed, too, of course. The frozen wilderness had – it must have, as a necessary complement to all its horrors – gold! Gold and the sea road to the golden East! There was, in short, emotion and the impure poetry of adventure in the early image of the North. Only later, much later, came a more rational opinion.

The Arctic, however, was not simply an obstacle to be overcome or evaded. It was a region, governed by natural laws of its own, which, if men understood, obeyed and used them, would enable them to survive there in good health. Before the nineteenth century was ended – that is, long after the first seamen had explored it – a Norwegian, Fridtjof Nansen, had deliberately driven into the ice a ship which another Norwegian, Colin Archer, had designed so that, when the ice squeezed, it did not crush the ship but lifted it. The truth was that the Arctic Ocean is more complex than its earlier explorers had expected. It is, first of all, a land-engirdled sea, with several narrow exits and one wider exit to the south, roughly the same size as the Mediterranean. The North Pole is situated in this sea, not in the middle of it, but nearer to Greenland and the Northern islands of Canada than to Siberia and Alaska. In any case, the Arctic region cannot usefully be defined by its relation to the Pole and the Arctic Circle. Its land area should

* Fridtjof Nansen, *In Northern Mists*, vol. II.

rather be thought of as the territory lying north of the tree line or, which is roughly the same thing, the line above which the average temperature in the month of July is not higher than 50° Fahrenheit. Roughly speaking, this line runs, at some distance inland, west to east through Siberia and the north shoreline of the Canadian mainland. It swings to the south-east so as to exclude from the tree-belt the territory between the mouth of the Coppermine River and the coast north of Churchill on Hudson's Bay. Then it curves again to the north, claiming Ungava and the northern corner of Labrador for the Arctic. The whole of Greenland and the north sections of Iceland are also, by this definition, Arctic territory. To the south of this is the sub-Arctic region, which the Russians call the *taiga*, a forest area in which the trees grow well-spaced out so that no tree filches the scanty sunshine from its neighbour's roots.

The Canadian Arctic, which was of most interest to the explorers who sought the North-west Passage, is divided into two regions. There is a sea area apparently without movement, under a pall of ice for all but a few weeks in the year, but not completely static – in fact, in constant, powerful but sluggish motion. The ocean ice is broken up by winds, currents and tides into floes which may be piled up along the shore of the mainland into ridges higher than ships' masts. Between the ocean and the continental mass the land is broken up into hundreds of islands. On these islands and the adjacent mainland to the south there are countless lakes, more lakes than in the rest of the world put together. These are not the only remarkable features of the area. Where soil exists in the sub-Arctic region, it is frozen to a depth of about two thousand feet and has been in this condition – permafrost – for tens of thousands of years. The permafrost prevents the moisture from draining away. And moisture is scarce. A great part of the North is a desert – with less snowfall than in Ottawa and with a third of its rainfall.

The landscape in the Arctic region varies from the high mountains which are found in the interior of Greenland to the flat, desolate islands off the Canadian north shore. And the fauna of the North? For the Arctic has wildlife – butterflies, beetles and, of course, mosquitoes and warble flies. It has eighty species of birds of which all but three winter in the south. The tern, smallest of the gulls, spends the cold months in the Antarctic, making a return journey of twenty thousand miles to escape the cold weather of the North. The biggest of the Arctic animals is the musk ox – if the polar bear is excluded, and the wolf is the largest carnivore. Caribou are there, relations of the European reindeer, hunted by wolves and maddened by mosquitoes on their annual migration, first to the Arctic coastlands and then – when the flies drive them from the shore – to the verge of the forests. Once the caribou could be numbered in millions and their migration – the 'Foule' (the horde) as the French trappers called it – was a flood of brown living beings filling the empty plain from one horizon to the other. But the caribou could not defend themselves against the rifle.

The Canadian Arctic region, in which rash, confident seamen were to search for the fabled channel to the East, was much larger and far more complex than they supposed. They thought that the North American continent tapered as it trended towards the Pole, somewhat as the South American continent does on the southern curve of the globe. They had no conception of the distances over which their search extended. But these distances were tremendous. From the north of Ellesmere Islands south-ward to Churchill where the tree-line begins is 1,700 miles. And measured from east to west, from the outlying rocks of Baffin Island to the mouth of the Mackenzie River, the distance is 2,000 miles.

Within this vast triangle of land and sea, ice and rock, explorers who did not realize the immensity of their tasks, were looking for the Passage. They were looking for a broad, open, easily recognizable channel. Nothing of the sort existed. What, in fact, lay before them when they crossed the Atlantic from the east, was a huge archipelago, a profusion of islands divided from one another and from the American mainland by channels of varying width and labyrinthine complexity. They found deep fjords which had the delusive appearance of straits, ice and fog which made it impossible for seamen to distinguish shore from sea, a sailing season which could be measured in weeks rather than months, a climate which could change in a night from pleasant warmth to the chill of a death-sentence. They were going to probe a dark and, as it proved in the end, an unrewarding mystery.

Incidentally, they were about to prove that the Arctic was a habitable region. Amid the hostile wastes they came upon a strange race of men who had found it possible to live where trees could not live. The discovery seemed unimportant to them. They were seeking gold and did not find it. They were seeking a way for their little ships between the granite shore and the floating mountains of ice. And when, at last, they found it, it could not be used for business or for war. But in the course of the search, they had found a new world and they thought, too hastily, that it was a dead one. They were mistaken. The Arctic is alive but is asleep, for its life goes on in slow motion.

Part One

The Search for the North-West Passage

Golden Cathay must Wait

'The said Islands abound in Gold, Rubies, Diamonds, Bolasses, Granates, Jacinets, and other stones and pearls.' *Master Robert Thorne, writing in Seville, 1527, to Sir Edward Lees, ambassador of King Henry VIII*

The first English expedition to the North since Cabot was led by a professional sailor of some experience, of considerable courage and of somewhat spotted reputation. His name was Martin Frobisher.

The Frobishers were an old Yorkshire family who had been settled in the parish of Normanton in the West Riding since the middle of the fourteenth century. They owned land, were entitled to bear arms, and made prudent marriages. Bernard Frobisher, for example, married a knight's daughter whose family name was York. In consequence, when Bernard died early, leaving a family of young children, Mrs Frobisher sent her son Martin (born about 1539) to London to be brought up in the house of her brother, Sir John York. Sir John was the Master of the Mint, and therefore an important personage in the realm. When Martin was fifteen, Sir John decided that the boy should go to sea. It seemed the best way in which he could discharge his duties as the guardian of a bold, quarrelsome, obstreperous youth. As it turned out, the choice of a career was admirably suited to Martin's temperament.

The sea offered many opportunities at that time to young men with a zest for adventure and no excessive respect for the law. Its dangers were correspondingly high, as Martin quickly came to know. His first voyage was made to the Guinea coast. From that expedition only 40 men came back to Plymouth of the 140 who had been in the ship's company to start with. Most of them had been struck down by disease. On his second trip, to the same part of Africa, the boy was more unfortunate. He was handed over by his captain as a hostage to the Portuguese. They kept him for nine months in the Castle at El Mina which, being one of the chief depots of the slave trade, was well provided with dungeons.

Martin returned from Africa hardened by his experiences and contemptuous of Portugal's claim to sovereignty over that part of Africa. With enthusiasm he took to a life of crime. Before many years had passed, he was looked on as one of the most reckless and unscrupulous pirates, prowling about the English Channel with a well-found, heavily armed ship and no inhibitions about whom he attacked. By the time he was twenty-five his name appeared on a list of malefactors which the King of Spain had drawn up, instructing his captains to hang at sight all those named on it. Next year he was arrested for piracy and brought before an English court. He explained to the bench that the whole business was a misunderstanding. While he was occupied in carrying coal from Newcastle-upon-Tyne, his brother, John, had taken his ship, the *Mary Flower*, to sea against his orders and had committed the outrages complained of. Whether the court believed this story or not, Frobisher was released from prison on his promise that, in future, he would not go to sea without a licence. This technical obstacle was, however, overcome without much delay. Cardinal Châtillon, a Frenchman, who in spite of his ecclesiastical title was a Huguenot, and was the brother of Coligny, the Admiral of France, leader of the Calvinist party in that country, gave Frobisher a commission to capture Catholic ships. To this document were soon added similar commissions from the Prince de Condé and the Prince of Orange. Frobisher had a sufficiently extensive licence. The trouble was, however, that he could not keep his hands off any likely-looking prizes that hove in sight, whether they were Catholic or Protestant, French, Spanish or even English. The town of Rye asked protection from him, pleading that no six of its ships could match him in a fight at sea.

In 1569 he was again arrested for piracy; cargo he had stolen was handed back to its French owners and Frobisher was sentenced to pay a fine of £900. At that juncture a man named Bowes came forward with a claim that Frobisher's vessel belonged, in fact, to him. This was important legally. It would be a bar should the authorities have a mind to confiscate the ship. At this point, as in so many narratives of that time, the story becomes more complex and obscure. The ship, it seems, was sold by Mr Bowes to Lady Elizabeth Clinton, who was not only the wife of the Lord Admiral of England but also a close friend of Queen Elizabeth. After this, the case against Frobisher was quietly dropped and the next thing we know of him is that he is in the Queen's service, on patrol off the Irish coast and capturing French and Portuguese ships under the most respectable auspices. Frobisher's career as a notorious – and convicted – pirate was at an end. He was destined for a more lawful kind of adventure. But hardly a less dangerous one.

In the meantime, he was lounging about Lambeth in idleness and, it seems, was willing to consider any reasonable offer of employment. The Irish Earl of Desmond, Gerald Fitzgerald, was at this time forbidden to return to his native land on the ground that, as the President of Munster put it, he was 'a man rather meet to keep Bedlam than to come to a new-reformed country'. Desmond was living in dignified exile in the house of Sir Warham St Leger in Southwark. St Leger, a Catholic, was an amiable gaoler, more inclined to enjoy a country life in Kent than to keep an eye on his noble guest. In Frobisher the earl thought he had found just the man for an enterprise he was minded to carry out. In the privacy of a Thames-side house, he explained to the Yorkshire mariner that his wife was about to have a child and that there were strong family and national reasons why no heir of the Fitzgeralds should be born on English soil. He suggested, there-fore, that Frobisher should buy a ship and anchor it below the guardships at Gravesend. Disguised as a fisherman, the earl would row over in an oyster boat, the ship's anchor would be raised and Frobisher would forth-with sail the ship to Ireland. In return for this service, the earl would make him proprietor of Valentia Island.

The proposition was one which appealed to Frobisher's business sense, while not affronting his patriotism too much. Besides, it seemed a fairly simple operation to one as familiar as he was with Irish coastal waters. However, the plot was betrayed and Frobisher had to argue his way out of trouble with the authorities by protesting that the earl had simply employed him to provide a boat. No more than that. Later on, Desmond was allowed by the Queen to return to Ireland. As was to be expected, he became first a rebel, and then a fugitive. When his retinue was reduced to a priest, two horsemen, a hen and a boy he was captured in the wood of Glenaginty by a fellow-countryman, Daniel O'Kelly, who cut off his head and sent it to England in 1582.

The abortive plot to rescue Desmond did not quite end Frobisher's flirtations with politics. In 1575 Desmond's unwatchful gaoler, Sir Warham St Leger, wanted very much to go over to Ireland to join forces with a Catholic soldier named Stukely, who was a cousin of John Hawkins. Stukely had taken the money of the King of Spain and was preparing to invade Ireland with a force of Catholic malcontents raised in England. Would Frobisher give him transport, in return for an Irish estate? Frobisher was considering the offer when, once again, the conspiracy was betrayed to the authorities. This time the betrayal was by Frobisher's wife, who had come to dislike St Leger.

Even then, the Spaniards did not lose hope that they could put the ex-pirate's talents to some use. Needy, idle, a spendthrift, a first-class mariner with a hint of the ruffian about him, he was just the man for them. Through an intermediary, the King of Spain approached him about a strategic project of the highest consequence, no less than the seizure of Flushing, a Dutch seaport in Protestant hands. But by that time Frobisher's mind was on other things. A vaster and more dignified scene had opened out to him. The summer of 1575 was a time when far-reaching adventures were being planned in England. Excitement was in the air. Down in Plymouth, Francis Drake was planning to fit out a flotilla for a voyage whose true, astonishing purpose was known only to a handful of men. And in London, Frobisher was trying to raise money for an expedition as far-reaching and audacious in conception as that of Drake. He was going to look for the North-west Passage.

But did anything of the kind exist? Sir Humphrey Gilbert had written – but had not yet published – a learned polemic which proved that it did. Gilbert, a man of property in Devon and a half-brother of Sir Walter Raleigh, was a typical product of his age, at once a scholar, a theorist and a man of action. So far he had been unfortunate, having been ignominiously routed by the Spaniards in a battle in the Low Countries. Since then he had lived in retirement at Limehouse, busy with various literary projects, above all, an ambitious polemical work which he called the *Discourse*. In this he had demonstrated by authority, reason and experience that there was a way to Cathay and East India on the north side of America. Ancient philosophers and the best modern geographers were assembled in chorus: 'All which learned men and painful travellers have affirmed with one consent and voice that America is an Island; and there that lyeth a great Sea between it, Cathaya and Greenland, by which any man of our country that will give the attempt may with small danger pass to Cathaya, the Molucca, India and all other places in the East in much shorter time than either the Spaniards or Portugals doeth or may do.'

Gilbert went on to tell of Europeans who had actually passed through a strait dividing America and Asia. Was there not a chart drawn by Sebastian Cabot and still to be seen in the Queen's privy gallery at Whitehall, which showed that Cabot had sailed west by north to 67°N, and found the sea still open? Then there was the historical fact that in the reign of the Emperor Frederick Barbarossa, Indians had been driven ashore by weather on the coast of Germany. How could they have come there save by a route northward of the American continent? The evidence piled up by Gilbert was eloquent if variegated, impressive if not conclusive. It was certainly enough to convince Frobisher, when he heard of it, that the search for the North-west Passage was an enterprise worthy of his skill as a navigator and his mettle as a man. It is, indeed, possible that he had from boyhood been haunted by the idea of the quest. During his first trip to West Africa, one of the captains had been a Portuguese named Antonio Pinteado who claimed that he had actually sailed through the North-west Passage. Pinteado's story was listened to with respect among the propagandists for the Passage. But Gilbert's arguments gave a new impetus to the whole thrilling conception.

Frobisher went into the City in search of finance. When the City looked coolly on the ex-pirate, whose reputation was not of the most respectable, Frobisher turned to the Court, where his pleadings fell on the ear of Ambrose Dudley, Earl of Warwick. What Frobisher was proposing was, of course, a wild speculation, a gamble. Its success depended on various guesses, reported at third or fourth hand, about the configuration of a coastline which nobody had traced through all its length, and which few had seen at all. The geographical ignorance of educated men at that time, eighty years after Columbus, was profound. On the whole, the best opinion was that Greenland and the far north of America was a part of Asia. But on the other hand, if the guesses of learned men were correct, if the Channel existed and were navigable, the wealth and power accruing to England would be beyond calculation. Provided, of course, that an English seaman found it!

It was a weighty argument in those days when the ultimate clash between England the Spanish monarchy still lay in the future, and when the power of Spain, although it had not yet been measured, was apparently much greater than that of England. In preparing the enterprise, Frobisher worked in close association with Michael Lok, a London merchant, a shipowner and an enthusiast for the North-west Passage, who as his partner helped him to raise £875 for a voyage of exploration. The Earl of Warwick not only put in money, but interested Lord Treasurer Burghley in the project and helped to persuade the Muscovy Company to pass over to a consortium of speculators its right to explore the North-west. Frobisher, whose 'courage and aptness' were acknowledged, was to command the expedition. Two small vessels were obtained: one, the *Gabriel* of 15 to 30 tons, was specially built for the voyage at a cost of £152. It was to have a

crew of 18. A second barque, the *Michael* (20 to 25 tons) was bought for
£120. Its crew numbered 17. Then there was a pinnace of 7 to 10 tons,
with a crew of four. In the end, when the £875 subscribed was not enough
to pay the costs of the expedition, the optimistic Lok agreed to make up
the balance. He had eventually to find £739.

The ships were tiny, the seamen few, but, on the other hand, the
navigational equipment and scientific books they took with them proved
that this was intended to be no mere escapade but a serious attempt to
extend man's knowledge of the world he lived in. Twenty compasses,
eighteen sand glasses, an armillary sphere, an adjustable sundial, a treatise
on navigation, an edition of the Zeno brothers' fanciful voyage, with a
map. And, of course, a large English Bible. Finally there was a blank chart
on which an outline of the British Isles had been sketched in by an official
of the Muscovy Company. The intention was that Frobisher should fill in
the empty spaces on the chart with the results of his exploration, the outline of any coastline he might discover, compass variations as he noted
them, and so forth. The famous astrologer and idealogue, Master John Dee,
spent some time instructing Frobisher's officers in the more occult mysteries
of navigation.

On 7 June 1576 his fleet of two small ships and their attendant pinnace
moved seaward from Ratcliffe to Deptford. Martin Frobisher, aged about
thirty-eight, was embarking on the voyage of discovery of which, as his
friend George Best said, he had been dreaming for fifteen years. At Deptford, the ships cast anchor in the river, the pinnace having fouled another
ship and burst its foremast. Next day, they left Deptford about noon and
paused opposite Greenwich Palace where the Queen was staying. There
they put out all the flags they could muster and fired a loyal salute which
was acknowledged by a gracious wave from one of the windows. In the
evening, one of the Queen's secretaries came aboard and gave the crews a
brief address in Her Majesty's name, bidding them be diligent, obedient
and successful.

The captain put on his smartest clothes and rowed ashore to take farewell of the sovereign whose sharp eyes told her – but she probably knew
already – that here was a man well-matched to a desperate adventure, ugly,
strong, bold and plainly endowed with a truculence which he kept in
check for so courtly an occasion.

Fifteen days later, the master of the *Gabriel*, the ship Frobisher was sailing
in, sighted Fair Isle between Orkney and Shetland. And two days after that
they had left Foula forty-five miles to the north, and were sailing west by

north. At this point in the voyage, a gale blew that lasted for eight days and proved too much for the pinnace, which disappeared along with her crew of four. On 11 July the two ships caught sight of the Greenland coast – Friesland they called it – rising like pinnacles of steeples and all covered with snow. At this point they had their first awe-inspiring glimpse of Polar ice. Frobisher took four men in a boat to row to the shore. It could not be done.

The ice interposed an absolute barrier. The cold was intense. The eerie light of the Arctic summer cast its spell on them. A fog at times fell to cover everything. The memory of the gale was with them. And all were aware of the danger that they might soon follow their four comrades, lost in the pinnace. All these melancholy factors worked so powerfully on the minds of Owen Gryffyn, master of the *Michael*, and his crew that they turned homewards. Seven weeks later they arrived in the Thames with the sad tidings that the *Gabriel* had been lost. And with her, presumably, had perished Frobisher and his shipmates.

The truth was less depressing, although sufficiently alarming.

Pressing on until she reached the southern tip of Greenland, the *Gabriel* had been struck by a violent storm which laid her on her beam ends. Water poured in at a hatchway and it seemed that all was lost. The crew gave way to outcries of despair but in this emergency Frobisher showed that, in truth, he was a man for the direst extremities of peril. Axe in hand, he worked his way along the ship's almost horizontal side, severing the braces that held the mizzen-mast. Shouting over the noise of the wind, he ordered the mast to be hacked through by axe-blows and thrown over-board. It was a desperate device but it proved to be enough. The *Gabriel* righted herself and bore southwards, with wind and sea behind her, until it was possible to pump her dry and rig a fresh mizzen-mast.

On 20 July, when the morning fog cleared, her master, a meticulous, observant mariner named Christopher Hall, sighted land with a great amount of ice heaped up before it. This he thought was Labrador: it was, in fact, Resolution Island, lying off the desolate south-east coast of Baffin Land. They sighted a lofty cape which Frobisher named Queen Elizabeth Foreland.

A field of pack-ice lay between them and the shore, within a cable's length of which no bottom could be found at a hundred fathoms. No anchorage here! No harbour! But some way further north there was a sight to gladden the hearts of men who had come through dreadful perils in search of the Passage to Cathay and were ready to greet it on the slightest provocation. Before them was a second headland on the further side of a 'great gulf, dividing as it were, two mainlands or continents asunder'.

Asia on one quarter, American on the other! Between them, a strait which the captain named after himself, following the example set him by Magellan at the other tip of the continent. Frobisher was convinced that he had found that avenue to Asia, so cunningly hidden behind the fogs and the ice floes, for so long sought in vain, so persuasively proclaimed by philosophers and historians. The North-west Passage!

Frobisher was however mistaken. His imagined 'strait' was only a bay, an indentation of the coast reaching about 200 miles into the wastes of Baffin Land. The coastline of America towards the north was infinitely more complex and extensive than he or any of his contemporaries supposed. But this was a disappointing truth which was not immediately disclosed to the eyes of the voyagers. For a time Frobisher and his friends believed that he had solved the great Riddle of the North.

Putting the matter to the test, Frobisher sailed about a hundred and fifty miles into the 'strait'. There he went ashore and was surprised by a 'mighty deer' – moose? caribou? – which attacked him without hesitation. He narrowly escaped with his life. More interesting, he saw traces of men ashore and, at sea, small floating objects which at first he took to be seals or porpoises, but which turned out to be men in canoes made of skins. The English visitors took careful note of the appearance of these strangers. They were like Tartars, with long black hair, broad faces and flat noses. They were tawny in colour, which suggested to the Englishmen that they were legitimate descendants of one of the three sons of Noah, unlike the Ethiopians who were, as all good Christians knew, the fruit of some forbidden union consummated after the Ark had grounded. The women were marked with streaks of blue colour down their cheeks.

The presence of these savages probably did not come as a surprise to the explorers. At any rate, in his narrative of the expedition, Captain Best proved – or, at least, contended – that 'all the land even unto the point directly under either Pole is or may be inhabited, especially of such creatures as are engendered and bred therein' (for he was willing to concede that, say, the elephant would not breed in a cold climate). With the Eskimos, Frobisher set up trading relations – seal skins and bear skins in exchange for bells, looking-glasses and suchlike toys brought from England for the purpose. As Robert Thorne had said half a century earlier, 'The preciousness [of commodities] is measured after the distance between us and the things we have appetite unto.' There was, however, no real trust between one side and the other in this commerce. The Eskimos waylaid five members of the crew who had been foolish enough to venture ashore too far from the ship. These stragglers never returned, although Frobisher spent two days in sounding trumpets and firing guns to let them know that he was still in the vicinity. He was ready to pay a handsome enough ransom for them, because by this time his ship's company were reduced to thirteen, some of them sick. With so few to work the ship there could be no question of going to Cathay.

Long before, a Norwegian seaman had warned his successors of some precautions they should take in dealing with the Eskimos of Greenland: 'Now if it please God they come to Greenland, then shall they set but two men on shore who shall take with them diverse kinds of merchandise – and let them observe whether men may there land or no, with the love of the inhabitants. And I counsel and charge those that shall trade for Greenland that they set no more folk on land but they keep men enough to man the ship.'

Frobisher found that a similar caution was necessary in doing business with the Eskimos of Baffin Land. For his part, he wanted very much to kidnap an Eskimo and take him back to England as a trophy or as a specimen for serious scientific investigation. This in the end he succeeded in doing by playing upon the Eskimos' fascination with the sound of bells. Promising that he would give a bell to the man who came close enough to take it from his hand, he enticed one unfortunate Eskimo to paddle alongside in his kayak. At the moment of exchange, Frobisher dropped the bell and seized the man, lifting him and his canoe on to the deck of the *Gabriel*. It was a remarkable feat of strength. The Eskimo, in his rage at being caught, bit his tongue through in his mouth but survived until he reached England where he died, supposedly having caught cold on the way. Later experience showed that these children of the wasteland were extraordinarily susceptible to the diseases of civilization.

So ended, pathetically, the first encounter between Englishmen of the era of discovery and the intelligent and, surely, attractive people who had come to terms with nature in a region of the earth where other men could not live. The Eskimo way of life excited the interest of the English, as well it might. Their kayaks, cunningly made of skins sewn together and fastened to a wooden frame, were light enough to be carried on a man's head. They were swift and silent in the sea, essential qualities in craft which were for the use of men who lived by hunting the creatures of the sea, walruses, seals, sea-otters, whales, etc. The occupant had in front of him as he paddled the tools of his trade, harpoons, darts and fishing lines, all fastened securely to his canoe by thongs of walrus hide. He himself was laced into the kayak by an apron of skins which fastened round his chest. It was waterproof. He was, in effect, part of the craft which, if it capsized, he could right again by deft strokes of his paddle. An Eskimo kayak was a very considerable technical achievement and to handle it in a heavy sea called for some skill. It was the most spectacular artefact of the Eskimos, more so even than the blubber lamp, or the bow which, in their homeland where no trees grew, they made from driftwood strengthened with plaited animal sinew, but it was not necessarily the most impressive feature of their culture.

Frobisher and his company made the acquaintance of the Eskimos during a brief summer on the tundra. There the landscape has a chilly, sharp beauty of its own and across it the wind never ceases to blow. The flatlands are brown, but they stretch between glistening cliffs, while here and there startling orange patches of lichen colour the rocks. But it is in winter, when everything is white, that the inbred gift of the Eskimo is revealed, the instinct on which his life depends. Then he finds his way over the waste in which there is no perceptible line dividing sky from land or frozen land from frozen sea; no outline anywhere, only plumes of snow whirling before the wind. By picking up features that are invisible to white men he can sense the slightest change in the direction of the wind. Wind! It is all-important to the Eskimo: one wind will carry the ice floes out, and it is time to hunt the seal; another wind will bring the floes back, then walruses will be the quarry. Driving his dog team, with his chin well tucked into his skin hood, the Eskimo need not look up to know that the wind has changed. He has observed it from the change that has occurred in the way the fur of his parka is being blown.

But Frobisher's sailors were not as impressed as they should have been by the ingenuity with which the 'savages', the 'cannibals', had adapted themselves to a bitterly hostile environment. They were too shocked by the Eskimos' habits, 'very strange and beastly', especially their practice of eating meat raw and of stealing any object that took their fancy – a length of old rope, a handful of nails. The Eskimos stole because their existence, beyond the margin where other races of men would have found life possible, excluded the idea of property. They were communists. As for their diet, they could eat raw meat but preferred it rotten. The stinking entrails of animals were delicacies on which they thrived. Only the liver of the polar bear was poison. What they ate might, indeed, be simple and even horrible to the sensitive stomachs of Europeans. But it had apparently one practical advantage. It enabled the Eskimos to stand up to the cold better than white men could. Travelling from Asia thousands of years before, crossing the Bering Strait on the ice or, perhaps, on a land bridge, they had worked their way northwards from the prairies, deeper and deeper into the Arctic land, learning how to hunt its animals – especially to hunt the seal from the ice – and defeat its cold. Nature, and necessity, had bred them as a special type of humanity, with shorter arms and smaller hands than Europeans. They spoke a language like no other on earth. There were, perhaps, 60,000 of them when Frobisher's seamen met them – perhaps a few thousand more, for they number 60,000 today and, in the intervening centuries, the contact with civilization has not been kind to the remarkable, talented, stoic race of Eskimos.

They were, of course, heathen who practised sorcery and, as the Englishmen thought, worshipped the sun. It was true that the Eskimos, as practical men engaged in a ceaseless struggle to keep alive, sought to obtain power over nature by spells and propitiations. It was a mistake, however, to suppose that they worshipped the sun, whom they thought of as a woman in contrast to the masculine moon. Their religion, if they could be said to have one was, like their cosmography, something that belonged to a race of men who were too busy to have time for useless speculation. The earth – was it not obvious? – was flat and round and a few weeks' journey in extent. The sky was a dome supported by four pillars. Under the rim of the earth was a place where sinful people went after their death. Above the dome of the sky dwelt the souls of the good. For the Eskimos believed in the soul, from the great Soul presiding over all to the souls that existed in fish and stones. But such esoteric realms of Eskimo thought could not be examined by a company of Elizabethan seamen during an apprehensive stay of a few weeks on a forbidding coast. If they had examined it at all, they would probably have remained fixed in the belief that these people were heathen, a prey to every kind of vice and beastliness.

After the kidnapping of the five sailors, Frobisher came to the sensible conclusion, therefore, that the time had come when he and his companions should make their way home. Golden Cathay must wait. The day before they left, each member of the crew was sent ashore to bring back any interesting object he wished to carry to England from the desolate land of which Frobisher had taken 'Christian possession' in Queen Elizabeth's name. Working in a hurry, for fog was coming down, one man picked flowers, another green grass and a third brought home a small, heavy black stone: marcasite? iron pyrites? – who could say? In England, more glamorous ideas about its nature soon found credence.

A month after leaving his 'strait', Frobisher reached Orkney and on 9 October dropped anchor in the Thames. He had been gone just four months; he had been reported lost. Now he was back, highly commended by all men for his great and notable attempt, but especially famous for the hope he brought back of the passage to Cathay. While the kidnapped Eskimo lived, he and his kayak roused extraordinary interest among the Londoners. The black stone was at first thought of no account until a piece of it got into the hands of a lady whose husband was one of the backers of the expedition. Probably by accident, she threw it in the fire and observed that it had not been consumed. More than that, when it was soaked in vinegar, the stone was seen to glitter like gold. Interest in it was at once aroused.

Frobisher's partner, Michael Lok, handed it over to the assay-master at the Tower, who reported that it was marcasite – pyrites – and when Lok was unwilling to accept this verdict, told him to show the stone to the assayers of the City. The first assayer who was consulted, Mr Wheeler, tested the stone. Marcasite. The second, George Needham, produced the same discouraging report. The third, a Venetian, Giovanni Baptista Agnello, was more optimistic. The stone, he said, contained a little gold. And he exhibited a little 'powder of gold' which, he said, had come out of it. When Lok, in whom credulity was fighting scepticism, asked him how he had found gold where nobody else had, the Italian answered, 'Ah, signor, nature needs to be flattered.' The answer was, at best, equivocal but England was at that time disposed to take an optimistic view of overseas exploration and its fruits. The rumour of Frobisher's gold ran through the City. The assayers had found that the sample brought back from the North was purest gold! Sir Philip Sidney wrote to an officer serving in Flanders that Frobisher had stumbled upon vast gold deposits. Another letter-writer was sure that Frobisher had found King Solomon's mines. Frobisher was sure of a cordial welcome when next he went down to court to kiss the Queen's hand. And it was certain that it would be easier to get financial backing for his next voyage. The only trouble was that, in the gleam and greed of a new gold rush, the grand purpose of these voyages, the discovery and navigation of the North-west Passage, might well be relegated to a secondary place. And so it was to prove.

The Hope Continually Increaseth

How Frobisher, in every coast,
    With flickering fame doth flie
A Marshall Knight, adventurous,
    Whose valour great was such
That hazardes hard he light esteem'd,
    His countrie to enrich.
            John Kirkham, in the praise of M. Martin Frobisher, 1578

'Let no wise man laugh at [Frobisher's] mistake, because in such experiments they shall never hit the mark who are not content to misse it.'
            Thomas Fuller, Worthies of England

Frobisher's second attempt on the Arctic was, therefore, an altogether more substantial affair than the first. A charter was obtained for a Company of Cathay, a joint-stock corporation whose shareholders elected Michael Lok Governor, and Martin Frobisher 'High Admiral of all seas and waters' of Cathay and other places of new discovery. In return for his work, Frobisher was to be given one per cent of all the goods which the Company might bring back to England. The ex-pirate from Yorkshire had moved far up on the staircase of dignity. The Queen subscribed £1,000 capital and, more valuable, a tall ship of her own. Sir Francis Walsingham, in spite of his scepticism about the value of the 'ore', a mere alchemist's trick, he thought, invested £200 or more. (It may be that he put money into this venture in which he did not greatly believe because some of the people who supported it had helped him to finance projects about which he was more enthusiastic, such as Drake's expedition to the Pacific.)

The ship which the Queen lent to Frobisher was the *Aid*, of 200 tons; its master was Christopher Hall, who had been Frobisher's master in the *Gabriel*. On this voyage the *Gabriel* was commanded by Edward Fenton, a gentleman of Lord Warwick's. There was also a third ship, the *Michael*, a barque of 25 tons, of which Gilbert Yorke, a gentleman of the Lord

Admiral's, was captain. Altogether 250 tons of shipping, and ships' companies which numbered 134 – sailors, soldiers, gentleman, miners, refiners – and six condemned criminals who were to be put ashore on Greenland to found a colony there. Food supplies were ample. Drink? Eighty tuns of beer for the men – a gallon a day – and five tuns of Madeira and sack for the officers. The sailing orders to the High Admiral showed that, in the year that had passed since the sailing of the first expedition, an important change of emphasis had occurred. This time, Frobisher's first task was to collect 'gold ore'; one of the smaller vessels was instructed to sail into Frobisher's 'strait', but not further than 500 miles; a party was to be left to winter in the 'strait'; and, only if no more promising ore were found, was Frobisher then to send back the *Aid* and try to make his way to Cathay with the two smaller vessels. It was a full programme.

The second expedition weighed anchor at Blackwall on 26 May 1577, and dropped with the tide to Gravesend where the ships' companies, like good Christians, received communion. At Harwich they took on some food and Frobisher, to his disgust, received letters from the Council strictly commanding him not to exceed his agreed complement of one hundred and twenty men. He had fourteen over establishment. Accordingly, he put enough men out of the ships – including the six convicts – to bring his numbers down to the permitted level.

He went ashore to pay his respects to the Queen, who was staying at Lord Warwick's seat in Essex. Then he returned to his flagship, the *Aid*, and gave the order to set sail. In a week, helped by a 'merry wind', they had arrived at Orkney, where the inhabitants fled 'with shrieks and alarms', painful experience having taught them that strange ships dropping anchor in their harbours generally brought pirates with them. However, with tact, the Orcadians were persuaded to do business with their visitors. The Englishmen found the islanders friendly and looked with compassion on the living conditions they found among them – no chimneys; peat fires; families living in the same cottage as their beasts, base money and the Presbyterian religion. To seamen fresh from the Thames-side maritime town, which stretched from London Bridge halfway to the sea, it was all very dreary.

For their part, the Orcadians, being mightily short of leather and rope, to say nothing of timber, were delighted to barter fresh food, which was plentiful in the islands, for old shoes and ropes. After this interlude, the expedition made off west-north-west and was soon out of sight of land. In this state the ships remained for twenty-six days. On 4 July the leading ship fired a gun believing it had sighted land for a moment through the mist. This seemed likely enough, for the sea had become black and smooth, a sign that they were close to shore. Later that evening – ten o'clock of a Polar summer's day – they saw the land plainly with a girdle of huge icebergs about it. It was Greenland – known to them as Friesland – in 60½° North. Comparing the coast with a chart made by the Zeno brothers two hundred years before, Frobisher found that the two agreed admirably. He could not be expected to know that the Zeno map showed an island, Friesland, which did not exist. Lying becalmed, they fished and caught a halibut so big that it gave the whole company food for a day. They marvelled, too, at the size of the icebergs, seventy or eighty fathoms below water and fresh to the taste. From this they conjectured, correctly as it chanced, that the floes were made not by the freezing of the sea but of melted snow or river ice which had reached the ocean from inland.

The ice-cap of Greenland, from which these icebergs came, is the biggest glacier in the Northern hemisphere, 700,000 square miles in extent. Fresh snow falling on older snow below squeezes it into ice, which is, in places, two miles thick. In time, the ice is forced outwards and so down to the fjords. Tens of thousands of tons of ice break off into the sea every day and float away to the south, profoundly affecting by their number the climate of Europe.

The scene among the icebergs was very different from that which greeted seamen who in other voyages had sailed southwards from England. Dionyse Settle, who told the story of this voyage, was a more colourful writer than Christopher Hall, the strictly factual chronicler of the first expedition. He was not a man to miss the chance of an outburst of rhetoric. 'Here,' he wrote, 'in place of odoriferous and fragrant smells of sweet gum and pleasant notes of musical birds, we tasted the more boisterous boreal blasts mixed with snow and hail, in the months of June and July, nothing inferior to our intemperate winter . . . All along this coast, ice lyeth, as a continual bulwark.'

During four days of cold and fog, Frobisher tried to find a way through the ice to the shore. In vain! The ships bore further west and, in spite of a savage two-day storm in which the *Michael*'s topmast was blown overboard, they arrived at Hall's Island, off Baffin Land, where the 'ore' had been discovered in the previous year. There with difficulty they found a landing place. But this time, the island yielded nothing to the miners, although other islands in the neighbourhood were more productive. Frobisher, who made a reconnaissance, was rowed back to the *Aid* with the promising news; he also brought eggs and a young seal shot by one of the crew. What was more, he had seen snares set to catch birds. The significance of this was plain: natives were about, people of 'subtle and cruel disposition', as he knew from his past voyages. Early next morning he led a party of forty gentlemen and soldiers to the top of a nearby hill. A cairn was built, a trumpet sounded, and, while everybody knelt, prayers were said by Frobisher so that, by their Christian study and endeavour, the barbarous Eskimos might be brought to the knowledge of true religion and the hope of salvation.

How great was the need for that knowledge, the missionaries were soon to discover. Making a tour of the country, noting how the stones sparkled – but 'all is not gold that glisteneth' as Master Settle prudently remarked – marvelling at a dead narwhal (the horn of which was kept for the Queen), they came upon a settlement of Eskimos whom they surrounded and attacked by land and water. The Eskimos fought desperately and, 'altogether void of humanity and ignorant what mercy means', drowned themselves rather than be taken. However, Frobisher's men were able to capture one old woman and a young one who could not flee because she had a small child to look after. 'The old wretch, whom divers of our sailors supposed to be either a devil or a witch, had her buskins plucked off to see if she were cloven-footed.' To English eyes, the older Eskimos were so unpleasing to look at that they were thought to be endowed with malign, magical powers. After that inspection, the old Eskimo was let go. But the young woman was carried off. The encounter ended when the sailors, overcoming their natural inclination to benevolence, set about plundering the Eskimos' tents.

On another occasion, Frobisher and Christopher Hall lured two of the 'savages' into conversation and, on a pre-arranged signal, laid hold on them, meaning to carry them to the boats. But the ground was slippery with snow and the Eskimos escaped. On this occasion, therefore, scientific enquiry was frustrated. In his retreat to the shore, Frobisher was wounded in the backside by one of their arrows. However, a shot from an English caliver, a light arquebus which was mounted on one of the boats, put the enemy to flight. Nicholas Conyer ran after them and, being a Cornishman and a good wrestler, threw one of them to the ground so heavily that his side ached for a month. This Eskimo was carried off as a captive, to be added to the 'bag' of one Eskimo mother, who with her child, was already in the ship.

In the meantime, a sudden storm had blown up, violent enough to prevent the boat parties from regaining the ships. Shivering with cold, they spent a miserable night on a small island. At sea, matters were no more tranquil. Through the negligence of a cook who allowed the kitchen chimney to overheat, the *Aid* took fire. Had it not been for one of the ship's boys who raised the alarm in time, the Queen's ship would have been destroyed, Frobisher would have been disgraced and the expedition brought to ruin. But this disaster was averted. After an alarming day spent in fending off ice floes, the men in the boats arrived back at the ships just as the storm was abating.

Digging trenches ashore in the search for gold to satisfy the 'greedy desire our country hath to a present savour and return of gain', avoiding the dangers from driving ice, landing in different places to explore the desolate country, the expedition had another concern. Frobisher had lost five of his crew to the Eskimos the previous summer; now he heard from an Eskimo that three white men were living with his people. Frobisher wrote the captives a letter, 'in the name of God in whom we all believe, who I trust hath preserved your bodies and souls amongst these infidels', telling them that he had a man, a woman and a child of the Eskimos whom he would give in exchange for them. Failing that, he would not leave alive an Eskimo in the country. This they could tell to their captors. 'And thus unto God, whom I trust you do serve, in haste I leave you . . . Yours to the uttermost of my power, Martin Frobisher.' This letter, along with pen, ink and paper, he handed over to Eskimos who, by pointing to the sun with three fingers, indicated that they would be back with an answer in three days. But no answer came in three days, or later; instead, there were new attempts to entice the English from their ships. The sport of hunting human livestock was one that both sides could play.

Frobisher's shipmates were lost, and for three centuries there was no clue to their fate. Then, in 1862, the story of their disappearance had a remarkable sequel. An American, Charles F. Hall, who spent two years in Frobisher Bay, heard from an aged Eskimo woman that long before, white men had come in ships, in three separate years. Five of the white visitors had been captured and had dug a trench on Kodlunarn Island (White Man's Island), which is in Countess of Warwick Sound. They had built a boat from timber left by the first expedition. And then they had sailed off. But the Arctic winter had killed them. That was the old woman's tale, told after three centuries. What importance can be attached to it? Is it an instance of folk memory of almost miraculous range? Was the old woman speaking of some wholly different incident? Or was she inventing a tale which she knew would interest a white man? Each can decide for himself which explanation he favours. All that can be said is that on Kodlunarn Island, a trench was seen and photographed in 1927 which is probably a relic of Frobisher's mining operations. There were also foundations of a 'house' which he or his companions may have built.

On 23 August, after a stay of a month, it was time for Frobisher to leave. Two hundred tons of 'ore' had by this time been brought aboard, enough surely to determine once and for all whether it contained a worthwhile amount of gold. The men were weary and some of them were injured. Their shoes were worn out. The bottoms of the baskets they used for loading were torn. And, most sinister of all, at night, ice was beginning to form round the ships. This was a warning that must be heeded.

So the tents they had pitched ashore were struck and packed away. A bonfire was lit on a hilltop on the island which is now called Kodlunarn but was named Anne Warwick Island by Frobisher. The company marched round with ensigns displayed. A last volley was fired. Then the anchors were weighed and the course set for England.

The homeward voyage was as dangerous as could be imagined. The wind blew a gale from the west, and the sea was high. One night there was half a foot of snow on the hatches. The master of the *Gabriel* was blown overboard – while the bosun was rescued only with difficulty, although the barque was 'laced fore and aft' with ropes breast-high. The *Michael* lost sight of the other two vessels and made her way home independently by way of Orkney. Then the *Gabriel* parted company with the *Aid* which, having the highest poop of the three, was driven with the greatest speed before the wind. Drifting on the sea under bare poles so that her companions might catch up with her, she was terribly battered by the waves. When a day of calmer weather came (2 September), her rudder was found to be torn in two. A dozen of the best crewmen were lowered into the sea to carry out rough repairs. When they had finished their work, they were more dead than alive. On 7 September, soundings showed that the sea bed was forty fathoms below the ship, 'sand, small worms and cockle shells'. From these clues they knew, as experienced sailors, that they were somewhere between Scilly and Land's End. As the wind prevented them from going up-Channel they made for the Bristol Channel and anchored at Padstow. There they were warned by the local people that it was a dangerous roadstead and made first Lundy and at last Milford Haven, a good harbour. This the *Aid* reached on 23 September, having been just a month on the homeward run.

The *Gabriel*, the sailors heard with joy, had stumbled into harbour at Bristol, with some help from a ship of that port. As for the *Michael*, it had at last dropped anchor at Yarmouth. Frobisher hurried to Windsor to tell the Queen of the success of the voyage and of the substantial amount of ore he had brought back. The hope of finding the passage to Cathay was, he said, greatly increased. The Queen decreed that the new land they had discovered should be named Meta Incognita, the Unknown Frontier.

So ended Frobisher's second attempt to find the North-west Passage, a voyage in which the quest for gold proved of more absorbing interest than the search for the elusive path which, as sailors believed and philosophers predicted, would lead through the northern seas to the wealth of the Pacific. The voyagers had accomplished something; they had combed the beaches of forbidding lands – with what results the gold refiners of London would now determine; they had reached relations of mutual distrust with the Eskimos: but, in spite of their claims, they had not advanced the quest for the North-west Passage by a mile. Frobisher had a shrewd notion that, in the minds of his backers, gold counted for more than geography. In any case, if he had doubts on that subject, the shareholders had representatives on board his ships who would speedily recall him to a sense of realities.

The expedition had brought three Eskimos to England with them, a man, a woman and a child. The sailors watched the man and the woman closely when they were first brought together, expecting heaven knows what sort of conduct from two infidels. What happened surprised them. At first, neither the man nor the woman spoke a word, as if the horror of captivity had taken away the use of their tongues. Then the woman sang a little, and the man spoke to her solemnly and at length. After that they settled down together, the woman looking after the man like a good housewife, keeping their cabin clean and killing the dogs for their meat. But they had no sexual relations and indeed were most careful not to allow their private parts to be seen. The behaviour of these unhappy captive Eskimos was, in fact, a model of dignity and decorum which deserved a better reward than the captivity that awaited them. The male Eskimo attracted great crowds at Bristol by his ability to bring down flying birds with his dart. Seeing Frobisher's trumpeter mount his horse, the Eskimo did likewise, finishing with his face to the horse's tail to the infinite amusement of the crowd. Both he and the woman were the subjects of careful watercolours by John White of the Painters-Stainers' Company of London who, by a happy stroke of luck, had accompanied Frobisher in the *Aid*.

The precious 'ore', obtained with so much labour and brought home with so much danger, was stored in Bristol Castle and the Tower of London. Preliminary tests were promising **or** dubious, according to the temperament of those who learned of the results, but before furnaces could be built to reduce the ore in bulk, the spring of 1578 had arrived. It was time to set out once more on a new attempt to probe the secrets or riches of the North, to bring back more of the precious ore and search for the passage to Cathay ('whereof the hope continually more and more increaseth'). Frobisher was eager to be off, goaded, it may be, by the thought that Drake had already vanished from Plymouth Sound on a mysterious and momentous assignment. The money – or the promise of money – for the venture was readily forthcoming. George Best, one of Frobisher's captains on his voyages to the Arctic, observed that the two main obstacles to exploration by the English had been lack of liberality by the nobility, and lack of skill in navigation by the seamen. Now one of these obstacles were removed; not only the Queen, but all the nobles were excited by the thought of new discoveries beyond the rim of human knowledge.

This time a fleet of fifteen ships, of which the Queen's *Aid* was once more the flagship, assembled at Harwich on 27 May. The captains all kissed the Queen's hand at Greenwich before dispersing to their ships. Frobisher was given a gold chain. In the fleet a suitable degree of protocol was imposed. Prayers were said twice a day. Card-playing and bad language were abjured. And at night, when necessary, the challenge was 'Before the world is God'. To which the reply was, 'After God came Christ His son'. This time there was not even a pretence of finding the sea channel to Cathay. Gold was the purpose of the new voyage.

The fleet set sail three days later, calling at Plymouth on the way westwards down the Channel. On the way the ships gave help to some poor men of Bristol who had been robbed by French pirates and needed both surgery and food. After that they cleared Dursey Head at the entrance to Bantry Bay on 5 June. Sixteen days later, they sighted the icebergs off the Greenland coast and Frobisher went ashore at one point where there was less ice than elsewhere. He came upon an Eskimo settlement without seeing any of its people, who had disappeared into the interior, warned of what they might expect by previous visitations of the Europeans. From the village, Frobisher took only a couple of white dogs, leaving in payment pins, knives and suchlike trifles. He stayed ashore long enough to declare Greenland a possession of Queen Elizabeth's with the name of West England. The last they saw of West England was a high cliff which they named Charing Cross.

Immediately afterwards, the ships were enshrouded in a sudden dense fog which compelled them to sound their trumpets and beat their drums day and night so that they would not lose touch with one another. There followed a dangerous storm in which one barque was so damaged by the ice that she sank, although her crew were rescued by their comrades in the other ships. The loss of this barque was particularly unfortunate because it was carrying the ready-cut timber for a house in which some valiant spirits intended to spend the following winter in the Arctic.

The crews, who thought that 'verily we should have tasted of the same source', were hard put to it to fend off the ice which drove against them before a south-west gale. They protected the ships as well as they could with oars, pikes, capstan bars and cables hung over the side as fenders. Every ship sought safety in its own way, some drifting where they found a little sea-room, some mooring to a neighbouring iceberg. Then, after a terrible night, the wind fell and the fog cleared.

This was followed by an incident in which Frobisher lost his way in a blizzard and the greater part of the fleet sailed after their flagship into what he called later the 'Mistaken Straits'. He and his ships were, in fact, in what was later known as Hudson Strait. They sailed further into it for twenty days, mostly in foggy weather, beset by a swift and contrary current so savage that ships were spun round violently as if they were in a whirlpool. The noise of the stream was as loud, they thought, as 'the waterfall of London Bridge'. The light was so bad that they could not measure the height of the sun above the horizon and for that reason could not be sure how far north they were. Frobisher sent his pinnace from ship to ship to ask the opinion of the captains and masters on this important point. The answers of these sages were dubious, although Christopher Hall, chief pilot of the expedition, was sure that they were not in Frobisher's Strait. He admitted, however, that as the trend of the coast was very like that of the Strait, the most experienced mariner might well be mistaken. After that, in persisting fog, the ships lost contact with one another, although most of them turned back hoping to find their way to the open sea. The danger from ice, water and collision was acute.

Some of the sailors were tempted to jump on an iceberg in the hope of prolonging life, others were prepared to make rafts of the ships' hatches, to supplement the boats, which would accommodate only half the company. Frobisher himself, with some accompanying ships, thrust more deeply westwards into the Strait, which he was confident was the highway to China. To his right was a continuous coastline. Ahead, he thought, was open sea. All the time, he kept a sharp look-out for an exit, somewhere in the shore lying to the north, which, by his reckoning, should take them back to his own 'strait' and the island where the 'ore' lay.

For a time he was tempted by the thought that he might sail on in the search for an explanation of a phenomenon that interested him greatly. He had noticed that in this channel the flood tide ran three hours to the ebb tide's one. This suggested to him that a vast sea lay somewhere to the west. It was an alluring thought. But, in the end, he abandoned the quest. Turning about, he made his way out of the Mistaken Strait, as he called it, against strong headwinds and a roaring rip tide. At one point in his journey there was no more than six inches between the ship's bottom and a reef. But prayers went up – 'Lord now help or never' – and were answered. By 24 July, Frobisher's storm-tossed flock gathered together in shelter.

One ship, the *Buss Emmanuel*, had suffered so much from the battering of the sea that she could only be kept afloat by 250 strokes of the pump per hour. Among the crews, murmurings – prelude to mutiny – were heard. Frobisher's stubbornness was criticized. Seamen were heard to say that they would rather be hanged in England for mutiny than fall a prey to death. Frobisher ignored this craven talk. He was going back to Countess of Warwick Sound where the 'ore' was waiting to be dug out. Failing in that, he would load all the ships' guns and, after a last salvo, burn the Queen's ships which were in his charge and himself with them! Rather that than have them become a prey or spectacle to the Eskimos, 'those base, bloody and man-eating people'. This desperate course did not prove necessary.

At last, after terrible hardships in gales, with snow lying a foot deep on the hatches and wetting the sailors to the skin so that a man needed five or six changes of clothes to keep dry – at last, on 30 July the fleet arrived at Countess of Warwick Sound.

There they found two of their consorts from whom they had been separated by the weather. And there the chaplain Master Wolfall held a service of thanksgiving. He was a brave and manly Christian who had left a pleasant parish, a wife and children, to be with his fellow-countrymen in these dangers. The two ships that had been separated from the flagship had marvels and alarms of their own to describe – ice so closely packed about them that men could walk from one ship to the other, bergs rising as high as 1200 feet out of the water and measuring half a mile round, rivers of fresh water running through the salt sea. All the wonders of the northern ocean.

Now the miners set to work digging for ore, while everyone else – the gentlemen in the lead – helped to load the ships one after another. They had arrived late and they left for home after no more than a month's stay. Frobisher's original plan had been to leave three ships and a hundred volunteers until next season. But when a council was held, protesting voices were raised. They had seen what the Arctic could do in summer. What would it be like in winter? In spite of this, a hundred volunteers were found ready to face the ordeal of a season in the snow. Promising reports of a new discovery of gold ore were heard. But, in the end, caution prevailed and the order to depart was given.

Already the ice was forming so thickly at night that they could hardly row their boats through it. They built a little house on Countess of Warwick's Island which they decorated with pins, laces, combs, mirrors, dolls and other toys which might persuade the 'brutish and uncivil' Eskimos to be more friendly to the next party of English visiting their shores. Master Wolfall preached a godly sermon and celebrated communion on the island. Then they were ready to go home, for the frost was growing more severe every day and, almost as serious, liquor was running short in the fleet, owing to untimely leakages in the barrels. They weighed anchor and set sail, taking with them memories of hardships and escapes, leaving behind the trenches which the miners had dug and which can still be seen.

After a voyage home as unpleasant as the outward passage had been, the battered ships returned one by one and re-assembled when the English coast hove into sight. It was just a month since they had weighed anchor. They arrived home between 24 September and 1 October, having lost 40 men by illness or exposure. It seemed that they had also discovered a new island never heard of before and never seen since. As it was sighted by the *Buss Emmanuel*, a vessel from Bridgwater, it was named the 'Island of Buss' and, such being the power of men to believe what they want to believe, Buss was depicted on mariners' maps for a century or more. To cartographers it came as a blessing, for it helped to fill an empty stretch of sea. Ever since then, it has been assumed that 'Buss' was a figment of the sailors' imagination. There is a possibility, however, that it existed in some form, thrown up by volcanic disturbance on the seabed as islands have been created more than once in those waters.

And now came the bitter dawn of disenchantment. The 'ore' of which the ships had brought back 1,000 tons to add to the 200 tons that had arrived a year before, was found to be worthless and, eventually, was used as road metal. The speculators had been deceived by dishonest assayers and all the money, £20,000, put up or promised by them had been lost. Frobisher's reputation, high at the moment of return, now slumped.

43

Ruined, he appealed to the Queen for help or employment but she, who had given him a gold chain in his hour of false triumph, would not go further than promise him a post in the Navy Office when it fell vacant. His barque, the *Gabriel*, was sold by creditors and fetched only £80. His troubles were domestic as well as public. His wife, Isabel, wrote to Walsingham to ask for relief, claiming that Frobisher ('whom God forgive') had squandered the money left her by her first husband. In consequence, she and her children were living in Hampstead and 'ready to starve'. Frobisher's only consolation in this depressing period was a chorus of praise from indifferent poets written before the truth about the ore was known.

Michael Lok had not even this comfort. He seems to have believed more firmly in the venture than anybody and certainly he put far more money into it than he could afford. Now, as partners are liable to do in the hour of failure, he and Frobisher quarrelled violently. Lok accused the leader of the expedition of wasting supplies and allowing his officers to steal them. He had failed to send two barques to find and explore the Passage. He had threatened Captain Fenton. And so on. In all, Lok's indictment comprised twenty-three items of accusation. Frobisher replied more succinctly: Lok had cheated the Cathay Company out of £3,000 and Lord Oxford out of £1,000. He had not ventured a single groat in the voyages. In short, he was a bankrupt knave. It is said (and it is likely enough) that Frobisher backed his accusations with violence. Bankrupt poor Lok was, beyond doubt. Pursued by creditors, he was thrown into the Fleet Prison from which, three years later, he was writing to the Council pleading for release so that he could support his fifteen children.

Those other victims of evil fortune, the mariners who had toiled and suffered on the third voyage, were still unpaid by December 1578 and, with Christmas at hand, were not a little discontented with their lot. The Queen ordered her fellow-adventurers to pay the men what they were due and this was done, with what reluctance can be imagined. Frobisher? He went back to his old trade of piracy in which he did well enough by 1581 to have £300 to risk in an expedition to Cathay by way of the Cape of Good Hope. At first, it was intended that this new expedition should be under his command and that, while giving priority to trade, it should seek in Asia for clues to the North-west Passage. Four ships were ear-marked in 1582 for the project and an imposing array of capitalists (eight peers leading the list) promised finance. Sir Francis Drake, who had recently returned from his voyage of circumnavigation and was now the most famous and, certainly, the wealthiest of English mariners, was put down for £700. This

44

sum was surpassed only by the contribution of the Earl of Leicester. In a letter to Leicester, Drake offered to supply Frobisher with experienced seamen who had served recently in his own ship's company plus 1,000 marks in cash although, he said, this would strain his credit. If Frobisher needed a ship, Drake had one available of 100 tons burden. Or he could supply a new little barque and two pinnaces. In either case, he would risk £1,000 of his own money on preparing and victualling the ships. However, the command of the expedition was taken from Frobisher and given to Edward Fenton, who made a botch of the business.

And so, in frustration and some ill-feeling, ended Frobisher's three-fold attempt to discover the North-west Passage. He had found, but failed to probe, a 'strait' which was in truth no more than a long inlet on the coast of Baffin Land. He had found, but again failed to probe, a strait – the 'Mistaken Strait' – which would have led him into that delusive expanse of water later called Hudson's Bay, which was to cheat so many future explorers. He had encountered the Eskimos and had maltreated them shamefully. He had found 'gold' and it had turned out to be worthless. But the deluding glitter of the marcasite – if that is what it was – had lasted long enough to inflame the greed of the capitalists and the sailors. And it had diverted attention from the Search.

Frobisher had, however, come to be recognized as the greatest living authority on the Arctic. The records of his Arctic voyages were translated into Spanish, although the Privy Council banned their export to Spain. Rivals must not share the fruits of English voyages. When he went to Copenhagen with an English embassy to present the Danish King, Frederik II, with the Order of the Garter, the King, who regarded Greenland as part of his dominions, listened with respect to the report of the famous explorer. It is even said that he asked Queen Elizabeth's permission to take Frobisher into his service. If that is so, nothing came of it.

The search for the North-west route to Cathay became the task of other men, and there was no lack of eager searchers. They could be found talking volubly in the quayside taverns of England, quoting learnedly from ancient authorities and pointing confidently to maps which showed, as did George Best's map in his *The Discourse* of 1578, that Frobisher's Strait ran into the Gulf of Anian which opened into the Pacific! For in those days the maps were often as enticing and as false as the ore that poor, disappointed, hot-tempered Frobisher brought home from Baffin Land. He thought constantly about exploring and colonizing America and even published a poem on the subject, although it is unlikely that he wrote it:

> A pleasant air, a sweet and fertile soil,
> A certain gain, a never dying praise;
> A easy passage void of loathsome toil
> Found out by some, and known to me the ways.

But never again did he go out to look for Cathay by a new way or the old way either.

However, he was not entirely in eclipse. He went as Drake's second-in-command in the West Indies Raid in 1585, in which he was assigned the dangerous task of neutralizing the Spanish fort at Cartagena. This he duly did. Three years later, in the fight against the Armada, he was given command of the biggest galleon in the English fleet, the *Triumph*. In that battle, Frobisher covered himself with glory by beating off the attack of four Spanish galleasses at a time when the English ships could not come to his help. It was a sea action quite in keeping with his tough, defiant character and, after it, he was knighted. Frobisher's death was that of a fighting sailor. He was wounded in 1591 at the head of a storming party at Crozon, near Brest, where the Spaniards had established a fort which they defended with fanatical courage against a large Anglo-French force, resisting until only eleven men were left alive out of four hundred. Frobisher was brought back to Plymouth and died a victim of incompetent surgeons. But so far as the North-west Passage is concerned, Frobisher's contribution ended in 1578.

The Land of Desolation

'I hope that now, being taught by their manifold losses, our men will take a more godly course.'

Richard Hakluyt

Seven years after Frobisher's third voyage to the North-west, the search for the Passage was taken up once more. This time the leader of the exploring fleet was a navigator from Devon named John Davis, son of a yeoman farmer. Up till that time Davis had escaped the limelight to a degree unusual in Elizabethan sailors, which probably means he had not been involved in any outstanding act of piracy or violence. After an unobtrusive life at sea, he had, seemingly, returned in 1579 to the farm in which he was born at Sandridge Barton on the Dart. Davis was at that time about 30 years old. In Devon, an important event befell him: he encountered Adrian Gilbert, his neighbour, whose brother was Sir Humphrey Gilbert and whose half-brother was Sir Walter Raleigh. The Gilberts, living in a beautiful house at Compton, were thus the most distinguished family in the district. They were grandees in the county and Walter Raleigh was on the brink of his meteoric and, finally, disastrous career at court. More exciting to Davis, the Gilberts were a power-house of ideas, for exploration, colonizing, education, adventure of every kind by land and sea – especially by sea. A year before John Davis returned to Devon, Sir Humphrey Gilbert had at last badgered the Queen into allowing him to plant a colony at the mouth of the St Lawrence anywhere between Labrador and Florida.

The fleet with which Gilbert proposed to accomplish this enterprise was quite a substantial one. Six ships sailed under his command with a crew of 365; a second flotilla, also of six ships, was under the command of Henry Knollys. But the two divisions were soon back in Dartmouth once more, violent disagreements having broken out between the commanders. Gilbert complained bitterly of Knollys' outrageous behaviour. Sir Humphrey was a man of abrupt opinions and tempestuous words. He had already been denounced in the House of Commons as a 'flatterer, a liar and a naughty man', and when he sought to answer those charges the House had refused to hear him. He was, in short, a man difficult to get on with.

Gilbert's second and fatal voyage began in 1583. By that time, his brother Adrian was deep in discussions with John Davis upon a matter which interested them vastly: the quest for the North-west Passage in which Martin Frobisher had failed but had, as they thought, nearly succeeded. While the preparations for Humphrey Gilbert's second expedition were being made, one Londoner, confident that he was seeking – and would find – the North-west Passage, said that he hoped to see the day when a letter written in London on May 1 would reach China by midsummer. Humphrey was an enthusiastic propagandist for the north route to Cathay. But now his purpose in sailing was a different one: he was going to found an English colony in the New World. On that voyage he lost his life when, in a storm, the pinnace *Squirrel*, went down with him on board. Sir Humphrey had refused to leave the ten-ton cockleshell for a larger vessel, saying with that arrogance which made so many men of his era such natural leaders, 'I will not forsake my little company going homeward.' He had sat aft with an open book in his hand calling out to a companion vessel each time it came within earshot, 'We are as near to heaven by sea as by land.' When midnight came, the pinnace was overwhelmed by the sea. So Sir Humphrey died, literate, dauntless, master of a phrase and a gesture, ill-tempered, and in the words of Edward Hayes, captain of one of the ships that survived, 'resolute in Jesus Christ'. He had left behind him a most elaborate polemic urging that the North-west Passage could and should be found. The venture was now taken up by his brother, Adrian.

One day in 1582, Adrian Gilbert took John Davis and Dr Dee, the great geographical theorist and mystagogue, to meet Sir Francis Walsingham. In a long secret discussion, talk opened about the North-west Strait which appeared to Dee one of the two probable channels to Cathay most worth investigating. The other was the route directly over the Pole. John Davis was present because Mr William Sanderson, an influential financier in the City who was fascinated by exploration, had said that he was the best man available to be the leader of the search if it were undertaken.

More important, Sanderson ('born a gent, bred a merchant adventurer') was prepared to back his opinion with his purse; he became the biggest shareholder in the enterprise in which a good deal of West Country money was also invested. The Queen gave a charter to Adrian Gilbert of Sandridge in the County of Devon, gentleman, and on 7 June 1585 John Davis sailed out of Dartmouth with two small ships, the *Sunshine*, of 50 tons and the *Moonshine* of 35. There were 24 men aboard, four of whom, James Cole, Francis Ridley, John Russell and Robert Cornish, were musicians. The ships had, to begin with, bad luck with the weather; they were driven back to the Isles of Scilly and kept there for twelve days by headwinds. Davis, a professional navigator if ever there was one, spent the time profitably by making an exact chart of the islands for the use of sailors who might come after him. When at length the ships set off westwards again in a calm sea and with a favouring wind, they fell in with a school of porpoises with which they had varying luck. The bigger fish carries away their tackle so they lost 'fish, irons, pastime and all'. Davis fought one with pike and boat-hook but in the end gave up, defeated. On 19 July the crews ran into a furious current which carried them northwards into calmer seas. There was a dense fog in which they heard a roaring noise which they thought must come from waves breaking on a shore that they could not see.

Alarmed by this, Davis ordered out the ship's boat of the *Moonshine* to take soundings. No bottom at 300 fathoms! In the *Sunshine*, he advanced towards the noise with infinite caution. The two ships kept in touch with one another by firing a musket at every glass (half-hour). Soon they were surrounded by ice floes; they realized, then, what caused the noise that had alarmed them. It had come from the floes grinding against one another. Before nightfall, the *Sunshine*, which had become separated from the *Moonshine*, rejoined its consort. By that time the deck was laden with ice which melted into excellent fresh water. The ships were now somewhere off the south coast of Greenland which, when first they glimpsed it like a white stripe showing above the fog, appalled them by its gloom. Disagreeably impressed by 'the loathsome view of the shore and irksome noise of the ice', Davis named it the Land of Desolation. They cruised along this coast without being able to reach the shore. For between it and them was an impenetrable barrier of ice. Five days after their first sight of land, they took their course to the North-west hoping in God's mercy to find 'our desired passage'. Four days later, they sighted land to the north-east. The air was mild, the sea free from ice. There were many islands all about them. A party which went ashore on one of these in search of water and wood found traces of human life – a shoe, sewn leather, a piece of fur. When Davis and two companions climbed to the summit of a high rock, they were seen by the local people who made lamentable outcries like the howling of wolves. The English shouted in reply and brought their four musicians from the ship to play while the sailors danced gaily on the rocks and made gestures of friendship to the Eskimos. There was no immediate response. The Eskimos may have remembered Frobisher's unmannerly behaviour a few years earlier. Then, after a time, ten canoes came out from neighbouring islands and two of these paddled closely enough to the rocks to exchange words with the English.

John Ellis, the master of the *Moonshine*, had the idea that by striking his breast and then pointing to the sun he would suggest the idea of friendship to the Eskimos. In this he had some success, for one of them ventured ashore. At that, the band played once more, the sailors began dancing once more and after that it was nightfall. Then the English, with friendly gestures of farewell, rowed back to their ships, confident that their diplomacy was succeeding.

Sure enough, next morning, thirty-seven kayaks came close to the English ships. An Eskimo, climbing a rock, displayed a sealskin; another beat an instrument like a timbrel. The English rowed ashore and there was a touching scene of fraternization in which John James, who was on the passenger list of the *Sunshine* and was Mr Sanderson's nephew (and, in all likelihood, his representative on the voyage), shook hands with one of the Eskimos. After that, a brisk barter took place, in the course of which the visitors bought five kayaks, and all the clothes the Eskimos were wearing whether sealskin or birds' skins, buskins, hose, gloves, everything – all of them beautifully made garments, for the Eskimo women were skilful with the needle. John James concluded that they were honest, guileless people although much in need of enlightenment as idolaters who worshipped the sun.

The explorers observed that the sea had brought a reasonable amount of driftwood to the shore and marvelled at the profusion of seals to be seen. The Eskimos promised to go inland and fetch more skins but the wind turned favourable and Davis would not wait. The ships set off to the north-west and, a week later, sighted land free from ice. They had crossed the Davis Strait and were on the coast of Baffin Land. To the north was a headland they called Cape Dyer, to the south another which they named Cape Walsingham. Between the two was Exeter Sound. They had made their landfall on the American coast about three hundred miles north of Frobisher's 'strait'.

They anchored in Totnes Bay as they called it, and spent a day or two hunting polar bears, which fought back gallantly and proved very hard to kill. About this time, the captain became aware of something disagreeable: the crew were murmuring: they had not enough to eat, not enough to drink. Rations were accordingly increased. Each mess of five men got four pounds of bread a day, twelve quarts of beer and six Newfoundland fish. Five days after arriving off Baffin Land they came, as they thought, to the southernmost point of the coast in that region which Davis named The Cape of God's Mercy. This, he thought, must surely stand at the entrance to the strait they had come to find. But in this he was mistaken. They were, in fact, in the long fjord which Davis named Cumberland Sound. They sailed another 180 miles to the north-west, finding the water of the Sound the same colour and quality as that of the ocean. And deep – deeper all the way as they advanced – 330 fathoms and no bottom! It must surely mean that they were approaching some vast body of water. Soon they had other evidence, equally cheering. They observed a school of whales which must certainly, as they thought, have come from the west for they had seen no whales to the east. And this strong tidal current setting from the south-west – what could it mean save that there was an open sea somewhere to the west? There is always something to persuade hopeful seekers that they are about to find what they have sought. If only they had time to stay and explore further to the west! But it was already 20 August. The season was late. And, ominously, the wind had swung round to the north-west. If they stayed longer, the ice might close in on them before the wind turned favourable again. As prudent seamen, they resolved to take the first fair wind for home. It came on 24 August and a month later they arrived in Dartmouth. Thereupon, Davis reported optimistically to Walsingham. He had found an isle of very great quantity, not in any globe or map described, yielding a sufficient trade of fur and leather. The North-west passage, he wrote, was 'a matter nothing doubtful' but to be passed at any time, 'the sea navigable, void of ice, the air tolerable and the water very deep.'

In the early summer of next year (7 May 1586) Davis set out once more, this time with a somewhat larger flotilla, four ships in all. The *Sunshine* and the *Moonshine* sailed again, in company with a ten-ton pinnace named the *North Star*. The captain flew his flag in the *Mermaid*, a ship of 120 tons, twice as big as the *Sunshine*. In the last days of June, after a stormy crossing, the ships arrived off the Greenland coast. Davis was delighted to see that there was no ice in the sea and little snow on the land. He ordered the carpenters to assemble a pinnace which he had stored in sections in the hold of the *Mermaid*. He meant to use it in the search for the Passage. Very soon, the Eskimos gathered in their kayaks, cheerfully greeting sailors whom they recognized from the year before. Davis and some business friends went ashore, giving away knives and refusing to take anything in return. Next day there was a constant stream of Eskimos bringing skins and fish to the ships.

While this was going on, Davis went in search of the native village. He did not find it. The Eskimos, who had already had some experience of these strange, blond invaders from the south, prudently kept their tents out of sight of the coast. Davis, who was intensely curious about the people, saw how they made fire by twirling a round stick between their hands. He noted that in a jumping competition, the English won, but that the Eskimos were the better wrestlers. The master of the *Mermaid*, searching for firewood, came on a grave with several bodies in it, covered with seal-skins. On top, a cross was laid. It was presumably a relic of the time when Christianity had been brought to that desolate region by Norsemen. Either the faith had died or the believers had been exterminated. The cross remained, however, a symbol with a meaning which had been forgotten or, at best, only half-remembered.

For, there could be no doubt about it, the Eskimos were idolaters and much given to witchcraft although, 'to small purpose, thanks be to God', as Davis said. Suspecting that a fire which the Eskimos had lit was for the purpose of sacrifice, he ordered one of the crew to stamp out the flames and kick the ashes into the sea. After this blow struck for Christianity, there was a marked deterioration in the relations between the two communities. Davis had soon to complain of an outbreak of pilfering by 'these miscreants'. In his absence, the ships were bombarded by slung stones, weighing as much as half a pound. When an anchor was stolen, Davis decided that the time had come to take reprisals. He captured an Eskimo and offered to release him as soon as the anchor was restored. But before that could happen the wind changed, with the result that the Eskimo was carried off on the ship. There he lived in the hold where Davis kept his supply of dry fish. He was soon, or so it seemed, reconciled to his fate and became a pleasant companion on the voyage.

On 17 July, after sailing further to the north in Davis Strait, the explorers came to a vast barrier of ice stretching across the ship's path as far as could be seen from east to west. It was so high that they thought it must be land. For thirteen days the ships cruised along the margin of this barrier without finding a breach in it. Ice coated the ships' sails and ropes. As for the crews, their strength failed and their spirits flagged. They came to Davis in a respectful but urgent deputation begging that he should not, through over-boldness, cause their widows and fatherless children to curse him. In this situation the captain decided to let the *Mermaid* go home; she was a chartered ship, and costing the shareholders £100 a month – he himself would proceed further in the *Moonshine* with a picked crew. This involved a change-over of provisions between the two ships, a task which was duly carried out, although the men who made the transfer were much troubled by a ferocious breed of mosquitoes. Davis left on 12 August working his way south by west across Davis Strait, where he became aware of a powerful current which was carrying the ship towards the west. On 19 August, when the *Moonshine* was off the south-east tip of Baffin Land, snow began to fall. When the weather cleared next morning, Davis went ashore and climbed to the top of a hill from which he could get a better idea of the country. What he saw did not raise his spirits. Land and sea were alike dreary. All round him were islands without a sign of habitation. Davis returned to his ship and weighed anchor. Then he shaped his course further to the south, where the 'Passage may be, through God's mercy, found.'

For a week he skirted the American coast, covering about 700 miles. At one point he seems to have passed the entrance to Hudson Strait without being aware of it. Landing on the Labrador coast, the English sailors found that they were among woods of fir, pine, alder, yew and birch, a typical sub-Arctic forest teeming with game birds. They killed many partridges and pheasants with bow and arrow. At the mouth of the Hamilton Inlet, Davis, ever hopeful, thought that at last he had found the Passage but, once again, strong headwinds defeated him when he tried to explore it. A day or two later, five young sailors he had put ashore to cure codfish were ambushed by 'the brutish people of this country' and, although Davis went to their rescue with musket fire, two of the young men were killed by arrows, two were badly wounded, while one resolute young man escaped, swimming to the boat with an arrow through his arm. That night their sorrows were increased by a storm so severe that Davis was forced to unrig the ship and make ready to cut down the masts. At the peak of the gale the cable of the sheet-anchor parted, and it seemed that all was lost. They would be driven ashore to be the prey of 'these cannibals'. But in this crisis 'the mighty mercy of God' came to their rescue. The wind changed, the anchor was recovered, and the ship was moored afresh. On 11 September, Davis set course for England, reaching the West Country in the beginning of October. His Eskimo hostage had not survived the crossing.

But what of the other two vessels, the *Sunshine* and the *North Star* – which, with sixteen men aboard, Davis had sent off on a separate mission to determine whether a way to the Far East could be found by sailing over the Pole? They had separated from the main fleet when the latitude 60° was reached and the ships were somewhere to the west of Shetland. Their intention was to sail north for another twenty degrees, if this were possible. The purser of the *Sunshine*, an employee of Mr Sanderson's named Henry Morgan, kept a record of what followed. On 11 June, they sighted Iceland. There they found the people living in stone cottages. They dried their fish in the sun, after which they packed it on top of their houses. Leaving Iceland, the *Sunshine* sailed north-west until, a fortnight later, she was sailing between two solid masses of ice. After a few days of that, the ship's master, Richard Pope, deemed it prudent to turn back towards Greenland. Soon they sighted it, very high, very blue – the Land of Desolation The ship could not reach the mainland for ice, which they skirted cautiously until on 3 August they came to Gilbert's Sound on the West Coast where they had a rendezvous with Davis and the rest of the fleet.

While they were waiting for the leader of the expedition to turn up, the sailors were challenged to a series of football matches by the local Eskimos. If the English report of these international matches is to be trusted, the visitors had the best of things: 'our men did cast them down as soon as they did come to strike the ball'. But perhaps there was some mutual misunderstanding about the rules of the game. (The ball was presumably made of some sort of fish-skin bladder.) At the end of August, after a bloody fight with the Eskimos over a kayak – Eskimo darts against English arrows – they decided that they could wait no longer for Davis and sailed for home with 500 sealskins and 140 half skins aboard. On 6 October after calling at Dartmouth the *Sunshine* entered the Thames and cast anchor at Ratcliffe, below the Tower. The main part of the fleet had arrived home a few days before them.

Although the outcome of the voyage had been scarcely remarkable, Davis was irrepressibly determined to try again. He told his chief backer, William Sanderson, that he would stake his own farmhouse to see an end to the business. The Passage must be in one of four places 'or else not at all'. To Walsingham he said that he had found a sea swarming with fish. Why not combine the two ventures of exploring and fishing? Walsingham advised him to send some of the fish he had caught to Lord Burghley, a man notoriously interested in promoting the English fisheries. There was some difficulty in raising fresh capital, for the Devon merchants pulled out of the venture so that Davis was thrown back on the Court and the City of London. But eventually he set out once more to solve the riddle. It was May, 1587.

On his third probe to the north, he took two small barques one of them his old ship, the *Sunshine*, the other a Dartmouth vessel, the *Elizabeth*. He also had a clinker-built pinnace, the *Ellen*, of London. As it turned out the *Ellen*, smallest of the three, was the ship in which Davis accomplished his most noteworthy feat in Arctic exploration. The fleet ran into trouble not many days after the ships put out from Dartmouth. First, the *Sunshine* sprang a leak, which meant shifting the ballast so that the hole could be worked on above water and stopped. Then it turned out that the *Ellen*, 'like a cart drawn by oxen', could not sail against a head wind. It was taken in tow by the *Elizabeth*. The next crisis was of a different kind – mutinous talk among the crew who wanted to go fishing instead of exploring. In fishing, they pointed out, there was good money to be made. After endless conferences, they agreed to accompany Davis as far as his landfall. When the three ships arrived at the west coast of Greenland, the old uneasy relations with the Eskimos – trading, sniping, stealing – began once more. In the wake of these difficulties came a worse one. John Churchyard, pilot of the *Ellen*, came to Davis as doleful as his name. The *Ellen*, while at anchor, in harbour, needed 300 strokes of the pump an hour to keep her afloat. What could be expected of her at sea? In this crisis, Davis showed his mettle: he would rather end his life with credit, he declared, than return in infamy and disgrace. The bolder spirits who had elected to stay with him were in agreement with this brave declaration. Accordingly, the fleet divided into two; a place and time of re-assembly was agreed and the two barques went off to fish. Davis took the *Ellen*, the ship which had needed so much work at the pump to keep her afloat.* In her, he crept northwards along the west coast of Greenland for a week or more until at last he came on a spectacle of breath-taking scale and splendour. Rising sheer out of the water to a height of 850 feet were cliffs on which a multitude of seabirds nested. In honour of his patron, Davis named the place Hope Sanderson.† It was 30 June; the sun at midnight was 5 degrees above the horizon. They had reached 72°12′ North, the farthest north that Davis ever attained. Probably on that June day he had sailed nearer to the Pole than any other European navigator before him.

But he did not stay for long, and he did not attempt to go further. For by this time the wind had swung round to the north and the *Ellen* ran west-wards more than 120 miles across Davis Strait without sighting land. The

*The passage in the record is obscure but 'the good ship which we all hazard our lives in' seems to refer to the pinnace in which Davis sailed.

†More fully, 'Sanderson, his hope of a North-west Passage.'

captain spent days trying in vain to find a way round the pack ice that blocked Baffin Bay. On one occasion he thought he had found a gap with clear water beyond it. He forced the *Ellen* through it by oar, but on the far side of the gap there was no outlet into free water. Instead, Davis found himself completely beset by ice-floes and only escaped, 'by God's help', two days later. Further south, off the coast of Baffin Land, he came on a belt of warm weather and a coast free of ice. Some of the sailors went ashore, taking hounds with them in the hope of sport. But they had no luck; the dogs had lived too long on shipboard. They had eaten too much cod and were too fat for the business of catching Arctic fox.

Resuming his way to the south, Davis passed the entrances to Cumberland Sound, Frobisher Bay and 'a very great gulf, the water whirling and weaving as if it were the meeting of the tides ... We saw the sea falling down into a gulf with a mighty overfall and moving with divers circular motions like whirlpools in such sort as forcible streams pass through the arches of bridges.' This was something quite extraordinary which suggested that it had an even more exciting explanation somewhere further west. It was, in fact, the entrance to Hudson Strait, but at that point in the voyage, with the Arctic summer near to its close, Davis could not spend time exploring it. His main concern was to avoid the ice pack, to collect the rest of his fleet and make for home. Searching the Labrador coast for the consorts he had left to fish there, he found no sign of ships, only a 'great sea, free, large, very salt and blue and of an unsearchable depth.' It was time to leave.

He was satisfied that he had established the fact that the 'Passage' was free towards the North. On another voyage, in another year, the matter could be put to the proof. From Sandridge he wrote to Mr Sanderson that he had reached 73 degrees north, finding the sea open and forty leagues (120 miles) between land and land. 'The Passage is most probable, the execution easy.' But by the time he arrived in Dartmouth it was 15 September 1587 and next year, English seamen had something to do more urgent than an exploration of the Arctic seaways. It was the year of 'the Spanish Fleet', the Armada, against which Davis sailed in the *Black Dog*, a small armed merchantman under the command of the Lord Admiral. And after that, Sir Francis Walsingham died and with him died one of the chief impulses towards northern exploration.

The upshot was that Davis never sailed to the Arctic again. But, by the careful observations he had recorded and by his book on the North-west Passage, *The World's Hydrographical Description*, he kept alive English interest in the Far North. In addition, the nautical instruments he designed, the backstaff and the quadrant, put the English science of navigation ahead of the rest of the world. It was a technical leadership of high importance. Davis had missed the chance of exploring Hudson Strait and thus was saved from discovering Hudson Bay, that vast cul-de-sac which he would certainly have mistaken for the Pacific. At the northernmost point of his third voyage he had approached the threshold of Lancaster Sound, at the north of Baffin Bay, which later turned out to be the beginning of the tortuous, ice-infested channel by which, one day, a ship would complete the crossing from one ocean to the other. But although Davis did not find the route himself, he was sure that one day it was to be found. After his three Arctic cruises, he retired from the quest, a baffled but undiscouraged man convinced still that the North-west Passage was something more than a figment of the imagination of mapmakers and theorists. That it was there in the North, behind the fogs and the banks of ice, waiting to be found and threaded by some lucky captain in a year when the Arctic summer was unusually benign – of that Davis was sure. But he would not be that captain.

After the Armada affair, John Davis and a ship of his, the *Desire*, came under the command of Captain Cavendish, who had just sailed round the world. As Davis described it, Cavendish's plan was to round South America and come back to England by way of the North Atlantic. This would have involved searching for the Pacific entrance to the North-west Passage. The expedition was a tragic failure. Attempting to thread Magellan Strait, the *Desire* ran into a series of violent gales which left her with only one anchor which had only one fluke. Three times the ship reached the Pacific and three times was driven back. At last, it crawled back into the Strait, defeated by the storm. The gale was one danger; starvation was another. Davis made salt by evaporating salt water and dried 14,000 penguins for food on the homeward run. Rations were down to 5 oz. of meal a week, 3 spoonsful of oil a day and 5 penguins a week for every four men. An epidemic of scurvy swept the ship and all the crew died but sixteen men. Of those sixteen only five were able to move. In the final stages of that frightful voyage, the *Desire* was worked by Davis, the ship's master, two men and a boy, and before long Davis and the master were too weak to go aloft. Topsails and spritsail were blown away. Davis and the master took turns at the wheel, the only two men aboard capable of handling a ship at sea. Disease was only one item in the tale of disaster. Nine of the crew had deserted and were killed by Indians; later thirteen men were killed on the Brazilian coast. On 11 June 1593 the *Desire*, with her crew of living skeletons, reached Berehaven in Bantry Bay at the end of a nightmare voyage which had lasted 22 months. She had set out with a crew of seventy-six; she returned with fourteen.

But the troubles of the sorely tried mariner were not over. Cavendish accused him of desertion. Davis defended himself effectively by pointing out that Cavendish had returned to England months before he did. Another trouble was of a more personal nature. When he hurried from Berehaven to Padstow by fishing boat, Davis found that in his absence, his well-connected wife, Faith, had taken a lover, a dissolute man named Milbourne who was accused of coining. Milbourne trumped up a charge against Davis and had him thrown into prison, a misfortune from which he was saved only by the powerful influence of Sir Walter Raleigh. In later life Davis, a scholarly but practical sailor, seems to have served as a ship's master under Raleigh in the Cadiz Raid in which the young Earl of Essex won so much glory. Then he was employed for a time by the Dutch. In 1605, at a time when he was acting as pilot in the *Tiger*, a ship commanded by Sir Edward Michelborne, they fell in with Japanese pirates at Bintang, east of Singapore. When the Japanese made a treacherous attempt to seize the ship, Davis fought the Japanese swordsmen and was slashed to death.

So died, thousands of miles from the chilly scenes of his greatest adventure, a sailor who had most faithfully served in the quest for the Northwest Passage. Davis is a man who, in spite of his professional ability, which was of the highest order, and his courage, which was amply proved, has somehow failed to leave his imprint deep on the history of the time. Perhaps he had no glamour; certainly he had not much luck. But he helped to keep alive the legend of the Passage and, after his death, another and even unluckier navigator followed in his wake, went more deeply into the labyrinth of the North and met his death in seeking the answer to the great riddle. Davis has not been forgotten by fame: his name is prominent in every map of the Arctic.

In April 1596 a chance encounter in Venice gave new life to the controversy. Michael Lok, the elder, the man who had lost so much money as a backer of Frobisher's voyages, was on a business visit there when he met John Douglas, an English seaman who was about to pilot a Venetian ship to England. In the course of conversation, Douglas mentioned to Lok that he had met a Greek in Florence who had an interesting story to tell. Lok listened and said that he would be glad to meet this Greek, and Douglas accordingly brought the two men together. The Greek was known as Juan de Fuca but it seems that his name was originally Apostolos Valerianos. He had been born on Cephalonia sixty years before and had been at sea all his life. Homeward bound with a rich cargo in a ship named the *Santa Anna*, he had been intercepted off Cape California by Captain Cavendish, who had robbed him of property worth 60,000 ducats. This was not, however, the part of the elderly Greek's story that was of most interest to Lok.

In 1591, it seemed, he had served as pilot with three small ships which the Viceroy of Mexico had sent out to find the Strait of Anian and fortify it against the English. For the English were known to be hard at work probing from the eastern side and they might at any moment burst on the Pacific scene. The Spanish expedition was, however, abandoned. The captain turned out to be a sodomist, the crew mutinied and the ships turned back to Mexico. In the following year the Viceroy sent out Fuca again with a caravel and a pinnace. He sailed as far north as the 47th parallel, as he told Lok, that is, to the south tip of Vancouver Island. There he found an inlet of the sea 90 or 120 miles wide at the entrance, which was marked by a high pinnacle of rock, like a pillar. The land trended north north-east. For twenty days, said the Greek, he sailed into this gulf, finding it grew wider as he went on. He went ashore and met people dressed in skins. The soil was fruitful. Coming to the conclusion that he had reached the 'North Sea' (the Atlantic) he sailed back and reported at Acapulco. There disappointment awaited him. No reward came to him from the Mexican authorities, who were either sceptical of his claims or, as he thought, no longer interested in the project. It seemed that the latest news from Spain indicated that the English had lost their enthusiasm for the Passage. Fuca was cold-shouldered by the Viceroy.

This was the situation at the time the Greek poured out his story to the English merchant as they talked beside the Lagoon of Venice. Fuca was ready to go to England and tell the Queen that, if she would lend him a ship of forty tons and a pinnace, he would sail through the Strait of Anian. It would take him no more than thirty days. Incidentally, he would claim from the English courts the 60,000 ducats Captain Cavendish had stolen from him. To this promising scheme there were only two obstacles. Fuca had no money. And Lok, pending the successful issue of the commercial dispute that had brought him to Venice, had no money either. Lok wrote to London for an advance of funds. But in the City, hearts were stony and imagination cold to his pleas. Fuca went back to his native island of Cephalonia where, before Lok had scraped enough cash together to send him to England, he died. But the Greek pilot's story, spun on a spring day in that fairy city, had not been told in vain. It lived on to add its layer of legend to the mythology of the Age of Discovery. In due course, Fuca was followed by other romancers. In Madrid, Lorenzo Ferrer Maldonado told an exciting story of how he had sailed through the Strait of Anian in 1588. It was fifteen leagues long, he said, and a quarter of a league wide and it had six turnings in it. In 1626 Father Salmeron reported that he had met a foreign pilot named Moreno who had sailed with Francis Drake through the Strait from east to west. It was a time when the taverns of Europe were haunted by bronzed mariners with glittering eyes and beguiling tongues who for a drink or a ducat would tell stories of voyages as marvellous as any of Ulysses or Sinbad. These imposters helped to keep alive the faith which would yet send many new dupes and martyrs to adventure and, sometimes, death.

In May 1602 Captain George Weymouth sailed from the Thames with two fly-boats, the *Discovery* and the *Godspeed*, on a mission which the Muscovy and the Turkey Companies were financing to find the North-west Passage. Weymouth would be given £500 if he succeeded and £100 if he failed. He carried letters from the Queen to the Emperor of Cathay. All went uneventfully apart from the expected hardships of frost and fog and the 'loathsome noise' of ice which they met in Frobisher Bay. Then on 19 July, while Weymouth was asleep, the crew mutinied and bore up the helm for England. What was more, they drew up in writing an explanation of their action which all of them signed.

Next day Weymouth called them to his cabin to state their case before himself, the ship's preacher, Master John Cartwright, and the ship's master, William Colbourn. The mutineers said that while no doubt they might winter in safety, it would be May before they were free of the ice again. It was, they thought, more sensible to sail back to England with the certainty of returning to these latitudes, better furnished with men and victuals, by the first of May. However, if Weymouth could find a channel further south, they would be glad to accompany him. Weymouth asked them who bore up the helm? They told him, 'One and all'. He ordered the leaders to be punished severely, but relented on the entreaties of the preacher and the master. After that, the two ships sailed shamefacedly home and sighted Land's End in September.

Needless to say the backers of the expedition, who had put £3,000 into it, were highly displeased with its total failure. But Weymouth put up such a convincing case for a new attempt that the blame for the mutiny was laid at the preacher's door. He was ordered to surrender the gown which he had been given for his expected audience with the Emperor of Cathay. Weymouth, however, was not sent out again on the quest. The two ships were put up for sale and the central figure of the next and tragic chapter in the story of the North-west Passage was a professional sailor named Henry Hudson.

The River of the Steep Cliffs

'For a transitory enchanted moment man must have held his breath in the presence of this continent, compelled into an aesthetic contemplation he neither understood nor desired, face to face for the last time in history with something commensurate to his capacity for wonder.'

F. Scott Fitzgerald, The Great Gatsby

Henry Hudson, who was probably born about 1570, the son of a London alderman, is first heard of in 1607 when he was appointed to command the *Hopeful* to 'discover the Pole'. He and his crew, twelve men in all, took communion with the 'other parishioners of St Ethelburga's Church' in Bishopsgate, London, a few days before setting out on their voyage. The twelfth man was Hudson's son, John, a boy of sixteen. Their purpose was to reach the Spice Islands by sailing due north. The task proved to be a little more difficult than was expected.

The idea was popular among the experts that in the region of the Pole the climate grew suddenly milder. Peter Plancius, for example, a Calvinist divine living in Amsterdam, and a passionate geographer, argued that, as the sun shone for five months continuously at the Pole, it was only reasonable that the weather should be warm. One had only to find a way through the intervening ice belt and, sooner or later, the magic perfumed isles of the East would show up on the southern horizon. As it turned out, however, there were complications on which Plancius had not reckoned.

After weighing anchor at Gravesend on 1 May, the *Hopeful* made its way slowly northwards, delayed by adverse winds, so that it was 43 days after leaving the Thames before the sailors saw through the fog a glimpse of land ahead. Greenland! The sails froze. The shrouds froze. The wind had so much strength that they were hard put to it to keep a sail in place. Through weather that was an unfriendly mixture of fog, rain and wind, they bore obstinately northwards, but all the time they were edged towards the east by the presence of the ice. On 28 June they arrived at Prince Charles Island, from which they groped their way towards Spitzbergen, where a powerful current swept them to the south. Hudson, a good observer, noticed that the sea, which had been a green colour on 6 July, was black on the next day and was therefore, in all likelihood, free from ice. On 11 July they were sailing through blue sea when suddenly it changed colour once more and turned green. Praying God to direct him, Hudson steered to the north for 30 miles. He was now approaching the group of islands which the Dutch called Newland. The sea was calm all of a sudden, with the sun setting on the ice, a great source of danger. It was foggy. Then deliverance came. A wind sprang up. The sky cleared and, from the crow's nest, William Collins, the bosun, called out 'Land ho'. In recognition of this, Hudson named the island they had come to Collins Cape.

Hudson's hope had been that if he could not find a way over the Pole he could at least sail west about round the north of Greenland and return to England by way of Davis Strait. He found he could do neither. There was an unbroken wall of ice between Greenland and Spitzbergen and there was no free sea between land and ice. On one occasion, the ship was in mortal danger, when, in dense fog, the sea was driving it westwards to the grinding noise of ice, ominous and growing louder. Hudson lowered the boat to tow the ship out of danger – a slim chance, it seemed. Then, in the nick of time, a favouring 'small gale' sprang up – 'God give us thankful hearts for so great deliverance.' Towards the end of July, Hudson decided that he had had enough of this flirtation with fog and ice. He turned homewards, arriving at Tilbury on 15 September 1607. He was by no means discouraged by his experience.

Hudson's second voyage, on which he sailed from St Katherine's on the Thames on 22 April of the following year, had for its purpose the discovery of a passage to China by the north-east, that is to say round the north of Asia. This had been attempted half a century before and the outcome had been a grisly tragedy.

Sir Hugh Willoughby had gone out in the *Bona Esperanza* and wintered on the coast of Lapland. When Sir Hugh failed to come back, the influential Muscovy Company, which had organized the expedition, sent a ship to look for him. What the search party found was graphically described by the Venetian Ambassador in a dispatch (1555) to his masters: ' . . . on the Muscovite coast with the men on board all frozen; the mariners now returned from the second voyage do relate strange things about the mode in which they were frozen, having found some of them seated in the act of writing, pen still in hand, and the paper before them, others at tables, platters in hand and spoon in mouth, and others in various postures like statues.' Whether true or improved by the imagination of the sailors, the story was alarming enough to discourage further English voyages in that direction for nearly thirty years.

The matter was not likely to die of neglect, however, because important issues of commercial policy were involved. The Muscovy Company's monopoly of trade with the White Sea was threatened by Dutch shippers who were pushing eastwards along the Siberian coast towards the River Ob beyond which, as it was believed, the sea was warm and the way to China open. To put the matter to the test, William Barents went out in company with Jacob van Heemskerk. They, too, observed how the sea could change its colour within a matter of a few miles from being as green as grass to a perfect azure like the skies. They decided that this change was associated with the presence or absence of ice. Dr Scoresby, who sailed these waters in the nineteenth century, noticed the same thing and came to a different conclusion. 'The colour of the sea varies from ultramarine to olive green, and from the most pure transparency to striking opacity. These appearances are not transitory but permanent, depending not on the state of the weather, but on the quality of the water.' The presence or otherwise of ice had nothing to do with it, he decided.

In Novaya Zemlya, Barents and his men built a wooden house* and spent the winter in a cold almost beyond endurance and suffering terribly from scurvy. Barents died on the way home. But, by that time, the Dutch were established in Archangel and the English were aware of a challenge to their trade with Russia. They knew that, at sea, the Dutch were formidable. After all, it was one of their admirals who captured some years later the supreme prize of the age, the dream of every freebooter on the seven seas, the Spanish treasure fleet on its way home from the West Indies. And it was another Dutch seamen who destroyed a Spanish fleet at Gibraltar. For the ruthless commercial business of that age, the Dutch East Indies Company commanded resources far exceeding those of the Muscovy Company. It owned forty ships, six hundred guns; it had 5,000 sailors on the pay roll. It was, in effect, a great maritime power. Plainly, it was essential for England to fight back against so able and energetic a rival.

In spite of the fact that Hudson's first voyage had ended in failure, he was at once sent to sea again, with instructions to seek a way to Cathay by

*Found 275 years later by a Norwegian, Elling Carlsen.

the north coast of Asia. On his return, he reported many remarkable happenings that had occurred during the voyage, including an occasion when two mermaids were seen by two of the crew. One of these creatures swam 'close to the ship's side, looking earnestly on the men, long hair hanging down behind, her skin very white, her tail speckled like a mackerel'. He reached Novaya Zemlya where, after a brief reconnaissance, he decided that there was no possibility of a passage to China by sailing east. There was nothing to do but return. Hudson dropped anchor at Gravesend on 26 August 1608, having been away just four months.

Already he had in mind the conception of a new and different voyage of exploration: to find and probe that passage to the north-west where John Davis on his third voyage had noticed 'the furious overfall', a current running at six knots. This strange and exciting phenomenon had been observed at the entrance to what is now called Hudson Strait. Brooding over this during the long summer days in the northern seas, Hudson became convinced that Davis had missed a wonderful opportunity. He thought, there and then, of sailing west and searching where Davis had turned back. But the wind was against him. And perhaps the crew were restive. For there is a puzzling sentence in Hudson's account of those days at sea. 'I gave my company a certificate under my hand, of my free and willing return, without persuasion or force of any one or more of them . . . ' It is a strange remark which suggests the very thing that Hudson is denying: that the crew had forced him to return – and had also forced him to give them a clean bill.

Hudson returned at a moment when English businessmen had momentarily lost their interest in exploration. Not so the Dutch. On the contrary, they were keener than ever. At all times there was a prize of 2,500 florins open in Amsterdam for the first captain to find the North Passage to the Far East. At this stage, the Dutch merchants invited Hudson to Amsterdam in order that they could pick his brains on the subject of the North-east sea route. Hudson replied that he thought it would be possible to sail over the Pole to the Far East. The Dutch listened and did not trust him. This was astute of them, for Hudson, in fact, was not disclosing to them the full extent of his thoughts about the Northern exploration. When the merchants had sent him away, Hudson called on Peter Plancius, the geographer, to whom he confided his true inner opinion, that the secret lay in the North-west.

At this moment the French, who were eager to have a bigger part in overseas trade, took a hand in the game. President Jeannin, French ambassador at The Hague, wrote at some length to Henri Quatre, telling him that he had heard about Hudson from a rich and friendly Amsterdam merchant named Isaac Le Maire. Hudson was convinced, as also was Peter Plancius, that there must be in the northern waters a passage corresponding to the one found near the South Pole by Magellan. Hudson said, too, that when he had sailed to the north as far as 80° he found that it became less cold; the land was no longer a savage waste haunted by wolves and bears; grass grew, and the sort of animals that lived on it. This had confirmed Plancius in his theory, that since the sun near the Pole shines continually for five months, its rays had sufficient strength to warm the ground. Le Maire was willing to send out a ship northwards to seek the Passage, provided the French King was ready to put up three or four thousand crowns. In reporting to Henri, Jeannin added a postscript, informing the King that the Dutch East India Company had now got wind of Hudson's secret negotiations with Le Maire and were making him an offer on their own account. Would the King instruct him what he should do? But, as it turned out, the French were too late.

Alarmed by this new development, the Dutch East Indies Company abruptly reversed course and signed an agreement with the Englishman. For a payment of 800 guilders (£65) Hudson was to sail north from Novaya Zemlya 'until he reached the Pacific or the fabled Strait of Anian'. There, according to Briggs, a contemporary mathematician of free-ranging fancy, 'are seated the large kingdoms of Cebola and Quirira whose houses are said to be five storeys high and to have within them pillars of turquoises'.

The Dutch, who were aware that their new employee, an opinionated individual, whom they already suspected, was tempted by the lure of the west, specifically limited Hudson to a search in the north and northeast. He left Amsterdam on 25 March 1609, in a small ship, the *Half Moon*, belonging to a type which the Dutch call a yacht. In his company were two old shipmates, Robert Juet of Limehouse, who had been master on Hudson's previous trip to the north, and John Colman, who had sailed with him to Spitzbergen in 1607. The *Half Moon*'s crew was mixed, part Dutch, part English. As might have been expected, the seamen quarrelled, and somewhere beyond the North Cape, in stormy weather, a mutiny broke out which Hudson settled by offering the men a choice: either they would look for the Passage between Virginia and the St Lawrence, or they would explore the channel where John Davis had observed the famous tide-rip. Either course meant abandoning altogether the enterprise as the Dutch had envisaged it. The outcome of the mutiny – if, in fact, there was a mutiny –

was that Hudson set sail across the Atlantic. He was now embarked on an adventure such as he had hankered after for a long time and which had been forbidden him. There was no more talk of Novaya Zemlya. The *Half Moon*'s head was turned south-west on 19 May. The crew passed the Lofoten Islands and Faroes and looked for Buss Island to see if it lay in its true latitude in the chart. They had sight of the first stars that night: the sea had changed colour to a pale green but of Buss there was no sign. By 8 July they had cast anchor on the Banks of Newfoundland, where they began fishing for cod. Four days later, they sighted ahead of them 'a low white sandy ground'. They were, probably, although they did not know it, off the coast of Maine. They tacked southwards, meaning to anchor near the shore. But fog closed in and they thought it wiser to stand off.

Five days afterwards, two Indian canoes came alongside and friendly, if wary, relations were established. These exchanges did not last long. Some of the more ruffianly members of the crew landed with firearms and set about plundering Indian huts. ('We drove the savages from their houses and took the spoil of them as they would have done of us.') Discipline on the ship was obviously at a low ebb, because Hudson was either irresponsible or had no authority over his men. The *Half Moon* made off to the South before the Indians could take revenge. It cruised southwards along the coast and then, turning to the north once more, arrived on 3 September at three in the afternoon at 'three great rivers' where, after careful reconnaissance, the English voyagers found a promising anchorage in five fathoms of water, two cables' length from the shore. The native people came aboard clad in deer skins and sometimes wearing feather cloaks. They exchanged tobacco for knives and beads.

The scene was enchanting. In the woods there was an abundance of tall oaks. In the sea were salmon, mullet and huge rays. Hudson had paused outside what afterwards became the harbour of New York. He anchored between Long Island and the New Jersey coast. The ship's chronicler, Robert Juet, decided: 'This is a very good land to fall with and a pleasant land tō see.' But the good land turned out to have dangers. John Colman, working in a ship's boat on a narrow river, to the west of the anchorage, was set upon suddenly by Indians in two canoes and killed by an arrow through the throat. After that incident, relations between the Indians and their visitors cooled. The sailors took two hostages and dressed them up in red coats. But seemingly they did not keep a close enough watch on them, for the pair slipped out of a port and swam off, making derisive noises when they reached the shore. Hudson was engaged by this time in a more exciting enterprise. He was making his way slowly up the Hudson River and hoping, for a few days at least, that it might be the channel to the west that he was seeking.

After entertaining Indian chiefs to wine and spirits, making one of them dead drunk to the alarm of his friends, he reached the point on the river where the town of Albany now stands. Five men in one of the boats rowed 12 miles further north. They brought back bad news. The stream, they said, became narrower and shallower. After all, this was not the way to Cathay.

On 23 September Hudson began to drop down the river towards the sea. He had turned just at a moment when, although he did not know it, he had reached the break between the Adirondack Mountains and the Catskills. He had sailed upstream about 150 miles from the sea. If he had followed the Mohawk River about the same distance to the west he would have stumbled upon one of the great, decisive secrets of American geography, the great lake system. Lake Ontario would have been revealed. The Indians had excited Captain John Smith with a story of vast waters somewhere to the west. That story would have been confirmed. And Hudson, beholding the Lake, would certainly have assumed that he had reached the Pacific. As it was, he rejected the proposal of his mate that they should winter on the American coast and make a new attempt on the North-west Passage in the spring. He distrusted the temper of his crew. The time had come to leave.

The *Half Moon* slipped out to sea down the river, the sailors picking out as they passed a 'very pleasant place to build a town on' (which may have been the site of the future New York). The ship arrived at Dartmouth on 7 November. Hudson brought back with him a story of the 'river of the steep cliffs', the Great North River, wide and navigable. It was momentous news which must, on no account, reach the ears of Britain's commercial rivals, for it seemed probable that the river of the steep cliffs might be, in fact, the way to Cathay. In the emergency, the English government acted promptly and with thoroughness. By Order in Council, no Englishman was to leave the country. The Dutch protested that the effects of this ban was that Hudson would not be able to report in person to his employers in Amsterdam. Not that this high-handed action by the English authorities came as any surprise to them. The English, said Van Meteren, the Dutch consul in London, 'are bold, courageous, ardent, and cruel in war . . . and very suspicious, especially of foreigners, whom they despise.' For their part the Dutch under-rated the importance of the river and suspected that

Hudson had not explored the American coast further north for the sufficient reason that he did not wish the Dutch to benefit from the discovery of the Passage which, they were sure, lay somewhere in that area. No doubt Hudson's mate, who was Dutch, was of the same opinion.

'Wickedness Sleepeth Not'

'The captains [for the North-west discovery] must be skilful mariners and good cosmographers, men of good reputation and of great resolution for their credits to perform such a voyage, and for their carriage not to be daunted at any disaster. Their commission must give them liberty to punish with death if mutinies or disorders arise.'

Sir William Monson

Having squeezed out the Dutch, the English speculators were not slow to take their place. In consequence, Hudson's fourth voyage was a purely English venture financed by Sir Thomas Smith, of the English East India Company, Sir Dudley Digges, a rich young landowner who had written a pamphlet on the North-west Passage, and a Yorkshire squire named John Wolstenholme. Digges argued the case for the search on the highest grounds of political and economic need. 'A glorious state and renowned Great Britain would be had the same discovered the North Pole and passage into the South Sea . . . there to set forth the name of Jesus Christ where plenty and abundance of many rich wares are to be had at low prices.' He was writing at a time when Englishmen were despondent about the poverty of their country, the prevalence of unemployment, the crime rate, etc. New, rich markets for British manufacturers must be found – and where more likely than in the Far East to which the North-west Passage was the route? Henry Hudson was appointed to command an expedition for which Digges and his associates provided the finance.

The ship, *Discovery*, put to sea from St Katherine's Pool, below the Tower of London, on 17 April 1610. It carried a crew of twenty men and two boys. Hudson had brought his son, John, with him. The rest of the ship's company are known by name and, before long, were known by their doings. Among them was a mathematician named Thomas Wydowse (? Woodhouse) whose presence gave an air of scientific gravity to the enterprise. Bennet Mathues was the cook; Abacuck Prickett, an employee of Sir Dudley Digges, was, it can be assumed, on board to look after his master's interest. Otherwise it is difficult to imagine what he, a former haberdasher, was doing there. Another landsman was aboard, Edward Wilson, a surgeon from Portsmouth. Sylvanus Bond was a cooper and Philip Staffs a carpenter. Over the seamen were Hudson's former shipmate, Robert Juet, the mate, John King, the quartermaster, Francis Clements, the boatswain, and Robert Bylot, a Thames-side man and a trained navigator.

Before the ship left the Thames two puzzling incidents occurred. A man named Colebourne was put ashore with a letter to the shareholders setting out the reasons why Hudson thought it necessary to get rid of him. And at Gravesend a young man named Henry Greene came aboard. Just why, it is hard to say. His name was not in the list of those who were entitled to sail. His embarkation has a somewhat surreptitious appearance. But it seemed that he had been living in Hudson's house in London in the town and, to the disgust of his respectable Kentish parents, he had been squandering his substance in a life of debauchery in the town. However, the youth was clever; he could write well and Hudson, through one Mr Venson, persuaded Greene's mother to spend four pounds on buying him clothes for the voyage. (Venson took care, however, not to trust Greene with the money.)

Greene was not long aboard the *Discovery* before it became evident that his bad reputation in London had been well-earned. At Harwich, he went 'into the field' with a man named Wilkinson, probably to fight, but perhaps for another reason. In Iceland, he picked a quarrel with Edward Wilson, the surgeon, and gave him such a beating that the surgeon would not set foot on the ship again until the crew insisted that he should, and no doubt gave him guarantees. In this matter, Hudson took his protégé's side, blaming the affair on Wilson's evil tongue. Juet, the mate, when drunk, told Staffs, the carpenter, that in his opinion Hudson had brought Greene with them to act as a spy on their loyalty. When this came to Hudson's ear, he was so angry that he could hardly be dissuaded from putting Juet on shore in Iceland to find his way back to England by fishing-boat.

Sailing to Greenland, Hudson was guided on his way by an old document which the eminent publisher, Hondius, had lent him. This was the sailing directions of Ivar Bardarsen, written in the middle of the fourteenth century, and for long used by Norwegian skippers on their voyages to Greenland. Bardarsen, otherwise known as Ivar Boty, had been a Greenlander, an important figure in the bishop's court there in the days when the

Norse settlement was still in existence. Bardarsen's treatise had been translated into German, then into Dutch, and, finally, from Dutch into English. The fact that Hondius lent this key document to Hudson indicates that he regarded the Englishman as an explorer worthy of respect. Already Hondius had given Hudson credit, in one of his maps, for discovering the ice-barrier between Greenland and Spitzbergen. Four days after leaving Iceland, Hudson sighted Greenland, beyond a barrier of thick, ribbed ice which prevented him from approaching close to the shore. They saw the mountains of Greenland shaped like sugar loaves and covered with snow. 'Much snow and ice,' Bardarsen had reported of it, 'but not so cold as Iceland or Norway.'

Several hundred miles further west, on the far side of Davis Strait, he passed Resolution Island and entered the strait which Frobisher had called the Mistaken Strait, and which Davis had not sufficiently explored. Now he was forced to the south by a stream of ice driven fiercely along by powerful currents. Before long, the *Discovery* was in Ungava Bay where it remained for three weeks, beset by ice and unable to break out. For a time, Hudson despaired that they would ever escape. But his next attempt to sail westwards was more successful, the torrent of ice having abated. On 2 August he sighted Salisbury Island and sailed south-west into 'a whirling sea'. He had entered what is now called Hudson's Bay. Abacuck Prickett tells the story. There were interesting sights to see on shore; there was trouble aboard, and the threat of more trouble to come. While they were still in Ungava Bay Robert Juet, the mate, had scoffed at Hudson's hope that he would see Bantam (Java) by Candlemas (2 February). Like Juet, the crew did not share Hudson's outward optimism. They refused to go further under the command of a captain who had plainly lost his way. In short, there was something like mutiny in the *Discovery*.

One seaman said that, if he had a hundred pounds, he would give ninety of them to be sitting at home 'in my dolphin chamber, at a round table, by a sea-coal fire'. But the stout-hearted carpenter, Philip Staffs, would have none of that craven talk: 'He would not,' he said, 'give ten of it to be back in England, but would think it as good money as ever he had.' In the end, Hudson reasoned the men into a better frame of mind and they set to work, powerfully aided by the danger they were in, to clear the ship from the ice. They hunted polar bears on the ice floes and on 10 September, they sailed between two imposing headlands, Cape Digges and Cape Wolstenholme, one of them two thousand feet high, the other a thousand, each rising vertically out of the sea and separated from one another by only two miles of sea. The crisis of finding a way into the Bay was behind them.

Hudson now dealt with the question of discipline. He called the men together after dinner and heard the case against Juet. It was said that the mate had told Bennet Mathues as they neared Iceland that he ought to be ready for bloodshed. Philip Staffs, the carpenter, and a seaman named Arnold Ludlow swore on the Bible that Juet had told them to keep their muskets charged and their swords handy in their cabins, because they would be needed before the voyage was over. During the days when they were 'pestered in the ice', he had encouraged gloom and dissatisfaction among the crew. After hearing the evidence, Hudson deposed Juet from his job as mate, appointing Robert Bylot in his place. Francis Clements, the bosun, was likewise dismissed and his post given to William Wilson, who was given half the bosun's extra pay; the other half went to John King, a quartermaster, who had behaved loyally. Hudson had acted less decisively and ruthlessly than, say, Drake would have done in similar circumstances. He lived to regret it.

After that, the *Discovery* made her way cautiously to the south through a sea, first of all like whey, and then in two contrasted hues, one black, the other white. They sailed for twelve or fifteen miles between the two colours. When Hudson sent off a boat to the land, the sailors came back reporting that they had found footprints of a man among the snow-clad rocks. The land was well covered with trees. But the inshore water was too shallow to make a good anchorage for the ship. By this time, the nights were long and cold and the snow was falling heavily. It was high time to find a place there they could spend the winter. On 1 November they found it and hauled the ship aground. By 10 November they were frozen in. They had food enough for six months, if they made prudent use of it. Hudson began a system of rationing and, in addition, offered a reward to any man who could add to the store by killing beast, fish or bird. Prickett, in his narrative, says that Hudson could have brought more victuals with him in the ship. The implication is that, for one reason or another, Hudson had cut things too fine.

One day in the middle of November John Williams, the ship's gunner, died. A gloomy event in itself, it brought greater misfortune in its train. For it happened that Williams had been the owner of a grey cloth gown to which the young man, Greene, had taken a fancy. But, like other events on board ship, this question is governed by a strict protocol of the sea. The tradition is that a dead man's belongings are put up for auction at the masthead and go to the highest bidder. Greene told Hudson that he would give as much for this gown as any man but that he wanted it. And Hudson agreed that nobody else should have it but Greene, a young man whom he liked. This – a breach with ancient maritime tradition – was ill-omened.

At that time Hudson had the notion that Staffs, the carpenter, should build a house on shore. He would not listen when the carpenter told him that it was no time of year to start building. Snow was lying thick on the ground and the frost in the air was sharp enough to kill. A man holding metal in his hand might well have his skin taken off. A month earlier, in October, it would have been different. Then would have been the time to think of building. But at that time, as Staffs reminded Hudson, he would not allow the house to be built. At this point Hudson flew into a rage and routed the carpenter out of his cabin, cursing him and threatening to have him hanged. In the end Staffs gave in, surly and resentful, and the house was built, somehow, and to no purpose. The following day Staffs went ashore, taking his fowling piece with him, to look for game and Henry Greene went with him carrying a pike. That was in accordance with orders; nobody was to go ashore unless he had an armed comrade with him. But for some reason, perhaps annoyance with Staffs, perhaps jealousy over young Greene – Hudson, whose nerves were on edge, was driven into a fresh transport of rage by this incident.

In a moment, it seemed, all his affection for Greene turned into hatred; he ordered that the dead gunner's gown should be taken from the young man and given to Bylot, the mate. Greene protested indignantly: this was the breaking of a promise! Hudson retorted that none of Greene's friends would trust him with twenty shillings, so why should he? What is more, Greene would have no wages at all unless he behaved as Hudson wished him to do. This was all very well but it was known to all the ship's company that Hudson had promised to pay Greene as good a wage as any other member of the crew and, what is more, to use his influence when they returned to London to have Greene made one of the Prince of Wales's bodyguard.

Grim beyond words was the plight of the *Discovery*'s crew. There they were, icebound on a desolate coast, in a remote corner of a vast and uncharted bay, with a tumbled mass of grey ice on one side, rocks on the other and snow everywhere, obliterating the outlines of the landscape, even the line dividing land from water. With God knows how many months of this freezing imprisonment before them and, at the end of it – what? Escape, a slow death from starvation (although until then game had been plentiful, it showed signs of tapering off) or a swifter end from cold? They knew, and recalled, how Willoughby's crew had perished. It was a crisis when men needed an iron frame of self-discipline which Hudson's crew did not possess or a stern, inspiring leadership which Hudson could not supply. Drake, about to thread Magellan's Strait, found himself facing an ordeal that called for every ounce of his moral and mental strength. Faced with an emergency even more savage, Hudson cracked. Swaying between affection and tantrums, he made more precarious a situation which was already desperate enough.

Winter ground on. Scurvy broke out. Francis Clemens, who had been bosun until Hudson demoted him, lost his toenails from frostbite. Hunting had been good – they shot a hundred dozen snow partridges – but when spring came near the game birds vanished and the crew were driven miserably to eat moss from the rocks and frogs from the ponds. Later, the ice began to break up and fishing became possible. On the first day they were lucky and caught five hundred fish as big as herring. It was, however, their biggest catch for many a day.

While they were busy with the net on that first day, the first seeds of a conspiracy were sown. Henry Greene and William Wilson suggested to some other malcontents that they should take the dinghy and make off. This scheme came to nothing, however, because Hudson himself decided to take the dinghy, along with the net and food for eight or nine days, and went off to the south. He hoped to meet Indians in that direction for he and the others had seen smoke in the sky: the Indians had set fire to the woods. Hudson was confident that they would sell him meat. He left orders for those who remained in the ship to take in water, wood and ballast in readiness for his return. But it did not work out as he had hoped. The Indians would not allow him to come near them. Worse, as soon as they sighted him, they set fire to the woods to drive him off. When Hudson returned, both he and the ship were in worse state than when he had left.

There was nothing for it but to set sail for home and measure out their miserable store of food as best they could over the months that the return voyage would take. Hudson, weeping, distributed the bread that was left – a pound of bread for each man – and five cheeses, where the men had thought there should be nine. Since the quality of the cheeses varied, Hudson shared them all out, the good with the bad, three and a half pounds per man to last a week. And so they left their winter anchorage and stood out to the north towards the mouth of James Bay. Then they dropped anchor in the uninviting expanse of Hudson Bay itself. Hunger by this time was making inroads on morale and discipline. The crew suspected that Hudson had a secret store of food hidden somewhere in the ship which he was keeping for some purpose which he did not divulge. Greene, who had given a shipmate half his fortnight's supply of bread to keep for him lest he should be tempted to eat it, came three days later and demanded it back. He could hold out no longer. The bosun ate his fortnight's bread ration in a day and was sick for three days thereafter. The crew of the *Discovery* were embarking on the suicidal follies of desperate men who have lost faith in their leader.

By 18 June the ship was again caught in the ice and misery and despair sharpened among the sailors. At this point Hudson committed another mistake, ordering the ship's boy, Nicholas Simms, to search the sea-chests to see if any food was hidden there. Simms found thirty 'cakes of bread'. They had been kept back by men who were sure in their own minds that Hudson had a private way from his cabin into the hold through which he brought in food to share with his favourites such as Woodhouse, the mathematician.

'Why does the master give meat to some of the company and not to the rest?' the bosun demanded of Staffs, the carpenter. 'Because it is necessary that some of us should be kept up,' said the carpenter. It was a fatal answer which, if it were true, could be used to justify all manner of horrors. On Saturday night, 21 June, Wilson and Greene came to Abacuck Prickett, lying in his cabin resting a lame leg. They told him that they meant to set Hudson and the sick men adrift in the dinghy to shift for themselves as best they could. There was less than fourteen days' food on board the ship. For three days they had not eaten. Now they were determined to mend it or end it. Prickett was shocked – or so he said afterwards – to hear such talk from men who had wives and children and were contemplating a deed that would exile them from England forever. 'Hold your peace!' cried Greene (who had neither wife nor child). 'I know the worst that can happen, which is to be hanged when I come home. I would rather be hanged at home than starved abroad.' As for Prickett, out of their good-will to him, they would allow him to stay on the ship. Prickett thanked them but he had not come aboard the ship to betray her. 'Then you must take your luck in the dinghy,' said Greene. 'If there be no remedy,' Prickett replied, 'the will of God be done.'

Furious at this equivocal remark, Greene went off, swearing that he would cut the throat of any man who gave them away. Left alone with Wilson, Prickett tried to persuade him to abandon the idea. It was no use. Wilson retorted that they must go on with their scheme while it was hot for, if not, their fellow-plotters would desert them and the mischief they meant to do Hudson would fall on themselves. At this point, Greene returned, demanding to be told what Prickett had said. 'He is at his old song,' said Wilson, 'still patient' Prickett asked Greene to postpone the deed for three days. 'In the interval,' said Prickett, 'I shall deal with the master so that all will be well.' Greene refused. 'Two days then,' said Prickett. 'Twelve hours!' Neither Greene nor Wilson would have it. It must be done out of hand—now or never! 'Wait until Monday, please,' Prickett pleaded. 'Then I'll join with you in sharing out all the victuals in the ship. And justify it when I get home to England!'

When the pair would not yield, he told them that they were contemplating something even worse than they had admitted—blood and revenge! Why otherwise were they preparing the deed at such an hour of night? At this point, Greene picked up Prickett's Bible that lay beside his bunk and swore – he who had already claimed to have no religious belief – that he would do no harm to any man. What he proposed to do was for the good of the voyage and nothing else. Wilson swore the same oath. After that, they brought the old man, Juet, into the cabin. For all his grey hairs, Juet was even more bloody-minded than the other two. John Thomas and Michael Perse, able-bodied seamen, followed – birds of a feather, says Prickett; and Bennet Mathues, the cook, and Adrian Motte, whom he asked whether they had seriously considered what they were taking in hand. They also took the oath which, it seems, Prickett had devised. No more conspirators appeared. 'Who will you cast away with the Master?' asked Prickett. 'The carpenter, John King, and the sick men,' answered Greene. 'You will need the carpenter,' Prickett pointed out. But Staffs, the carpenter, was condemned because he was suspected of unfair dealings with the food. And King, an illiterate man, had taken Bylot's place as mate. That was *his* crime. Prickett thought that finally he had persuaded them to spare the carpenter.

'It was dark,' said Prickett, later on, 'and they in readiness to put this deed of darkness in execution. I prayed them to stay until morning. Now every man would go to his rest, I hoped, but wickedness sleepeth not.' Whatever else may be said of Abacuck Prickett – such as liar, weakling, double traitor, mutineer, or witness to the truth – he could in a phrase, summon up the atmosphere that night among those famished seamen, whispering in the darkness in that lost ship off that desolate shore. When he was criticized later on for his part in the oath-taking, to defend himself he gave its terms: 'You swear truth to God, your prince and country. You shall do nothing but to the glory of God and the good of the action in hand, and harm to no man.'

All this time, Henry Hudson lay fast asleep in his cabin while Henry Greene watched close at hand lest the Master wake up and, hearing a suspicious noise, bring all to ruin. There was another danger. Where was King, the mate whom Hudson had appointed in Bylot's place? Was he with Hudson? Were they talking together? To their relief, the conspirators found that he was talking to the carpenter, who was sleeping on the poop. When he came down, Bylot, who shared a cabin with him, met him as if by chance. They went into the cabin together. The rest slept in their usual places. Bennet and the cooper, both disabled, lay in the cookhouse, and Woodhouse, the mathematician, who was sick, lay outside it on the starboard side with Sydrack Funer near him. Then came the surgeon and Henry Hudson's son, John, Wilson the bosun and Arnold Ludlow. Juet and John Thomas slept in the gunroom. On the port side of the ship were two seamen, Michael Butt and Adrian Moore, who had been disabled ever since a violent storm which swept away the ship's anchor. Bylot and Prickett lay outside the gunroom. Amidships, between the capstan and the pumps, were the boy, Nicholas Simms, and the arch-villain, Henry Greene. Thus, within the space of a few yards, the murderers and their victims lay huddled together with the creaking timbers of the *Discovery* about them.

At the first grey light of dawn, Mathues, the cook, rose and went with the kettle to fetch water. John King left his cabin and climbed down into the hold. Somebody shut the hatch above him, so that he could not get up. While Greene and one of the seamen kept the carpenter in talk, Hudson emerged from his cabin. The moment for action had come. The trap was sprung. Mathues and John Thomas, the seamen, leapt upon the Master, and overpowered him while Wilson pinioned his arms from behind.

'What does this mean?' cried Hudson.

'You will know when you are in the dinghy,' they told him.

Hudson shouted for help to the carpenter, telling him his hands were tied. No answer came. Juet went into the hold to deal with John King who, however, kept him at bay with a sword. He might have killed the old scoundrel if others had not come to Juet's aid. At that moment, the ship's dinghy was brought alongside and the sick and crippled men were hauled out of their cabins and told to get down into the little craft. Hudson was forced by Thomas and Mathues to do likewise. From his place in the dinghy he called out to Pritchett who, dragging himself on his knees from his cabin, begged the mutineers to do as they would be done by. But they ordered him back to his cabin where, a few minutes later, he spoke to Hudson throught the window that gave light to the cabin. 'Juet will overthrow us all,' said Hudson. 'Nay,' said Prickett, 'it is that villain Henry Greene.' Bylot stayed below deck and later declared that he thought they meant to hold Hudson in the dinghy only long enough to search the ship for the food they believed was hidden in it. Mathues and Thomas, who had been the first to attack Hudson, were with him in the dinghy and Greene, doubly treacherous, seems to have thought that it would be a good idea if they stayed there and were lost with the captain. In the meantime, the sick men were being pushed into the dinghy. At that point, Mathues said that Bond, the cooper, who was a friend of his, should not go, while Thomas insisted on saving his friend, Francis Clements. In their place, Arnold Ludlow and Michael Butt who, shortly before, had been loud in abuse of Hudson, were manhandled into the boat. The mathematician, Woodhouse, was another castaway. He went, lamenting, to his doom. Staffs, the carpenter, was set free as Prickett had advised he should be. He turned out, however, to be a man with a conscience. He would not stay in the ship, he said, unless he was forced to do so. 'Go then,' said the mutineers, 'for we will not keep you.' 'I will go,' he said, 'provided I can take my chest with me and all that is in it.' They put it aboard the dinghy while Staffs went down to take his leave of Prickett. 'If you stay,' argued Prickett, 'you may arrange things so that all will be well.' But Staffs had been persuaded that there was nobody left on board who was capable of sailing the ship back to England. He added, 'If you reach the capes' – meaning the two tall cliffs which stand at the entrance to the Bay – 'before the dinghy does, leave some token that you have been there at the place where the birds breed.' At that, the two men parted, with tears.

In the end, there were nine in the dinghy. One of them was Henry Hudson's son, John, who appeared in the crew list as a ship's boy. The only food allowed to the castaways was some meal, but Staffs had succeeded in taking with him a fowling-piece, powder and shot, pikes and an iron pot. When the ship was all but clear of the ice, the rope holding the dinghy to the stern of the *Discovery* was severed, topsails were set, the ship stood towards the east in a clear sea. And the dinghy dropped further and further back in the ship's wake and, at last, was lost to sight. The mutineers were by this time too busy to think of the men they had condemned to a miserable death. They were rifling the ship, breaking into sea-chests and looting what they came upon. Some food they found – two firkins of butter, a peck of meal, twenty-seven pieces of pork, two hundred biscuits (in Hudson's cabin) and a butt of beer. In the midst of their rummaging, someone raised the cry that the dinghy was in sight once more. It was as if their consciences had caught up with them. In a panic, 'They let fall the mainsail and out with their topsails, and fly as from an enemy!' . . . There was no going back on the decision to abandon the poor wretches in the dinghy. Rather than that, Greene, Wilson and their accomplices would run up the skull and crossbones flag and turn pirate.

The *Discovery* went on its way to the north under the nominal charge of Robert Bylot, although Prickett was installed in Hudson's cabin – protesting that this was rather a place for Juet, a seaman, than for himself, a landsman. But Greene insisted that Juet was to have nothing to do with Hudson's journal or the charts which were kept in the cabin. The best of Hudson's belongings were reserved for Greene himself. Troubled by ice, starving, so that they were glad to eat grass, plagued by ceaseless bickering between Bylot and Juet about the course they should sail, nagged at constantly by the thought that they would never get out of this dreadful bay, never see England again (and if they did, what then – the gallows at Execution Dock?) the *Discovery* and her crew of murderers made unsteady progress to the north.

Prickett had an additional cause for anxiety. He came to the conclusion that Greene, knowing him to be a reluctant mutineer at best, would prefer to have set him adrift along with the other nine in the dinghy. If they returned to England, Prickett might be an inconvenient witness. He was no sailor. He was disabled. He was, in short, just the sort of man the mutineers were anxious to be rid of. One fact may have protected him. He was the employee of Sir Dudley Digges, one of the chief promoters of the voyage, and the mutineers may well have counted on him to plead their cause with his master when they reached England. But knowing what a desperate character Greene was, Prickett was by no means easy in his mind. Greene, he thought, was subtly trying to involve him in a search for goods that Greene himself had stolen. In the course of the search, thirty loaves of bread were found which Greene told the others had been stolen by Prickett. By that time Greene had established an ascendancy over the others. More and more, the crew treated him as captain of the ship and, more and more, Greene declared that he would return to England only when he had the King's promise under the royal seal that his life would be safe. 'They had many devices in their heads,' wrote Prickett, 'but Henry Greene in the end was their captain.'

When the ship arrived at the two capes, Digges and Wolstenholme, which stand as sentinels at the entrance to Hudson Bay, a fresh dispute broke out between Juet, who wished to sail west, and Bylot who steered to the east. After that, they made contact with a community of Eskimos with whom they tried to barter articles from Hudson's cabin for deer-meat. Greene was convinced that they had nothing to fear from the Eskimos. He, Wilson and Thomas showed looking-glasses and Jews' harps to the 'savages', while Perse and Motte gathered sorrel on the rocks to eat. Prickett, a lame man, stayed aboard the ship's boat. Suddenly, the peace was broken. Prickett tried to chase off an Eskimo who insisted on entering the boat, but at that moment the Englishman was attacked by another Eskimo who had a knife. The first blow cut Prickett in the arm and grazed his chest; the second blow he warded off with his hands, the third wounded him in the thigh and all but severed his little finger. At this point, Prickett had recovered from his surprise and fought back on more equal terms. Looking round for a weapon, he saw one he had forgotten in the excitement of the struggle, the dagger he wore at his side. This, with all the strength he had left, he drove into the Eskimo's throat.

Meanwhile, the shore party was under savage attack from the Eskimos. Thomas and Wilson were wounded in the bowels. Perse and the ringleader, Greene, tumbled into the boat. Greene was gravely wounded. Motte scrambled over the rocks and swam until he was able to cling to the stern of the ship's boat. He was pulled aboard by Perse, who held off the attacking Eskimos with a hatchet. Crying 'Coragio!', Henry Greene laid about him with a truncheon. The boat was being cleared of the shore when Motte, shouting to his comrades to wait for him, was pulled aboard it at the last minute. Now the Eskimos fitted arrows to their bows and loosed a volley. Perse was wounded. Prickett had a cruel arrow wound in the back. Greene was killed. All this happened out of sight of the *Discovery*. On the way back to the ship, Perse fainted but Motte was able to attract the notice of those left on board. Greene's body was dropped into the sea. The Eskimo who had attacked Prickett died that day. So did Thomas and so, 'cursing and swearing in a most fearful manner', did Wilson. Perse died two days later. The Eskimo attack had made almost a clean sweep of the men who, according to Prickett, had been the ringleaders of the plot against Hudson. This might be a coincidence. It was undeniably convenient for those who survived, and, on their return to England, would have a great deal of explaining to do.

The *Discovery* crossed the Atlantic with favourable winds and a starving crew – driven to eat birds' bones fried in candle-grease. Every man had as his ration a pound of candles every week. They were too weak to stand at the helm. For this reason, the crossing was longer than it need have been. Steering was faulty. Robert Juet, last of the leaders of those who had cast Hudson adrift, died of want before the cry went up, 'A sail, a sail!' It was a fishing boat from Fowey and it brought them, more dead than alive, into Berehaven in Bantry Bay, where they pawned the ship's cable to buy food. It was 6 September, seventeen months after the *Discovery* had left St Katherine's Pool on its disastrous voyage.

As soon as they arrived in London, Bylot and Abacuck Prickett presented themselves at Muscovy House where they told Sir Thomas Smith their sorrowful tale of mutiny, murder, famine and death. Twenty-two had sailed and only eight returned. Four men had been killed fighting with Eskimos. One had died of hunger. Nine had been deliberately left by their shipmates to perish of cold or starvation. And what was to happen to those who returned? The penalty for mutiny was known. The penalty for murder was known. What fate could the haggard and haunted survivors expect when they appeared before the Court of Admiralty? In particular, what view would be taken of the conduct of Bylot, who had brought the ship back, of Prickett, a man of some education, who, by his own confession, had been in the confidence of the mutineers, and of Edward Wilson, a surgeon? But although the cloud of suspicion against them was dark indeed, there was one point in their favour. They were the survivors; they could speak and write. The dead could not be witnesses at the trial. Prickett's version of events was the only coherent account of the voyage.

The Masters of Trinity House might say that Prickett and his two companions, Bylot and Wilson, deserved to be hanged, but Prickett's story was plausible enough. Luke Foxe might say, after reading it, 'Well, Prickett, I am in great doubt of thy fidelity to Master Hudson,' but Prickett's story had no competitor. It argued that Hudson, by injudicious and dishonest behaviour, had provoked the mutiny. It accused Juet, William Wilson and Henry Greene – above all, Greene – of plotting and leading the rebellion in the ship. And, as it chanced, all of these men were dead. Prickett's manner might be sanctimonious, his narrative might not reveal the whole truth about these appalling winter months in Hudson Bay, it might be too convenient to be true, but there was no rival to its testimony. Besides, there was another factor.

Prickett and Bylot had returned to England convinced that they had found the North-west Passage. Working their way out of the great Bay on the homeward run, they had gone aground on a rock near Digges Cape, at the point where they had turned eastwards into Hudson Strait. Then a 'great flood or billow *from the west*' had freed the ship. Such a flood could have only one reasonable explanation. On this point mariners, merchants and geographers were all agreed! An ocean lay to the west. The officials of Trinity House now asked themselves three questions: Must not the Great Bay be fed from the Western Ocean? Does that ocean lie to the North-west of Salisbury Island on the North of the Bay, and in the throat of Hudson Strait? Is not the Western Ocean the same as the South Sea (the Pacific)? After long thought, it was decided that the answer to the first question was, No, and that the Channel should be sought north-west of Salisbury Island. These conclusions should have brought to an end the exploration of Hudson Bay. They did not.

The disastrous voyage of Henry Hudson had one substantial result: a new company was formed – 'The Discoverers of the North-west Passage'. In its list of 288 members, most of them rich and respectable City merchants, occurred the names of Bylot, Prickett and Wilson. And when, in May 1612, two ships were sent out on a new adventure, the *Discovery* and the *Resolution*, Captain Thomas Button was in command of them and Bylot and Prickett were members of his ship's company. They sailed at a time when a serious charge was still hanging over them. But probably they had little fear that their necks were in danger. Mariners who had first-hand experience of the Arctic were too precious to be sacrificed on some legal punctilio.

Button's was the first of a new series of expeditions to search and find out a passage by the north-west of America to the Sea Sur, commonly called the South Sea. Meanwhile the Court of Admiralty continued its lethargic enquiries into the death of Henry Hudson. In July 1618, Abacuck Prickett, William Wilson, Bennet Matheus and Francis Clements appeared in Southwark to stand their trial for piracy. They were charged with putting Henry Hudson, master of the *Discovery*, 'out of the same ship with eight more of his company into a shallop in the Isle of America without meat, drink, or other provision; whereby they died'. The accused were found not guilty.

But how, it may be asked, did Hudson die? What happened after the *Discovery* with its panic-stricken, conscience-stricken crew of mutineers had set the mainsail and hurried away from the men they were murdering? The evidence is inconclusive and, such as it is, comes from the accounts given by fur-traders. There is, however, one clue coming from another source. Captain James, an explorer backed by the Bristol merchants, spent the winter of 1631–2 in James Bay. There he found a row of stakes, sharpened by axe, and driven into the ground above a sandy beach on Danby Island. These were certainly the handiwork of a European. They were perhaps the work of Philip Staffs, carpenter of the *Discovery* and the only man who joined the castaways of his own volition. If that is so, they were the last relics of an honourable man.

Henry Hudson is, like Willoughby, Cabot and Magellan, one of the tragic figures of the Age of Discovery. He was a failure for two reasons, once because he could not dominate his unruly crew and again because he did not find the northern seaway to Asia. Indeed, he was even more unfortunate. For, convinced that he had found the secret, he led succeeding explorers on a false trail. Hudson's Bay was a vast trap for a stream of hopeful, deluded mariners of whom Henry Hudson was only the first. There is something appealing about him. He seems to have lacked the iron-hard qualities of the great commander who can maintain discipline among a surly and doubting crew in a tense situation. But his devotion to the task of exploration has an intensity which makes him at one in spirit with the men who sought to reach the Pole or the summit of Everest. He may have suspected before dying that the Passage, if he found it, would not be a commercial proposition. If so, it would certainly not have convinced him that the voyage had not been worth making. His ship brought back a chart of the North American coast which greatly enlarged the knowledge of the cartographers of Amsterdam. That was an achievement which would have given him solid satisfaction. With this accomplished Hudson might have been willing to spend the rest of his life ashore, in the company of his wife, Kate. She was as it chanced, a remarkable woman. When the *Discovery* came back without its captain, she found herself left a poor widow. Far from being discouraged by this disaster, she travelled to India for the East India Company and made a respectable amount of money trading in cloth at Ahmedabad.

A Swelling Sea out of the West

'Observe well the flood. If it aim to South-west, you may be sure the passage is that way.'

Henry, *Prince of Wales, to Thomas Button in 1612*

After the drama of Hudson's expedition, it was obvious that other navigators would be eager to explore the Bay in which he had perished and which, as those who had returned from his last voyage asserted, held such promising hopes. His voyage raised many questions and left the most exciting of them unanswered. If the Bay was not an arm of the great South Sea itself, might it not at least lead to that sea? The western shore of the Bay was still uncharted, unknown. It must be searched. That was the first necessity. In the month of May 1612 a Welsh captain from Glamorgan, named Thomas Button, set out with two ships (and Bylot and Prickett aboard) to put the matter to the proof.

Button was a well-connected man who had entered the English naval service in the year after the Armada. He was, apparently, a high-spirited young man and had no pedantic attachment to the niceties of the law. In January 1600 he came before the Glamorgan magistrates on a charge of robbing the house of a widow named Anne Harris. A serious offence, but it was, perhaps, not a time for the justices to take too grave a view of the misdeeds of a promising young naval officer, especially if he had influential relations living in the neighbourhood. Button was pardoned by the magistrates. In the following year, he distinguished himself at the siege of Kinsale, in Ireland, in which a substantial Spanish force was compelled to capitulate. Button was rewarded for his service with a pension of 6s. 8d. a day. Eleven years later, he had advanced in his profession; he was under royal patronage. The instructions to him before he sailed to the Arctic were signed by Henry, Prince of Wales, and his task was to enter Hudson's Bay and find a through route to the South Sea. If winter overtook him, he was to seek southwards for a suitable harbour, 'for we assure ourself by God's grace you will not return, without either the good news of a Passage or sufficient assurance of an impossibility'. He was to devote himself single-mindedly to the search until the happy day arrived when he could send his pinnace home with the good news that he had arrived in the South Sea.

Button picked a naval vessel, the *Resolution*, as his flagship. It was accompanied by Hudson's old ship, the *Discovery*, in which sailed Bylot and Prickett, the lucky survivors of the mutiny. By that time the *Discovery* had been in home waters for only a few months. The ships were provisioned for a voyage of eighteen months. After Hudson's experience it seemed hardly enough.

On entering Hudson's Bay, Button lost five men in a fight with Eskimos who were legitimately annoyed because Button had taken four of their canoes and had returned only two of them. The 'savages' may have been given confidence to fight when they remembered their encounter with English interlopers in the previous year at that very place. After that encounter, Button sailed westwards across the Bay and decided to spend the winter in a creek near Port Nelson, which he named after the master of the *Resolution*, who died there. Winter came, so severe that many of the crew died, being ill-prepared against extreme cold. When, at last, spring broke up the ice, Button and the survivors of that dreadful winter steered to the north and west, convinced that the Passage, if it existed at all in those parts, must lie somewhere west of Southampton Island, on the channel which he named Roe's Welcome. But by the time he had explored that Strait as far as 65°N, Button decided that there was no hope of finding a way out in that direction. He was convinced that Hudson's Bay was a wide land-locked sea and that it did not hold the secret of the Passage to the West. Button made a quick homeward crossing and was in the Thames towards the end of September 1613.

He had still an honourable career before him. With benevolent relatives to help, he became Admiral of the King's ships on the Irish coast and was knighted by his cousin, Sir Oliver St John, Lord-deputy in Dublin; after that he was appointed rear-admiral of the fleet which unsuccessfully attacked Algiers under his kinsman, Sir Robert Mansel. In the twenties of the seventeenth century, he was engaged in an official enquiry into the state of the navy which earned him a great deal of unpopularity with the Navy Board. However, from these difficulties, Button was rescued by the powerful nobleman who had now become his patron, the Duke of Buckingham. It was in vain for the Navy Board to complain that Sir

Thomas would 'take notice of no order unless he received the Duke's immediate command'. Buckingham's influence saved him. But Button's embarrassments were not over. While the Admiralty charged him with various kinds of financial misconduct, he alleged that his pension had not been paid. And by that time Buckingham had been assassinated. When Button died, in 1634, these tiresome issues had not been decided. What is certain is that after 1613 he did not sail to the North-west again. He did not believe that Hudson's Bay was the entry to the Channel. What he had seen had convinced him of that. But the belief that Button had lost still exerted its spell on others. Robert Bylot, who had brought Hudson's ship home after the murder, was still a believer. He was sent out on the search again in 1615, this time with William Baffin as his pilot.

There was a group of capitalists in the City of London who were fascinated by the problems and prospects of Arctic exploration. They had imagination as well as energy; they had the means to back their enthusiasm. Nor were they the sort of men who were easily discouraged. There was Sir Thomas Smith, son of a Wiltshire yeoman known as 'Customar Smith', because he had been for years Farmer of the Queen's Customs. Sir Thomas was a member of the Muscovy Company. As an ambassador he had gone to Moscow in 1604 to negotiate on trade questions with Boris Godunov. He was the first governor of the East India Company and of the company founded in 1612 to discover the North-west Passage. Equally important was a younger man, Sir Dudley Digges, the part sponsor of the Hudson Expedition, active as a businessman, diplomat and politician (hostile to the Court). Sir John Wolstenholme, also a director of the North-west company, another wealthy patron of polar discovery, had also sponsored Henry Hudson.

It was Wolstenholme who was responsible for advancing the career of William Baffin, a Londoner, and a sound practical sailor, who had served as pilot when Sir Thomas Smith and three other financiers sent ships to Greenland in 1612 under the command of Captain James Hall. This venture ended badly, however, when Hall was killed in a skirmish with Eskimos. The year after, Baffin, by this time in the service of the Muscovy Company, sailed as chief pilot in a fleet of seven ships with the task of seeing that England's monopoly of the Spitzbergen whale fishing was respected. In 1615, Smith, Digges and Wolstenholme appointed Baffin pilot of the *Discovery*, that historic, ill-fated ship, in which Captain Robert Bylot was once again to search for the North-west Passage. Baffin was said to be skilled in the technical side of his business rather than in words, but he flattered his patrons as eloquently as could reasonably be expected: 'What need I spend time herein,' he said, 'when never-dying fame hath, and will, enroll your names in Time's chiefest chronicle of Eternity.' On 16 March, the ship weighed anchor at St Katharine's and ten days later was at the Isles of Scilly where, however, bad weather drove it to Padstow. When Baffin and his companions set off again, on 19 April, they had a good passage and sighted the coast of Greenland on 6 May. After that they sailed on a southerly course to avoid the ice which beset the coast in floes, some of them as much as 200 feet above the water. Bylot asked Baffin whether he thought the ship should sail into the ice at this point. Baffin thought that, first, they should go further north. But Bylot said that this was the moment to go into the ice and Baffin acknowledged that Bylot knew more than he did about ice conditions in these parts. In a little, the ship seemed to be fast set in the ice but, from time to time, the ice opened a little and they were able to move, not to the north-west as they had hoped, but to the south. They were, at this time, at the southern approaches to Davis Strait, in weather that was turning colder. Snow fell heavily, freezing on the shrouds and tackle. When the weather cleared, they sighted Resolution Island, about 13 leagues to the west. It was 27 May. Three days later, they had turned the south point of the island and were within Hudson Strait, moving westwards; the wind was favourable and the vessel was not too much encumbered with ice. Hugging the north shore of the Strait, they continued slowly to the west, hearing the howling of dogs on shore, seeing tents and boats but no people until, after prayers on 8 May, Baffin and seven others ventured ashore. There he found a group of Eskimos and uttered the few words of their language he knew. Neither side trusted the other, but a cautious system of barter began. Baffin observed that these Eskimos were more uncivilized than the Greenlanders.

At the end of July they sighted Salisbury Island, which lies at the point where Hudson's Strait, Foxe Channel and Hudson's Bay meet. They found themselves in the midst of a great number of islands divided from one another by channels through which the tide rushed with such incredible volume that 'unless the Lord Himself had been on our side, we had surely perished, for sometimes the ship was hoisted aloft, and at other times, she, having got the upper hand, would force great mighty pieces of ice to sink down on the one side of her and rise on the other.' Three days after they had escaped from this peril, Bylot noticed that, as they went northwards, the water became shallower and the ice muddier. He decided to sail further east until he knew how the current ran. His first intention was to make for Nottingham Island, but that night – it was 8 July – the wind blew from the nor'-nor'-west and a great swelling sea came out of the west – 'which put us in some hope'.

So Bylot gave up the attempt to reach Nottingham Island. Soon they saw land to the west (Southampton Island), ending in a promontary which they called Seahorse Point, because of the large number of walruses on the ice. Further to the north and west was another headland, Cape Comfort, under which they came to anchor in a little cove. All the time they were watching the movements of the tide, hoping for some indication of a channel opening to the west. When they found nothing that convinced them, Bylot asked the crew whether they would prefer to go hunting walruses or study the currents at Nottingham Island, where the survivors of Hudson's voyage had reported the existence of a current coming from the north-west. After debate, they chose the latter which, after all, was the purpose for which they had been sent out.

During ten days of bad weather, the *Discovery* cruised round Nottingham Island before crossing southwards to Digges Island. By this time, Baffin was convinced that the notion of a flood from the north-west was an illusion, due to the eccentric behaviour of the tides in those waters. He concluded that doubtless there was a Passage, but probably not in Hudson Strait. With no further delay, the *Discovery* set sail for England and came to anchor in Plymouth Sound on 8 September. No lives had been lost on the voyage.

In March 1616, just a year after their previous departure, Bylot and Baffin set out once more in the good ship *Discovery* of London. There were seventeen aboard her. Their instructions this time were to sail northwards along Davis Strait until they reached 80°; at this point they were to steer south and west to 60°. It was believed that by doing so they might reach the northern coast of Japan! In that event, they were to kidnap a specimen Japanese and bring him back to England. The explorers did what they could to carry out these instructions. Two months after leaving Gravesend, they had reached Hope Sanderson, the impressive cliff on the Greenland coast which was the furthest north Davis had reached. They sailed on, putting the ship into the ice, which was very thick in those parts.

They passed Eskimo settlements on the way, people who were living as well as they could on raw seal meat; they rejected European food when it was offered to them. But this time they found themselves embayed in a wide sound infested by whales and, for that reason, named Whale Sound by the seamen. They had reached latitude 77°30'N. A few days later, sailing to the north, the channel they were sailing through narrowed; they named it Sir Thomas Smith's Sound (78°N). Baffin was surprised by the wide variation of the compass – as much as 56° to the west – that he found in that area. But there was no time to investigate that puzzle: time was running short, the seas were rising and they could find no anchorage. They stood to the westward in an open sea and in ten or eleven days were close to land at the entrance of a 'fair sound' which they named after Alderman Jones, one of their patrons. Two days later, helped by an 'easy gale' at eastn-orth-east, they ran along the coast southwards until they came to the opening of another and wider sound and named it Sir James Lancaster's Sound, after a city magnate who was an enthusiastic supporter of Arctic exploration. This sound they did not enter, for by now their hopes of finding the way to the northern coast of Japan during that season were diminishing fast. Sailing due east, greatly troubled with ice which prevented them from reaching land when they saw it, they reached the Cumberland Isles on the coast of Baffin Island. By that time they were 800 miles south-east of Lancaster Sound and had seen no sign of what they were seeking. Baffin admitted in his narrative, 'Hope of passage could be none.' After crossing to the Greenland coast, they traded with the Eskimos for salmon peal (young salmon), paying in glass beads and small pieces of iron 'which they do as much esteem as we Christians do gold and silver'. Then, blessed with a north wind and fair weather, they headed for home. Twenty-four days later, they dropped anchor in Dover Roads.

Baffin lost no time in telling Sir John Wolstenholme his opinion: there was no passage or even hope of a passage in the north of Davis Strait. The Strait was nothing but a great bay. 'How many of the best sort of men have set their whole endeavours to prove a passage that way! Yes. What great sums of money had been spent on it!' The vainglorious Spaniards would not have circulated so many false maps if they had not been confident of a passage. If it had pleased God that a passage had been found, the praise of its finders would have eclipsed all other adventurers and discoverers. For his own part, Baffin said, he would hardly have believed the contrary until his eyes became witness of what he desired not to have found. 'How vain the best and chiefest hopes of men are in things uncertain!'

There it was, then, plain and forthright, in the words of a manifestly honest and experienced navigator. No way through Davis Strait! What then? Baffin thought that there was more hope of finding the Passage if the search were begun at the Asiatic end. He went out by way of the Cape in the service of the East India Company. In 1620, as master of the *London*, he took part in an action at Surat where four of the Company's ships fought a combined force of Dutch and Portuguese. Two years later he was serving with an English force which the Company sent out to help the Shah of Persia to expel the Portuguese from Ormuz. While reconnoitring a castle wall in 1622, Baffin was shot in the stomach 'wherewith he gave three leaps and died immediately'. His widow, a 'troublesome impatient woman', pestered the East India Company with demands for money until 1628.

Not everybody shared Baffin's gloomy views of the North-west project. He had not entered Lancaster Sound. And he was wrong in one important respect. Baffin Bay was not sealed-off to the north. The search went on. Men more sanguine than Baffin took up the task.

North-West Foxe

'Worshipful Gentlemen and Foster Fathers of my Academie, I present you
here neither with Jason's voyage to Colcos, nor the Golden Fleece as yet,
but with the best of my endeavours to the North-West.'

Luke Foxe

If one had to embody in a single figure the strange enthusiasm for the discovery of the North-west Passage which overcame English seamen during
several generations, Luke Foxe would be just that man. He was, like
Frobisher, a Yorkshireman, born in Hull two years before the coming of
the Armada. He was proud and touchy about his origins: 'To those who
saith that I am but a north-country coaster and hath but been brought up
in small vessels, I wish their pride to know that God's mercy is over all His
creatures and hath created as good men in the North as in the South.' Like
his father before him, he became a sailor – a sailor with a single governing
idea, as fixed as the Pole Star. 'At the return home of all ships from thence'
[i.e. the North-west] I enquired of the masters, mates and others that were
that way employed, whereby I gathered from reports and discourses and
manuscripts how far they had proceeded.' The inquisitive boy from Yorkshire grew up to be a well-read, opinionated student of the growing science
of navigation, who haunted the shops of globe-makers and publishers of
books on seamanship. Eventually, he attracted the attention of a fellow-
Yorkshireman, Henry Briggs, Savilian Professor of Astronomy at Oxford,
and a distinguished mathematician of the time.

Briggs, an enthusiast for the idea of a North-west Passage, had remained
steadfast in the faith when Baffin had returned from Hudson's Bay a sceptic.
Briggs had drawn a map to illustrate Baffin's brief account of his voyage
and on it he had roundly declared that north of Hudson's Bay was the
entrance to the nearest and most temperate passage to Japan and China. For,
whereas, in the bottom of the Bay the height of the tide was only two feet,
at Port Nelson, further north and six hundred miles further west, the tidal

movement was 15 feet or more. What was the explanation of this phenomenon? Briggs had no doubt at all: 'The nearness of the South Sea.' So he drew his map, argued his case and, when he came across Foxe, recognized a zealot like himself. The two men, the mathematician and the sailor, talked together earnestly and at length.

With the help of Briggs, Foxe presented a petition to King Charles I, asking for 'a small sum of money towards the discovery of a passage to the North-west to the South Sea, Hudson and Sir Thomas Button having discovered a great way and given great hopes of opening the rest'. At the same time, Foxe obtained the support of Sir Thomas Roe, an able diplomat in the bold Elizabethan tradition, who had lately returned from a successful embassy to the King of Sweden.

When the King's interest had been obtained, Lord Dorchester, one of the Lords of the Admiralty, wrote to Sir Thomas Button in January 1630 asking him if he thought there was any likelihood of the venture succeeding, 'yea or noe'. Button replied from his home in Cardiff: he had no doubts at all that if a brave and experienced man were given 'the managing of this unparalleled business', success would come. But there must be no wasting of time in Hudson's Bay as both Hudson and he had done, on instructions. Whoever was chosen to lead the new expedition should, on reaching the west cape of Nottingham Island, follow the current which Button was confident he would find there. This was the only way to discover the Channel which Button was as confident existed as he was that there is one 'between Calais and Dover'. Button volunteered to bring the journal of his voyage to London for the King to see. At the same time, he took the opportunity to remind Lord Dorchester that he had not been paid for his services in the past, and, in consequence, was worse off than he had been ten years earlier, with a wife and seven children to support. Button came to town, and gave his advice in person, although it is not known whether he obtained any cash from the Exchequer.

The outcome of these conferences was that in 1631, Luke Foxe was given command of a small, elderly naval vessel, the *Charles*, of about 70 tons. 'The truth is,' he wrote later, 'that I had been itching after it ever since 1606 . . . Here my ambition soared a pitch higher than my ability, as time hath made me to know.' In 1606 Foxe was only twenty. The *Charles* had a crew of twenty men chosen carefully for their godly conversation and none of them more than thirty-five years old: if possible, with experience of frost-biting voyages. There were also two boys, 'beardless younkers'. Provisions were carried for a cruise of 18 months. The ship's master, whose name Foxe disdains to mention (it was Dunne) was appointed by Trinity House. Foxe, who begins his narrative by saying 'Gentlemen, our Yorkshire proverb is "Plain dealing is a jewel",' describes the master as 'the most arrogant bull calf that ever went as master, and the most faint-heartedest men'.

The *Charles* left Deptford on 5 May 1631 and five weeks later, on Mid-summer Day, Foxe had his first glimpse of ice and read to the crew the article in his commission which reminded them to look diligently for ice. All night, a man was to sit watching in the fore-top. So the *Charles* continued on her way westwards until she came to the headland which marks on the north side the entrance to Frobisher's Strait. Foxe's narrative at this point is somewhat confused because, like other navigators of his time, he believed that Frobisher's Strait, which as we know is an arm of the sea, ran through Greenland. In spite of his muddled notions about the geography of the region, however, he found his way to Hudson Strait and, entering it, made the difficult course between islands and capes, troubled by strong currents and eddies which reminded him of the behaviour of the stream rushing between the arches of London Bridge and meeting the incoming tide. The collision of the two currents there caused such a disturbance in the river that the watermen could not keep their boats steady, 'the counter tide wheeling on one side, the eddy coursing on the other, not joining their separation but going as it were distracted above Coldharbour . . . We are safer at sea.'

Foxe made fast to an icefloe and went to bed, as also did the rest of the crew, the watch excepted. He now wanted to press on to the west and, to his annoyance, found that Dunne, the Master, 'a proud fool and insolent', saw no need for haste, while the Master's mate would not so much as stir out of his cabin to look at the situation the ship was in, all beset by ice. This was a moment for speed, Foxe believed; later, there would be time for leisure. As he put it, he was like the mackerel men in London who must hasten to market before the fish stink. It seems that Dunne and the mate, Yourin, had been appointed against Foxe's opposition. They had no liking for the work and it is obvious that they disliked Foxe. 'Not one word passed between him and me,' Foxe reports of the Master. 'Nor have we drunk to one another since he told me he cared not for me.' But the mistake had been made in London and could not be remedied in the Arctic.

The Master and his lethargic mate prevailed, and the ship lay quietly all night among the ice. Next morning the wind blew strongly from the east-south-east and the ice began to break up. Foxe made one floe fast with two grapnels, meaning to tow it at the ship's stern as a drag to slow the vessel down as they were blown before the wind to the north-west, where Foxe expected the strait to be less impeded by ice. This state of things lasted for one day only, whereupon the strength of the wind broke the grapnels. In this crisis, Foxe heartened the ship's company by telling them that he expected to find the ice would become thinner as they went further into the strait.

The company replied by presenting him with a written demand for an increase in their liquor allowance. Their situation at that moment was so spectacularly perilous that a man's natural courage might well need to be reinforced. The strait was crowded with icebergs of enormous size, like cathedrals, and composed of fresh water, and floes – flaked ice, as Foxe called them – about an acre across, salt, and no more than a couple of feet above water. Yet ships might lie snugly among ice of that kind, although, says Foxe, let the mariner have a care to his rudder when the tide turned and the grip of the ice loosened! While they continued thus for a few days, the master and his mate annoyed Foxe by making a series of dismal prognostications: 'I would with all my heart they were changed, and others in their places,' wrote Foxe.

It was certainly no time for faint-hearted counsellors. There was an instant of frantic alarm when an iceberg, sixty feet above the water, drove straight at the ship. The masthead watch had given no warning of its approach and, for an instant it seemed that it would either crush the vessel or fall over on top of it and sink it. Fortunately, however, in the capricious way of floating ice, a few floes came across the path of the advancing berg and diverted it. The weather changed rapidly after this – black fog, which the sun dispersed; then, fair weather and calm. Foxe sent the Master's mate out in the boat to try the tide. When he returned, and clambered aboard he was surly and insisted on making his report to the Master and not to Foxe who thought gloomily: 'I fear a mutiny or hindrance to the voyage.'

All this time the *Charles* was making her way westwards along the Hudson Strait and was about to enter the Bay. One day they came upon a sea unicorn, shaped somewhat like a mackerel with a head like a lobster and a twisted black horn six foot long. More serious, Foxe was much troubled by the eccentric behaviour of the compass, which seemed to have lost its magnetism. He thought that this was due either to the 'sharpness of the air' which dulled 'the power of his determination' or else to the presence in the mountains nearby of some minerals which 'detained the nimbleness of the needles'. At Nottingham Island, which lies at the entrance to the Bay, he sent a boat's crew ashore who found the foundations of an old tent but nothing else of any interest. Next day, the crew of the *Charles* spotted a polar bear on a floe to which the ship was moored and hunted it from floe to floe until the Master killed it with a lance. 'We made about twelve gallons of oil of him.' Boiled, his meat was like beef but, roasted, it tasted oily and smelt rank. The night of 19 July was the first for many days that they saw stars and, on the horizon to the north, the aurora borealis appeared, sign that a storm was coming. There was endless bickering between Foxe and the Master about the course the ship should follow. Dunne said that, while Foxe might be a desperate man, he, Dunne, had a life to lose. 'So have I,' said Foxe, 'and mean to be careful of it for the sake of the voyage.' When Yourin intervened with some sharp words, Foxe told him he expected work from him, not impudence. Labour relations on the *Charles* were none too smooth.

After a time, continuing on their way further to the west, they arrived at an island which they thought must be a cemetery of the Eskimos. The corpses, none of them longer than four feet, had been laid out on stones or the wooden sides of old sledges. Where were the trees of which these sledges had been made? Where were the tools that had smoothed the wood? And where were the men who had left their dead in this place? They must, thought Foxe, have been nomads who had paused for a time and then passed on their way. There was what seemed to be a place of ceremony made of big stones laid in courses. This shrine – if that is what it was – was haunted by wild fowl and ravens bigger than those Foxe was familiar with in England. The visitors robbed the graves to make their fires and took away as souvenirs Eskimo darts, one of which had a copper head 'which I took to be the work of some Christians'. Foxe named the island Sir Thomas Roe's Welcome.

Then he stood away towards the south-west. All this while, he was cruising along the west shore of the Bay. A hundred miles further south he sighted a low island all of white marble where the crew went ashore and caught swans and the ship's dog brought a reindeer to bay. But, as it chanced, one of the quartermasters, Peter Nessfield, who had followed the chase, had neither gun nor lance to dispatch the beast – or else was overcome with pity when he saw it shed tears. Moreover, the dog had hurt his feet so much on the sharp stones that he could not go on with the chase. And so, rather ineffectually, the hunt ended.

Meantime, the weather was improving; indeed, by the first week of August it was as hot as anything Foxe had ever felt. By that time, they had passed the mouth of a great river with a white cliff standing at its entrance.

Foxe had now two main concerns on his mind: he wanted to find a tree in the forest suitable for a mainmast, and he wanted to assemble a collapsible pinnace which he had brought out with him from England.

By 9 August he was approaching Port Nelson, taking soundings anxiously as he went along, for the two rivers that run into the Bay at that point form a single estuary which is only five fathoms deep, shoaling to two. At length, he found an anchorage at a place where there were small woods on both banks and a clay cliff to the north. Exploring on land, he came upon a valley where he could set up a tent and put the pinnace together. Very soon he realized that he was not the first white man to visit these parts. An English ship, probably belonging to Sir Thomas Button's expedition, had been there before him. He found hogsheads, a main top, a top-gallant mast and other relics. Next morning the parts of the pinnace were brought ashore and Foxe, the carpenter, the quartermaster, the gunner and the cooper set to work assembling her. Meanwhile one of the seamen, Sam Blades, and the surgeon were sent out to look for a tree big enough to make a main yard. They came back having failed, but reporting the discovery of broken anchors, a broken gun, a quantity of round and crossbar shot, a tent and a cross that had fallen down, its inscription erased. That night it was very hot and there was a great display of lightning. Meanwhile, work went briskly forward and in three days the pinnace was all but finished, although the men who laboured to get her ready were impeded by a sudden deluge of rain.

Rowing up the river with the Master and others, Foxe came upon a dense forest of small spruce. Peter Nessfield, who had been put out of the boat so that Foxe could take her into shallower water, went exploring in the woods and reported that he had come upon the footprints of a man. But when they went back to look, they could find nothing. In this area, blackberries, strawberries, and gooseberries all grew in abundance. By the time they returned to the ship they found that the pinnace was ready to be sailed. In the days immediately following, Foxe was at pains to restore the cross he had found, nailing to it a new inscription in lead which informed anyone who chanced to read it that the land was called New Yorkshire.* Then one Sunday after prayers he and his companions left for the south-east, working their way along the coast.

The weather was calm with some showers of rain and Foxe thought of his friends at Whitby, wishing them as good weather for the hay-harvest as he had. He noticed an infinite number of wild geese flying to the south.

*Button had already named it New Wales.

Four days later came a day so cold that Foxe recognized it as the harbinger of winter. The land in those parts was low, well covered with trees and the wind was against the ship. And then, suddenly, about seven o'clock one evening, they spied a sail. It was Captain Thomas James who had left Bristol in the *Henrietta Maria* three days before Foxe and his crew left the Thames.

James sent his lieutenant over in his dinghy to invite Foxe, his Master and the Master's mate to dinner. He and Foxe had been sent out on the same mission in ships of the same tonnage and with crews of the same number. Foxe was backed by London merchants, James by Bristol money; both had the King's commission. One captain was bound to feel that the presence of the other in these waters was embarrassing and unnecessary. That they had met was an extraordinary coincidence. Two little ships of seventy tons in an expanse of water half as big again as the Baltic Sea. Yet they fell in with one another at the mouth of what is now called the Winisk River, half-way between Port Nelson and James Bay. The meeting between them promised to put something of a strain on good manners and mutual tolerance unless they were exceptionally congenial to one another. As it chanced, they were not. Foxe was a Yorkshireman, quick to suspect a slight; James was Welsh, from Monmouth, a member of the Inner Temple, where, in the records, he is described as 'a younger son of James apJohn apRichard Herbert'. He was, it seems, something of a mathematician.

Up to that point, the adventures of James and his crew had been more alarming than those of Foxe. A month after leaving Bristol in the early summer, the *Henrietta Maria* was for days in danger of being crushed in the ice off the Greenland coast. Sailing further westwards, still troubled by icebergs, some of them higher than the masthead, they ran into stinking fog and a black sea. They heard at night 'a hollow and hideous noise' which, at first, they took to be the roar of breakers on an unseen shore. It turned out to be the sound of waves beating on a bank of ice stretching between them and the land. They were at the entrance to Hudson's Strait.

When a wind from the west threatened to drive the ship ashore, James made fast to the side two large icefloes, drawing ten fathoms. They were to serve as fenders. The ship's boat was sent out to look for a safe anchorage but was at once in danger of being crushed and destroyed. Her crew hauled her like a sledge from one floe to another. At this moment, the two floes broke loose from the ship, carrying with them the small anchor which had kept them in place. In this emergency, James signalled to the boat's crew to hurry back. When they did so he replaced them with fresh oarsmen and sent the boat out again to retrieve the anchor. All this time, the ship was being driven closer to the land so that, very soon, James could see rocks underneath the keel and all about. He took a bold decision then, putting out more sail so as to force the ship in among the rocks.

There he had the good fortune to run against a big floe that was fast to the shore, and thus deadened the impact of grounding. Even so, the shock broke the main knee of the ship's beak-head and tore away four of the main shrouds. Fifteen feet of water between them and a rocky bottom, the ice driven hard by the tide against the sides of the ship and the boat, with a third of their company in her, lost somewhere in the fury of the sea! Lost – and perhaps shattered to fragments. No! There she was, glimpsed in the turmoil of seas amidst the rocks bringing back the kedge anchor. All that evening and through the night that followed, the crew worked desperately to ward off the ice which was pounding against the ship, driven by a blizzard blowing from the west.

Next day, in spite of all they could do, the ship settled on a sharp rock and, when the tide ebbed, heeled over seawards; although they sought to hold her upright in place with cables stretched taut between masts and rocks, as the water ebbed the gunwale of the fo'csle was soon in the water. The sailors were unable to stand upright on the deck. Having done all they could and done it in vain, they jumped on a floe and fell to their prayers while waiting for the ship to capsize. Almost at once, prayer was answered. The tide turned. The ship righted herself. They had time for a prayer of gratitude but not for much more. The danger from the ice floes, some of them 300 paces in circumference, continued day after day and had to be fought off with axes, iron bars and anything else that would serve. In a respite, James clambered ashore and built a cairn surmounted by a cross. He named the place The Harbour of God's Providence, prematurely, as it seemed. Next day he went out to seek a better anchorage and reached the top of a hill from which he could see the ship almost hidden behind an iceberg that reached halfway up the mast. At that moment, the ice broke with a terrifying report and James hastened back to the ship expecting to find that all was lost. But – 'God be thanked' – the ice had broken off in a direction away from the vessel. James warped her to a cove, not a mile distant, which promised to give better shelter.

Going ashore, he found neither tree, plant nor grass, nothing but rocks and ponds which had not thawed yet so that no wild fowl frequented them. In one place Eskimos had made hearths – why he could not think, for there was no wood on the land nor fish in the sea. Then, when a fair wind sprang up from the east, the *Henrietta Maria* sailed out of the cove, between icebergs twice as high as the top of its mainmast. After that, with a changing of the wind, they were caught again among the floes until, in a day or so, the ice opened somewhat and they could prise a way through for the ship. James had hoped that they could explore to the north-west, but the ice barred the way and threatened to destroy the ship. He must wait until next year, if he lived to see next year. In the meantime, he gave orders to his ship's master to steer west by south. But a fortnight later they were still fighting off the ice, heaving the ship forward with their shoulders, while they hacked at the edges of the bergs with mauls and crowbars.

Seeing that the morale aboard was weakening, James exerted himself to keep the men's spirits up. One day he made everybody get out on the floe and drink the King's health, although the deserted ship was moving, with all sails set, through the ice. At the same time, he prudently rationed the amount of fuel that the steward delivered to the cook every day. Through weather good and bad, the ship kept on her course south-west and Captain James became increasingly convinced that there was no hope of reaching the Passage through the Bay. Then, on 13 August, in the course of a hazy afternoon, it seemed that final disaster had come.

The ship struck a hidden rock. Two swelling seas carried her over the reef into three fathoms of water. All sails were struck, an anchor was dropped, the pumps were manned. But the disaster was not complete; the ship was making no water. The boat was sent out to reconnoitre but was, almost at once, lost in the fog. After two hours, it returned, guided by shots fired into the darkness. Following the lead given by the boat, the ship was brought to an anchorage which served during that night indifferently well. At noon of 17 August, James thought they were twenty miles south of Port Nelson. But three days passed before they could see land. Then, in the calm of the evening, they dropped their anchor. The calm, however, did not last. The ship dragged on its anchor, the wind blew hard and a choppy sea was leaping at the spritsail yard. While they laboured at the capstan to wind in the anchor cable, a series of misfortunes overtook them. A small rope, which had fouled the cable, wound itself about the Master's leg. With difficulty he got clear. Two mates were hurt. One of the strongest crew men was struck in the breast by a capstain bar and lay sprawling, helpless. Worst of all, the gunner had his leg caught between the cable and the capstan. His foot was torn off, the flesh was stripped from his leg, the shinbone was shattered. And so he lay screaming, poor devil, until his shipmates recovered their wits enough to pull him clear. He was bundled down to the surgeon who took off his leg at the 'gartering place'.

After this calamity came some days of variable winds with fog which cleared to show them that they were in a little bay. There they anchored while James sent out the boat with the orders that it should be back by sunset. When dusk came and there was still no sign of the boat, they fired shots and lit flares. At last an answering fire was lit on the shore. The ship approached it warily knowing that the fire might have been lit by savages. It had, in fact, been lit by the boat's crew who were sternly rebuked by James on their return. Why had they been absent so long? Their answer was that they had been stranded by the ebbing tide on a sandbank and only released when the water rose again. They reported a great amount of drift-wood on the shore, tracks of deer and bear and many wild fowl. There were no signs of people. Two days later, after a battle with stormy winds that tested to the limit James's skill as a seaman, they caught sight of a ship a dozen miles to leeward. They made sail and bore up with her. It was the H.M.S. *Charles*, Captain Foxe in command, lying at anchor.

Foxe took advantage of the arrival of the seaman from the *Henrietta Maria* to find out where James had been, how far to the north he had voyaged and how long he had spent in the ice. Next day he went on board the *Henrietta Maria* where James entertained him well on roast partridge. They dined in the open air between decks, the main cabin being too small for them. During the meal the ship took so much water that Foxe, who had a talent for disparagement, decided they would not have lacked for sauce if their dish had been roast mutton. He was led on to speculate what might happen if James carried out his plan of spending a winter in the Bay. If he and his companions were shut in by the ice, they would be kept from putrefaction by the cold air. If, on the other hand, they were on the open sea, then they would be pickled every day. These agreeable thoughts occurred to him as the meal progressed and the ship behaved like a duck, as he thought, her nose no sooner out of the pitcher than in it again!

Meanwhile, Captain James talked learnedly about mathematics, to Foxe's irritation. Foxe wanted to know why James had allowed himself to be fobbed off with a ship as unsuitable as the *Henrietta Maria* if he were determined to spend two winters away from England. And why, for that matter did James insist on flying his flag. 'Because,' said James, 'I am going to the Emperor of Japan with letters from His Majesty and I will not strike my flag, not for a forty gun ship of the King's.' 'Keep it up, then,' said

Foxe, who likewise carried a letter to the Emperor, 'but this is not the way to Japan.' James tried to persuade the Yorkshireman to find a harbour for his ship but Foxe would have none of it. He had come, he said, not to do as much as other men, but more – indeed, he had already done so. He was particularly annoyed when James suggested it was his duty, under his commission, to spend the winter in the Bay. Only the fact that he was a guest prevented Foxe from making some angry retort. Whether James was patronizing or not may be in doubt. But Foxe was certainly prickly and conceited, forever looking for a cause of offence.

However, the parting of the two captains at six o'clock next morning was civil enough. Foxe handed over the James ten muskets and a falconet. Then, his farewells made, he bore off to the south-west carrying as much sail as masts and ship could bear. He had no wish to remain any longer than he needed to do in James's company. By nightfall he had put thirty miles between him and their meeting place and had dropped anchor off a river mouth with low, wooded country on either bank. There he spent the night in fair weather with an easy wind.

Having shaken off his rival, Foxe was more determined than ever to carry out his mission. He was sure, as Sir Thomas Button had been sure, that the Passage existed, 'as there is one between Calais and Dover'. His was the knowledge of his time. For instance, he thought there was an island named Friesland between Iceland and Greenland – was it not recorded in Zeno's map? He thought that the northern part of Greenland was joined to Asia. Above all, he thought that Hudson had been on the right course when he went exploring in the great Bay. Now he, Foxe, unwearying student of maps and inquisitor of returned navigators, would follow in the wake of that great, unfortunate man. For those (and apparently there were some) who were inclined to question his fitness for the task as a North-countryman who had served only in small coasters, Foxe had a sharp reply: 'Let no man be disdained.'

If Foxe seems unduly touchy, he had some excuse. His encounter with James had been a disturbing experience. By the time the two ships took their separate ways, Foxe was convinced that James, although an expert in mathematics, was no navigator. He himself worked his way along the shore of the Bay to the east and then to the north until the beginning of October. Nottingham Island, where Button had hoped that he might find a way to the north-west, turned out to be disappointing: a great mass of ice barred the ship's way.

By that time, Foxe had already detected the first signs that winter was coming. The men began to 'hurkle' with the cold and some of them were no longer willing to come out on deck. The nights were clear, the pettie dancers (aurora borealis) brilliant and sinister. There was a great deal of wind and 'hoary frost hung on our ropes'. The crew were taking bets that Hudson Strait would be solid with ice and that they would not get home that year. The Master, coming out of his cabin for the first time in a week, as Foxe sourly noted, encouraged this dispiriting talk. So, too, did 'that rogue', the bosun, who had once been to Greenland, and reported that the ice in these parts never melted. He thought that the speculators who had put money into the voyage should be ashamed for sending them to look for a needle in a bottle of hay. Breaking in on this gloomy talk, Foxe had a quarrel on a point of navigation with the Master, 'upon my soul, he is the most unpleasant fellow that ever kissed his Majesty's hand'. Next day, after prayers, the sun shone and thawed the crew – 'You will not believe,' said Foxe, 'how a little clear and shine did stir up' their spirits.

After that, Foxe and the Master were not on speaking terms for a time. Rather pointedly, the Master avoided attending prayers, thus setting a bad example to the men, Foxe thought. The weather was very cold and freezing hard and complaints were continuous from one or another. To cheer things up, Foxe named two capes after the King and Queen. Drink flowed; toasts were drunk, much comforting the sorely tried seamen. By this time the *Charles*, leaving Hudson Strait on the starboard side, was forging northwards into a channel which had never before been penetrated (Foxe Channel) where he was hopeful of finding the Passage, 'for certain those great tides must have recourse to another ocean'. On 20 September he crossed the Arctic Circle.

But plainly he could not hope to do more that season. The wind was high, the weather was growing more severe. By 1 October, he decided that it was time to make for home. 'The Lord for his mercy sake, look upon us, for we are all in weak state.' One group of islands he called 'Briggs his Mathematic', in gratitude to the scholar who had been his benefactor. When the wind slackened, snow began to fall heavily, and trouble broke out among the crew. In spite of all the care with which Foxe had picked the ship's company, some of them had broken into the store of liquor. Foxe's impulse was to punish them for this misdemeanour by keeping all drink from them until the thieves owned up. The crew as a body said they would rather have nothing to drink than have any man punished, and, to Foxe's annoyance, the ship's Master, whom he already suspected of currying favour with the men now that the homeward run was beginning, sided with the crew on this question. He said that Foxe did not know how to treat men as human beings and, generally, he lined up with the malcontents. By 5 October the *Charles* had doubled Cape Chidley against a sea so heavy that her bowsprit and spritsail yard were often under water.

The ship's rigging glittered with icicles and, as Foxe put it, 'snow showers were sent from Boreas's frozen forge which searcheth our very beards . . . for three weeks no novelty'. The mate took to the bottle and was 'all wamble'*; the crew, too, were 'pretty pleasant' having been making free with the sherry casks in the hold; the cook, whose gimlet had been used to let acqua vitae out of a cask, was a-bed. What with one thing and another, Foxe thought it was just as well he had given the order to go home at the first sign of snow. Very soon he was guiding the *Charles* towards the Scillies, for although the route by Orkney was shorter, the weather was cold, the nights long and the moon 'decayed'. As it was, the homeward voyage had its anxieties, with the Master and his mate laid low, the gunner not often on deck and the sick men able to do nothing. Happily, they encountered no icebergs after passing Cape Chidley.

One day Foxe had a dispute with the Master, who wanted to open another tierce of sack 'for the good of the men', the last tierce having improved their spirits so much. 'I told him,' said Foxe, 'I had no quarrel to a drop of sack,' but the crew's needs could be satisfied without wasting the shareholder's money. 'Put on bonnets to hasten home,' cried Foxe, bonnets being additional pieces of canvas which could be laced on to the bottom of the sails to give the ship more speed. 'Well,' said the Master, 'I will look well to the sack.' 'I believe him,' said Foxe drily. The *Charles* reached the Downs on the last day of October, 'not having lost one man nor boy nor any manner of tackling, having been forth near six months, all glory be to God.' With the warmer weather, the crew's health had greatly improved. How different it might have been had adverse winds in Hudson Strait driven them back into the grip of the ice!

All things considered, Foxe thought he had reason to be pleased with what he had done, even if he had not found the way to the east. Not everybody shared his satisfaction. Above all, he was criticized for coming home so soon. Sir Thomas Roe, for example, wrote a letter to the Merchant Venturers of Bristol, in which he remarked that Foxe had not called on him, 'whether for shame or (as he pretends) to make his cause perfect'. From the interrogation of the Master and his mate, Sir Thomas had learned

*staggering.

that Foxe had not searched for the North-west Passage beyond Cape Comfort, but had 'run down into the Bay'. He had made a worse mistake by following the current round Nottingham Island to the north-east – 'But I never knew men seek a North-west Passage on a North-east shore.' Roe concluded, 'So all our hopes now rest upon Captain James,' who is resolved 'not to come home like a sluggard and say a lion roars or was in his way.' Obviously, the Master and his mate had taken their revenge on Foxe by maligning him to Roe. And Roe, in accepting their version of events, was being hard on the captain who, with recalcitrant officers and an undisciplined crew, had probably been wise to come home when he did. But the fact was that Foxe had returned, while James, the barrister-mariner, had stayed on to face winter in the Bay. If Foxe's narrative has a strident, defensive tone, then, the reason is not far to seek. Even when Foxe went to Court at Oatlands to deliver his report to the King, he was reminded that his rival was thought to have played the more splendid rôle. On the way back to London by river, one of the King's gentleman told Foxe that Captain James had reached the Pacific and would come home by the Cape of Good Hope.

'If he does,' said Foxe, testily, 'may I be severely punished, as I will deserve. If Captain James has not done as much as I have, may I be rewarded with what I have saved, to wit, eleven months' victual and pay and £75 a month.' It need not be said that, when James did return, Foxe was easily convinced that the Welsh captain had not achieved as much as he himself had done.

A Winter in the Forest

'Ye marine worthies! How many anxious and painfully sleepless nights must have been yours! What suffering from cold and scanty fare! What discomfort from your small, fragile pent-up vessels!'

Declaration of the Indies, Robert Thorne

'I wish that some learned man would write of [scurvy], for it is the plague of the sea and the spoil of mariners.'

Richard Hawkins, 1622

What, in fact, had happened to the Welshman during his sojourn in the Bay?

A little more than a month after parting from Foxe, James was overtaken by winter while exploring the southern shore of the Bay. He was then not far from Charlton Island in the south part of what is now known as James Bay. The perils of his situation – snow, storm, rocks, shoals, and sinister grinding noises which persisted through the night – inspired him to prayer and even to poetry:

> 'Oh, my poor soul, why dost thou grieve to see
> So many deaths muster to murder me?
> Look to thyself; regard not me; for I
> Must do for what I came, perform or die'.

His crew, who did not have his ability to seek comfort from verse, were weak by this time and some of them were ill. James rowed ashore to look for help but there he found only a few berries for the sick. The snow fell; ice came, forming on the bow of the ship and the cable, as thick as a man's waist. He could use the sails no longer; they were frozen stiff. The seamen had a great deal of difficulty in rowing to the shore through the ice. Then the sick men raised their heads from the pillows to ask that a house should be built for them on land. James accordingly put the carpenter and other fit men to work hewing down trees and rough-squaring them with the axe. The sails were thawed over a fire in the hatchway; after that, some of them were stowed away between decks while the mainsail was used to cover the new-built house. Hunters went hopefully out into the forest with two greyhounds: one party came back with a small deer; on a second expedition the gunner's mate was taking a short cut across a frozen pond when the ice broke beneath him and he was seen no more.

Meanwhile, the gunner, 'an honest and strong-hearted man', who had lost his leg in the accident with a cable, died of cold in the gunroom, having asked that, for the little time he had to live, he might drink sack and nothing else. A pan of coals was kept burning in the gunroom beside him. But nothing would raise the temperature. 'His plaster would freeze in the wound and his bottle of sack at his head.' And so the gunner died, like a Christian and full of sack, and was committed to the sea a good distance from the ship.

The day after the gunner's death, the ice increased extraordinarily and the snow lay in flakes on the water as it fell. Freshly formed ice, in sections two inches thick and at least a quarter of a mile across, drove against the ship, putting cable and anchor under heavy strain. James fired three musket shots so that the men who had gone ashore to build a house for the winter should come to his aid. They heard, answered, but could not reach the ship before ten o'clock on the following morning, wading part of the way through water that was thickening to ice. Seeing that no anchor would hold the ship, James gave orders to run her aground. It was a risky manoeuvre, for she might sink so deeply into the sand that she could not be dug out again. Or the ice might tear away so much of her planking and iron-work that not enough material would be left to make a pinnace for the voyage home if the *Henrietta Maria* had to be abandoned. At one moment, the ship was in danger of being smashed on the rocks ashore. At the next, there was a change of wind and they were hard put to it to hold her to the shore with an anchor. Sooner or later, it seemed, the ship would be crushed in the driving ice at sea or smashed to fragments between the incoming floes and the rocks. James remembered with foreboding how, years before, Sir Hugh Willoughby and all his crew had been driven out to sea and had perished of starvation. Now he had to resort to a desperate expedient which in its mixture of ruthlessness, boldness and technical logic can be classed with the most extraordinary actions of that iron age.

Calling his officers together, he told them he proposed to put the provisions ashore and sink the ship. After debate, the officers agreed. Then the crew were consulted. They, too, approved. Their store of bread, a hogshead of beef and packing cases full of provisions were lowered into the ship's boat and rowed to the shore through the thickening water. The wind turned to the north-east, filling the harbour with ice and encouraging James to hope, throughout the whole of a day, that the ship would be frozen in where she was riding and that there would be no need to sink her. But at daybreak on the following day (28 November) the wind swung round to the west, clearing away much of the ice between the ship and the shore, although not enough to allow the boat to be rowed to the land. In these conditions the ship would certainly be battered to pieces. It was time to make ready for the last project.

James put the carpenter to work, cutting a hole, five inches square, in the ship's hull four feet from the keel. Only the sheathing was left between them and the water. At the same time, the remainder of the bread was brought up into the main cabin along with all the gunpowder. At five o'clock in the morning of 29 November, the wind began to blow very hard from the west-nor'-west and James sent the cooper down into the hold where the casks were stored. The full casks should have their bungs hammered firmly in, the empty should be brought up on deck or, if that were impossible, should be staved in. The cables were coiled on the lower tier of the hold, with the spare anchors laid on top of them. By seven o' clock, it was blowing a full gale from the north-west and there was a danger of the *Henrietta Maria* being driven so far up the shore that they would never get her off again. James was resolved to sink her there and then, rather than risk her taking any more damage. By nine o'clock, she began to roll under the force of an unusually great sea: 'This was the fatal hour that put us to our wit's end.' James went down to the hold, accompanied by the carpenter and, with his auger, bored a hole in the sheathing and let the water pour in.

By ten o'clock, the lower tier of the hold was under water, but the ship was pounding with increasing violence against the shore. James and the carpenter could neither work nor stand in her. Nor was she sinking as quickly as they wished. Worst of all, she was beating against the shore so hard that James thought she could hardly last another quarter of an hour. Two hours later, the lower tier of the hold came loose and floated up inside the hull where it began to beat with such force against the bulkheads of the bread-room and the powder-room that everything was smashed to pieces. Rising higher, it made havoc between decks; chests, loosened from their fastenings, flew about so that James feared the ship would break in pieces at any minute. At one o'clock, the rudder was torn off and lost in the sea. But not until two more hours had passed did the ship begin to settle. By that time, the water had reached the upper deck. Gone were most of their clothes, most of the bedding and the surgeon's chest. The men who had gone ashore stood looking on, almost dead with cold and sorrow, at 'our misery and their own'. The men on the battered ship looked back at their comrades with woeful hearts. At the approach of darkness, James ordered the longboat to be hauled alongside and commanded his companions to board it. But this they refused to do unless he went with them. In fact, he had meant to do so. 'Thus, lastly, I forsook the ship,' he says.

So there they were in the boat, 'seventeen poor souls, cold and wretched, with the tide ebbing seawards fast, the water as thick as soup with ice.' Four oars were double manned; four more men sat ready to row. With the tide on the ebb and the water so thickly congealed with snow, they thought it certain they would be carried out to sea, unable to row against the movement of the water. But at last they reached the shore, hauling the boat after them. There they met the four men who had all this time been working on the house. Neither party could recognize the other. All were caked with ice and snow, faces, hair, clothing. And voices were unrecognizable.

In the house, before a good fire, they thawed out and began to discuss their future. James asked every man to speak his mind freely. The carpenter thought that the ship was so damaged that she would never sail again. There was no creek or cove in the neighbourhood where she could be beached so that he might repair her. Besides, the rudder was lost and he had no ironwork on which another rudder could be hung. Other speakers thought they had hauled her up so high on the shore that they would never be able to get her off again. Already she was embedded three feet deep in the sand. Others again said that, as she lay within the movement of the tides, the ice would tear her to pieces. There was another matter, too. Two of their anchors were under the ice, which would certainly shatter them when the spring came and the ice broke up. Thus, they would be left with no anchors for the homeward voyage – if there ever was a homeward voyage!

James brought the gloomy debate to a close with a few godly and optimistic words. 'My masters and faithful companions,' he began, 'be not dismayed by any of these disasters, but let us put our whole trust in God. We are as near heaven here as in England.' If the ship was foundered – but he hoped not – other Englishmen, when wrecked, had built a pinnace, why should not they do so? No doubt those other Englishmen had to deal with more friendly climates but nothing was too hard for courageous minds! Responding to this display of leadership, the crew, led by the carpenter, recovered their cheerfulness. James promised the carpenter ten pounds worth of plate if he built a pinnace. More than that, if he sailed home in the pinnace, the carpenter should have it for his own, freely, plus fifty pounds in cash. It was decided that the frame of the pinnace should be made from the trees growing round about them in the island and, if the *Henrietta Maria* was not found to be serviceable in the spring, her planks could be used for the pinnace.

Next morning, all of them, led by James went to the surgeon to have a haircut and be shaved, for their beards had proved an intolerable nuisance when icicles formed on them. After that they got down to work. The crew was split up into working parties. One-third, under the master, were sent back to the ship to get things out of the hold, a third – the coxswain's party – were to bring them ashore by boat, and a third, led by James himself, were to carry them half a mile through the snow to a place where they meant to build a storehouse. The heavier goods would be left on the beach. That afternoon, when the tide was at an exceptionally low ebb, the boat was manhandled into the water and rowed towards the grounded ship. They hoped to bring more goods out of the ship's hold. James watched them from the shore, anxious lest the boat should be carried out to sea by the retreating sea and lost. But in due course a fire was kindled on board the ship as a signal that the boat party had arrived safely. The trouble was, however, that with darkness falling, the members of this party did not dare to return to the shore. They spent the night, famished and shivering, on a bed in the main cabin. By next morning, the temperature had fallen so low, freezing the sea, that they were able to carry bedding and clothing on their backs over the ice.

Milder weather came next day and some of the seamen, who had trusted to the ice, fell in and were rescued with difficulty. They could land nothing that day by boat or on foot. The following day, the boat, when loaded, drew four feet of water and could not be rowed within 'a flight shot'* of the shore. In consequence, men were forced to wade through the icy water and carry everything out of the ship on their backs. When it was obvious that the longboat was too firmly caught in the ice to be any more good as a ferry, they tried to hoist her on to the ship. but in this they failed. They were forced to leave her by the ship's side. Days passed, during which the cold was extreme; snow fell heavily, and noses, cheeks and hands were frozen as white as paper. Ice stove in the side of the longboat, but on the other hand there was one piece of good news: in the woods the carpenter

*Roughly the breadth of the Thames above London Bridge (Leland).

found timber suitable for making a keel and a stern for the pinnace. After twenty days, when at last they gave up all attempts to get the provisions out of the ship, they left there five barrels of beef and pork and all their beer, firmly frozen in. One morning, when they were trying to run the longboat further up the beach on its oars, they were surprised by a sudden descent of fog as black as night. They could not see further than a few feet ahead of them and found their way back to the dry land with difficulty.

After that, they gathered in the house, frozen and miserable. Many of them, who had come too hastily to the fire, developed blisters as big as walnuts on their hands. By this time their troubles were multiplying fast: the well had frozen; when they drank melted snow-water, it made them so short of breath that they could hardly speak; all the sherry, vinegar and oil was frozen as hard as wood and had to be cut with a hatchet. But once again they had good luck as well as bad. On an earlier reconnaissance, James had found a well about three-quarters of a mile from the house. Now he sent men to look for it; they found it, flowing strong and clear under the snow. All through that winter the well kept them supplied with good water. When bedding, provisions and firewood had been gathered, it was time to celebrate Christmas Day 'in the joyfullest manner we could'.

The house in which their festivities took place was built a bow-shot from the sea among thick trees and sheltered by a south bank. There was a fine white sand underfoot; and, two feet below that, they came on water. This prevented them from hollowing out a cellar, as James had originally intended. The house was twenty foot square, a size which the mainsail would cover. Strong six-foot stakes driven into the ground were closely wattled with branches to form the walls. Two holes were left to let the light in and the smoke out. Outside, three rows of bushes were stuck upright in the ground as close to the house as might be. At a distance from the hut, tree trunks were piled to a height of six feet. A low door was left open so that they could creep in and out; in front of it, trunks were heaped up as a windbreak. A big tree, stripped of its branches, formed the roof frame of the house; over it the mainsail was spread. Bonnet sails were hung round as wall coverings on three sides. Bunks were erected in two layers and filled with branches on which the spare sails were laid, with the bedding on top. In the middle of the hut was the hearth, with planks laid on the ground about it to prevent the damp from striking upwards. Twenty feet away from the house a second, rather smaller, hut was built on much the same principles. In it, food was prepared and the lower ranks of the crew lived.

Further off was the storehouse where they kept their reserves of bread and fish.

By Christmas Day all the three huts were hidden in snow which lay waist-deep on the ground and was methodically trodden into paths so that they could go from hut to hut and take exercise when they needed to.

And so James and his comrades faced the winter of 1631–2, in hard conditions which, as time passed, they made more comfortable. James, being an observant man, made copious notes in his diary. One day in January he recorded that the sun rose in an oval shape, twice as long as it was broad, and only recovering a circular shape when it had risen higher above the horizon. The ground, he noticed, was frozen to a depth of ten feet. In February, he reported the arrival of scurvy, that arch-enemy of the long-distance voyage. Swollen gums, loosened teeth, swollen legs, weak backs – showing these symptoms, two-thirds of the crew were under the surgeon's care. But the work must go on, fetching firewood and bringing food from the storehouse, although most of them had no shoes to wear, having scorched them on their feet before the fire. As for the spare shoes, they had all gone down when the ship was sunk. Binding clouts about their feet, they got about as well as they could. James distinguished three degrees of cold: in the hut, the roof beams were hung with icicles, there was hoar frost on the bedclothes and the water in which the cook was seething meat would be frozen solid in the tub at night. The surgeon's medicines were frozen in the bottle. In the woods, the cold froze their faces; but, worst of all, was the cold they felt out on the ice when they went to visit the ship. It would freeze the hair on their eyelids so that they could not see. In a few hours, it would have stifled a man. So, at least, James thought.

But, somehow, they survived and spring came, slowly. After St David's Day which James, as a good Welshman, kept 'after the manner of the ancient Britons', with prayers for Charles, Prince of Wales, one of the crew thought he had seen a deer in the woods and went after it with some companions. They returned in the evening without the deer but with massive blisters on their feet. These took a fortnight to heal. The cold continued, the snow was as deep as ever. True, they had wood and could make a fire. But, says James, 'I must tell you how difficult it is to have wood in a wood.' Axes and hatchets were soon damaged, and could only be roughly repaired; green wood made so much smoke in the fire that men would rather shiver for cold than burn it; dry wood, being full of turpentine, made so much soot that they looked like chimney-sweeps. The men whose task it was to find crooked timbers for building the pinnace were forced to crawl through the snow and, when they had found a likely timber, light a fire beside it to thaw it so that they could cut it out and drag it home through the snow.

Easter Day, which was extraordinarily cold, they observed as religiously as God allowed them to do. Sitting round the fire they took stock of their plight. By this time, scurvy was striking harder. Five men, one of them the carpenter, growing worse all the time, could do nothing through sickness; the bosun and many others were invalids. Only five men were fit enough to eat their daily rations. Nor did they look to the future with much hope, believing, as they did, that the ship lay under the water with enough ice in her to burst her seams, while the pinnace, on which rested so many of their hopes of getting back to England, was still in need of a great deal of work before it could take the water. And what hope was there of that, with the carpenter manifestly in failing health?

Listening to all the doleful talk, James reached a decision: as soon as the weather turned milder, they would clear the ship of ice, although they had only two iron bars and four broken shovels with which to do it. Meanwhile, the snow fell more heavily than ever, but moister, not dry like fine sand as it had formerly been. A fortnight later, the sun shone, the mist lifted and they could see a small island about twelve miles away to the south. They remembered seeing it the year before. James put some of the crew to work clearing the snow from the upper decks of the ship and lighting a fire in the main cabin. Others were set to work to find the anchor in the shoal water and, when they found it, to search for the rudder. This was a harder task; indeed, the best opinion was that it was lost irretrievably beneath the sand. Three men asked to be allowed to sleep on board, which would relieve them of hearing the night-long groans and lamentations of the sick. A week after the clearing of the ship began, there was good news: a cask in the hold was pierced and found to be full of excellent beer (although admittedly it tasted a little of bilge-water).

By the end of April, they began to work the pumps in the ship because, by that time, it was plain that the carpenter was a dying man and there was little hope of finishing the pinnace. Worse still, there were only four men fit to make the journey through the snow and over the ice to reach the ship or the half-finished pinnace. But they were encouraged to find that when they dug out the sand round the ship the water did not rise inside. It seemed the hull was sound enough. James set to work thawing the pumps with hot water as a preliminary to pumping water out of the hold. With admirable resilience, on May Eve the working party returned to the house late from their work and made merry, ceremoniously wearing ladies' names in their caps as if they had been in England for the feast. They fared as well as they could. They had lived through the winter on beef boiled with oatmeal, with pork and pease pudding for Sunday dinner. When they were lucky enough to trap a fox, they boiled it into broth for the weakest of the scurvy victims, men who could eat neither beef, pork, fish nor porridge and – in the worst cases – could not so much as turn in their bunks without help. Those who were slightly less crippled were able, with the help of hot fomentations, to go out through the snow as far as the ship. But by night-fall they were as bad as ever and must be bathed and anointed before they went back to bed, while the surgeon cut away the dead flesh from their gums. James had prudently reserved a tun of Alicante wine for this time. Heavily diluted with water, it made a poor sort of beverage, hardly better than water. The weakest of the invalids were allowed a pint of neat Alicante plus a dram of aqua vitae.

Suddenly the cold made a brief, but savage return, and the sick grew worse, fainting when they were taken from bed and only brought back to life with difficulty. The chief mate's master died on 6 May and was buried ('in the most Christian-like manner we could') on the top of a bare sandy hill which they called Brandon Hill after a height at Bristol. Meanwhile, the work of clearing ice out of the ship went on. They came upon five barrels of beef and pork, plus four butts of beer and one of cider – none of them any the worse for having spent a winter under water. After that, they discovered their stock of spare shoes which they dried out at the fire. The ship seemed to be sound enough, although Will Cole, the dying carpenter, insisted that this was simply because the ice was keeping the water out. Let her begin to labour in the sea and she would undoubtedly open, he thought. And, true enough, they could see daylight through her seams between wind and water. What worried them most, however, was the loss of the rudder. James sent men off after wild-fowl but, having no shot save what could be improvised from old pewter and the sheet lead covering the touch-holes of the guns, they had only indifferent luck. The cooper, weak as he was, set to work repairing casks. The hope was that cables, fastened to the casks, might be passed under the ship's keel to buoy her up.

In addition, the captain manured a patch of earth that was now bare of snow and hopefully sowed it with peas. On 18 May, Cole, the carpenter, died and was buried that evening on the hilltop beside the chief mate's master. While he was still able to work, he had brought the pinnace – 27 feet on the keel and 10 feet on the beam – to the point in construction where she was ready to be bolted together. She was a well-proportioned vessel of twelve or fourteen tons. When they made their way back from burying the carpenter that evening, the Master went aboard the ship and saw something that made his hair stand on end with horror. The body of the gunner, buried at sea close on six months earlier, was floating in the icy water just outside the gunroom ports, head downwards, his one leg upwards, the bandage still at his wound. This grisly visitant must be removed without delay. The gunner's body ('as free from noisesomeness as when we first committed him to the sea') was dug out of the ice and buried beside the other corpses on the hilltop. That day, too, George Ugganes, a handyman, finished the pinnace as well as he could.

By this time, the ponds in the woods were thawing fast, although when the sailors climbed a tree which they called their watch-tree, they could still see no sign of a break-up of the ice on the frozen sea. That Whitsunday was a mournful feast, with health getting worse, game birds proving elusive, and no bird or leaf eatable in the woods. The bosun took to his bed with such a terrible ache in the thigh that all expected him to die. The weather was unnatural – spells of unendurable heat by day, freezing hard at night. All around, the ice cracked with terrifying reports. Amidst this misery there was, however, one flash of joy. It came during the early days of June when David Hammond, a seaman, poking about in the ice with a lance, found the lost rudder! 'Oh!' cried James recalling it later, 'this was a joyful day to us all!' They were greatly in need of good news at that time, for when they tried to eat their salt fish on the last day of May, only James and the Master were able to chew the food.

When there was a stretch of clear water between the ship and the shore, James set about the task of hanging the rudder on the stern. The work needed patience and fortitude. The youngest, strongest men took turns in the water, raking away sand from under the stern so that there would be deep enough water to fasten the rudder to the stern post. Half of a quarter of an hour was as much as any of them could endure in the water at a time. It took them six days of work in these terrible conditions before they completed the task, watched closely by their comrades all the time lest they should faint. In the meantime, ten tons of ballast had been heaved overboard, while other heavy articles had been taken ashore so that the ship should be as light as possible and might be floated out into open water one day at high tide. At the worst, James was prepared to cut her down to her lower deck, take out the masts and buoy her off the shore.

By this time, the victims of scurvy were growing stronger and were now on a diet of 'vetches' which they found growing on the beach. When boiled in oil and vinegar these made 'excellent sustenance and refreshing'. Soon men's teeth were firm enough in their gums for them to be able to chew beef. Bears, foxes and birds had vanished from the area but in ponds speckled frogs multiplied and the woods were alive with flies of every kind – butterflies, butcher flies, horseflies and 'an infinite abundance of blood-thirsty mosquitoes', worse torment than the frost had been. By this time, it was mid-June. But so far as they could observe from the watch-tree, the sea was still a solid mass of ice. The cooper, although hardly able to drag himself about, fastened cables to the empty beer and cider casks. Passed under the keel, the cables could help to raise the ship clear of the mud. One day, at high tide, the crew were able, heaving together, to pull the ship through the sand so that she was afloat at low water. It was a triumph. Two days later, James, from the top of the watch-tree, could see open water to the north. Soon the sea ice would break up.

In the meantime, they found that under the ship's keel were stones as big as three foot high. God had indeed been kind to them for if, when they forced her ashore, she had struck one of these stones, she would have been lost. They towed her to the place where she had been moored a year before.

On 24 June, James attended to more ceremonial tasks. He made a large wooden cross to which he fixed pictures of the King and Queen, doubly wrapped in lead. In addition, he fastened to the cross a list of the king's titles, the royal arms, the arms of the City of Bristol, a shilling and a six-pence. This symbol of British sovereignty was duly set up on the hilltop where they had buried their dead comrades. Next day, the bosun began to rig the ship. At nightfall, James took a sailor with him and lit a fire on a prominent height. He watched from a treetop to see if any answering fire was visible, meaning to ask anybody in the neighbourhood if they had any information of a way out to the ocean. Nobody answered. James told his companion to set fire to some bushes nearby. Unhappily, the sailor lit trees to windward of them and these, in the hot, dry weather, blazed up like flax. James had to hurry down from his watch-tree. Not only the bushes, but the ground moss, too, had taken fire. Before James had scrambled halfway down his tree, the trunk was ablaze. The two men had to quit the place as fast as they could, leaving their weapons to the flames. When day broke, the conflagration was still burning furiously and threatening the huts where they had spent the winter.

James ordered the beef and the powder to be carried aboard and then, after an inspection of the fire, ran back to the camp and ordered the ship's new set of sails to be taken down to the waterside, while the houses were to be dismantled. At noon, the wind swung round to the north and the sentry whom he had left to watch the fire ran in, shouting that the fire was following hard at his heels like a train of powder. At that, the work of taking what they needed out of the houses went forward at a frenzied speed, which became faster as the fire swooped towards them with a terrible rattling noise and on a front a mile across. No sooner had the last objects of value been carried to the water's edge than the blaze reached their huts and swallowed them in a minute. The dogs first sat on the sails and howled, then ran into shallow water and stayed there. At last, there was a change in the wind and the fire went off elsewhere. The officers and men of the *Henrietta Maria* spent the night aboard the ship.

When James went up to the hill-top on 1 July, he saw that the fire had burnt its way for sixteen miles on a track as wide as the island. That evening, after prayers, they paid a last visit to the graves of their dead comrades where James, leaning on one of the tombs, recited 36 lines of rhymed verse he had composed. It 'moved my young and tender-hearted companions with some compassion'. In addition to his redoubtable talents as a man of action, he had a sense of occasion. After his recitation, he fastened a copy of the poem to the cross, along with an account of their stay on the island. Next day they left for home.

The voyage was long and dangerous. The ship worked northwards along the coast in fog and ice as far as Cape Henrietta Maria where the crew went ashore and made ineffectual attempts to kill deer, tiring the dogs and wearying themselves all to no purpose. James was disgusted by what he regarded as the ingratitude of the dogs, who had been kept all winter and forgiven many misdemeanours such as stealing meat out of the steeping tubs, in the hope that they would be useful. They were dogs of a very good pedigree, which made their failure all the more disappointing. Hardening his heart, James left them ashore in Labrador where, since they were a dog and a bitch, their descendants may survive.

Terribly battered by the ice day after day, and troubled with leaks that kept the pumps going every half watch, the ship could make headway neither north nor east because of the ice. James heard some murmuring among the crew; men said they would be happy to see him buried for otherwise their fate was to starve on a piece of ice. He waited in patience for a better humour to come. But the situation was desperate, and James, always a man for extreme remedies, was prepared to sink the ship for a second time. When he dropped anchor, a big floe struck the cable a heavy blow. The anchor dragged, and, in consequence, the ship was driven into shoal water on a foul and rocky ground. Only a change of wind saved her from disaster. By this time it was August and the nights were beginning to close in. In a fortnight of arduous labour, they had made only thirty miles of progress to the north-east and, now, in one stormy night, they lost all the distance they had covered. With the wind steadily in the north-west, they were in constant danger of being driven on to the reefs that lay to the east. In this emergency, the empty casks aboard were filled. The ship was left unpumped. Everything was made ready for a new sinking. And it was impossible to get clear of the shoal water, for the offshore ice was too thick for them to sail through. Not until 17 August, when they had been six weeks in almost hourly danger of death, could they make sail to the north and get clear of the ice. By that time the worst was over, although another week passed before the keener-eyed members of the crew sighted land six miles away and James knew that it must be Nottingham Island, which stands at the point where the great bay turns into Hudson Strait.

The bad weather continued, and they were driven so fast to the north-west that, when the lead was heaved, the ship was past it before twenty fathoms of line were out. One afternoon – it was 25 August – the sea became suddenly smooth and, while they wondered what this could portend, they ran in upon flat ice again. In alarm at this, James summoned a council of his officers – master, lieutenant, surgeon and so on – who gave him their advice in writing on 26 August. It was simple enough. 'Go home without delay. The nights are long and so cold that we can hardly handle the rigging. The weather is stormy. We doubt whether Hudson Strait can be passed before we are frozen up. The ship is leaking and the men are weak.' James accepted the verdict. He took it, with a sorrowful heart, as he says, but, no doubt, with complete agreement. He ordered the helm to be borne up and the course shaped for England. Just under two months later, the *Henrietta Maria* arrived in Bristol Road. When she was hauled on dry land, the damage to her was found to be considerable. Her cutwater and stern, along with fourteen feet of the keel, were torn away; much of her sheathing was lost; her bows broken and bruised; while, under the starboard bulge, a sharp rock had cut through sheathing and plank and had penetrated an inch and a half into a timber that it met. For the miracle of their safe return James and his companions went to church and gave thanks.

As a result of his perilous and not unheroic voyage James had come to one important although negative conclusion: there was no passage by way of Hudson's Bay to the South Sea. It was all fantasy, a dream conjured up by 'the vicious and abusive wits' of Portuguese and Spaniards, supported by lying or inaccurate maps which showed sea where there was known to be mainland and land where there was known to be sea. Even if 'that merely imaginary passage did exist,' said James, 'it would be very narrow, beset by ice and longer than the route to the East by the Cape'. These were the disenchanted views of the returned explorer when he anchored at Bristol on 3 October 1632. A year after his return, James was serving in the Bristol Channel against pirates and had some success. In the beginning of 1634-5, he wrote to the Admiralty reporting that, through sickness, he was unfit for duty. He made his will, forgave his elder brother, John James, his debt of £250, and left his property to his widowed sister, Katherine Lacey. Soon afterwards, it seems, he died, for his will was proved on 4 May 1635.

Unlike James, Foxe did not lose his belief that the Passage existed and that he had been looking for it in the right place. However, he was never given command of another expedition to the North. His backers, Briggs and Sir Thomas Roe, died, and Roe, it seems, had lost faith in him long before. It may be that Foxe, too self-assured, opinionated and jealous, became in time a man with a chip on his shoulder and, probably, a bee in his bonnet. Sitting in his room in Hull he wrote his account of his voyage, the raciest of narratives of Arctic exploration of that era. His last sentences showed that the old explorer who, by this time had lost his money in the war, had not lost his faith in the Search. God would send some happy man to pluck the fruit, for 'here lieth the way to Colchos and he that finds the same brings home the Golden Fleece . . . My pen and self is now grown weary and, hoping some other brave spirit will enter the lists and attempt the enterprise, I rest.'

But it was 1635. In five years' time the Long Parliament would be summoned. Englishmen had nearer and different matters to think about than a search among the floes and islands of the polar seas for a way to the fabled East. North-west Foxe, as he called himself, was, although he knew it not, writing the epitaph on the wonderful first surge of English exploration of the North. It had begun with the voyage of Cabot a hundred and forty years before. It had ended with the return of Captain James. It had accomplished – what? Not a great deal, be it acknowledged. The Strait of Anian had not been discovered, nor had it been firmly obliterated from the maps. The geographical relation between Friesland (which did not exist) and Greenland on one side and Asia on the other had not been cleared up. Was Greenland one island or two? That was not finally settled. On the other hand, Davis Strait had been probed, Hudson Bay had been mapped along a great stretch of its coastline, and Foxe had voyaged northwards along the Channel that bears his name and left the hope that, some day, another explorer would go further. He passes out of the story with a gleam still alive in his eye which would be reflected later. In the meantime the search for the North-west Channel passes from the sea to a river. After the English chapter in the story comes a French one. Jacques Cartier had a successor.

Part Two

Mr Gooseberry and M. Radisson

'They of Canada say that it is a month's space to saile to a lande where cinamon and cloves are growing.' Epistle Dedicatory to the Right Worshipful and most vertuous gentleman Phillip Sydney Esquire.
Divers Journeys, London, 1582

While the English sailors persisted in their attempts to find the way to China through the labyrinth of the Arctic, an ambitious French enterprise had been launched on the St Lawrence River, six hundred miles due south-west of Captain James's wintering place on Hudson's Bay. The colony of New France, first permanent settlement on North American soil north of Florida, had been founded at Quebec. Trading in furs with the Algonquins and the Hurons living to the west, the French settlers were inevitably drawn into projects of westward exploration as bold and exciting as anything planned in London or Bristol. One Frenchman above all others was a man of heroic stature and statesmanlike vision.

On the day Martin Frobisher was mortally wounded while storming the Spanish fort at Crozon, near Brest, a French sailor of twenty-seven or thereabouts took part in the action. Samuel Champlain was possibly, as his Old Testament first name would suggest, born in a Huguenot family. He came from Brouage, a small seaport near the Protestant stronghold of La Rochelle and had fought under Henry of Navarre. Son of a captain, he went early to sea. As he later wrote to Queen Marie de' Medici, 'The art of navigation . . . has impelled me to expose myself to the impetuous waves of the ocean.' It was no exaggeration. Four years after the fight at Crozon, Champlain was demobilized and, through the influence of an uncle in the Spanish service, sailed for the West Indies in a ship which the King of Spain had chartered.

In the course of that journey he crossed the Isthmus of Panama and, like Drake before him, set eyes upon the Pacific. The thought occurred to him then, as it had done sixty years earlier to the counsellors of Charles V, that 'if these four leagues of land . . . should be cut through, one would come from the South Sea to the higher sea and shorten the journey by more than 1,500 leagues.' Unfortunately, however, the Isthmus belonged to Spain, the mortal enemy of France. If a Frenchman wished to find a route to the Pacific he must look in another direction. But Champlain never forgot what he had seen that day on the isthmus and never entirely lost the illusion that the American continent might, after all – and not only at Panama – be narrower than was sometimes supposed. The trouble was to find the right place.

By 1603, after many adventures in Mexico, he returned to France, and soon afterwards set out on a new voyage which took him to Canada. Champlain, at thirty-three, had been appointed geographer to the Lieutenant-general of New France. For this official post he was well fitted by training and experience, although, as it turned out, empire-building rather than map-making was to be his true mission.

From the moment he landed in Canada, Champlain devoted himself to establishing a French settlement in the region. For this project, Henri Quatre was an enthusiast. The King was as confirmed an optimist about Canada as his great minister, Sully, was a sceptic. 'One never draws great riches from anything north of the fortieth parallel,' said Sully, who was as good an artillerist as the King was a good leader of cavalry. The one was cautious as the other was impetuous. As a propagandist, Champlain argued that the way to China, that goal as ardently sought for by men of his time as the philosopher's stone had been by their fathers, probably lay along the course of the St Lawrence: if one followed that river towards its source in the west, one would almost certainly arrive at Cathay. So while, as a colonial politician, he made peace with the Algonquin and Huron Indians and war on the Iroquois, as a geographer, he carried out a series of journeys of exploration in the course of which he discovered Lake Champlain. Then, one day in 1603, he heard from Indians of a great lake (Ontario) and of a waterfall a league broad (Niagara). Beyond that, it seemed, that there was another lake (Erie) and, although his Indian friends could only report it by hearsay, a third lake (Huron) so vast that no man would venture to put out into it.

The water of this lake was very salt, like the sea! And where, Champlain enquired, did the water of these distant lakes flow? Eastwards, to the St Lawrence? Not at all, replied the Indians. Champlain thought that, in that case, the most distant of the lakes they spoke of might be the South Sea itself. But he could not be sure; the evidence given by the Indians was confusing. Some of them denied that the farther lakes were salt, while others persisted in saying that, four hundred leagues to the west, lay a great water the end of which no man knew. The only thing that was certain was that there were great stretches of water in the interior of Canada and that one of them might be the Ocean itself!

Champlain drew up a report to Henri IV in which, after conjuring up a glowing picture of the wealth of Canada, he said that the way to the Kingdom of China, 'whence great riches could be drawn', was to be found by following the channel of the St Lawrence farther to the west. The proposition seemed reasonable enough; it was certainly exciting. As it turned out, however, Champlain was diverted from the search for the road to China for reasons similar to those that had diverted Frobisher a generation before him. His life was spent in a series of journeys through the wilds which, occurring at the same time as Henry Hudson's fatal voyage to the Great Bay, probed more deeply into the Canadian interior than any Europeans had gone before. But he did not reach Cathay.

Champlain accomplished something which has proved to be more important than the discovery of the North-west Passage would have been. He is the true founder of New France, of French Canada. As for the road to China, to the end he believed it would be found by following the course of a Canadian river. The route favoured by the English, further north through the icefields of the Arctic, he dismissed. Either it did not exist or, if it did, it could not be traversed by ships. No! In the west, where, as his Indian friends told him, there were people as white as any Frenchman, there surely lay the answer to the riddle that had baffled generations of explorers. 'Thirdly,' he wrote to the King of France in 1618, 'the Sieur de Champlain undertakes to discover the South Sea passage to China, to the East Indies, by way of the river St Lawrence . . . which issues from a lake about 300 leagues in length, from which lake flows a river that empties into the said South Sea.'

It was a magnificent dream but Champlain could never find a financial backer for the journey to the west to which he pinned such glittering hopes. It was, perhaps, just as well. But he went on hoping and he did not hope alone. His interpreter, Jean Nicolet, who spent ten years wandering among the Indians, carried with him wherever he went a flowered robe of Chinese damask in readiness for the day when he should meet a mandarin and find that he had crossed some unmarked border and was in Cathay. For he firmly believed all along that, roaming in Canada, he was already in some outlying province of the Middle Kingdom. By the time Champlain died in 1635, his dream still unfulfilled, he had founded Quebec. His widow being a rich young woman, he left his property to the Virgin, and his last counsel to men of his own kind. 'The advice I give to all adventurers is to seek a place where they may sleep in safety.' His widow became a nun. And Champlain sleeps safely enough on a hill above the St Lawrence, his journey to the west unachieved. If his own most cherished dream was unrealized, another dream has been turned into spires and ramparts all about him, but after Champlain's time: when he died, there were only 85 adult inhabitants in the fort of Quebec.

In France there was not a great deal of public interest in Champlain's visions of a great colony beyond the Atlantic, a real New France, little interest, except among the Jesuits, in the missionary projects of this ex-Huguenot (if that is what he was). There was no practical interest at all in his hope to find the short route to China beyond the Great Lakes. Furs, and the monopoly of the fur trade through Quebec – that was a sufficient prize for the French merchants. Furs and not the spreading of the Faith. There was, indeed, one argument against urging on the work of proselytizing too vigorously. If the Indians became Christians and went no more on the warpath, they might neglect to hunt the beaver and the otter – and, for that matter, if too many Frenchmen settled as farmers in Canada, they might absorb all the pelts brought in by the trappers, so that none were left for export! There were – as there usually are – good reasons for leaving well alone. The trouble was, however, that some matters cannot be left alone. Canada was one of them. The French were not the only hunters and traders in the Northern frontiers. There were also the Dutch. There were, above all, the English . . .

The English were for a time fully absorbed by the Civil War. They endured the Commonwealth and breathed fully again in the Restoration. When the Plague struck London in the month of June 1665, the Court moved to Oxford. It was there, then, that King Charles II received two French visitors and, with his usual affability, listened to their story. The story was worth hearing, although His Majesty had already been told the gist of it by George Cartwright. Cartwright had returned from one of the colonies on the Atlantic seaboard which Captain John Smith had named New England half a century before. He had given the Earl of Arlington an account of what he had heard from some Frenchmen who had talked in Boston about 'a passage from the West Sea to the South Sea and of a great trade of beaver in that passage'. Cartwright had thought that the best present he could make the King was to persuade the Frenchmen to come to England. So here they were, as picturesque a pair of adventurers as even that age could show. The King heard their story with insight and sympathy. After all, he was himself an adventurer.

They were Médard Chouart, Sieur des Groseilliers, better known to the English as 'Mr Gooseberry', and his brother-in-law, Pierre Esprit Radisson. Already each of them had behind him a life of danger, hardship and enterprise. Groseilliers, born in a village on the Marne, had emigrated from France to Canada as a boy, and had become a *coureur de bois*, a hunter and trapper, living in the wilds among the Indians. At a time when the Iroquois had imposed a blockade on the French colony, Groseilliers had been sent on a perilous mission to the Indians living further west. If he could do so he was to persuade them to defy the Iroquois and bring their pelts for sale to Montreal, a trading post which Champlain had planned on the St Lawrence on a site first seen by Jacques Cartier. Groseilliers had travelled far into the hinterland, where he bought enough furs to make his fortune, and had returned with exciting stories, picked up from his friends, the Crees, of a 'Bay of the North', a vast sheet of water stretching beyond the tree-line, extending into the unknown, and with an incredible wealth of fur-bearing animals on its shores.

His companion, Radisson, born in Avignon, had also gone to Canada as a boy. He had been captured by a party of Mohawk Indians and adopted by one of their families. He had escaped, was recaptured, and was tortured, as was customary. But his adoptive family had successfully pleaded for his life. For a time after that Radisson had lived as a Mohawk, speaking the Indian language and going on the warpath with his foster-brothers. After a time, he had made his way back to the area of white settlement and, by way of France, had returned to Quebec. From there, in 1659, he and Groseilliers set off together to the North where the Bay was to be found. They travelled secretly, for the colonial government frowned on their enterprise. Although it appears that they did not actually reach the Bay, they returned with a rich load of furs. In Quebec they had the unfriendly reception that is reserved for those who successfully defy a bureaucracy. They were heavily fined and, in addition, were taxed on the pelts they brought back. Indignant at this treatment, they sailed to France to complain to the authorities there. But they found no redress, and no interest for their tale of the prospects awaiting hunters who made the long, hard journey to the Great Bay. Frustrated and resentful, Groseilliers and Radisson took their story to Boston in New England where it awoke greater interest.

There they found enough financial backing to furnish a ship. But once more misfortune overtook them, for the captain was too frightened by the weather conditions in Hudson Strait to go on with the voyage. After that, they fell in with Mr Cartwright, the Englishman who was the means of bringing them to Oxford and to the audience with Charles II.

The proposition which the two Frenchmen put to the King that day was simply this: the path by sea into Hudson's Bay offers a better way to reach the natural wealth of the Canadian wilds than the route by river up the Gulf of St Lawrence, which was a French monopoly. King Charles was sufficiently impressed by what those far-travelled and daring Frenchmen told him to give each a pension of 40s. a week. They accompanied him back to London when the Plague scare was over. Results followed in due course. In June 1668, two ketches with a total burthen of 97 tons sailed out of the Thames, Mr Gooseberry in one, M. Radisson in the other. The captains had orders to treat the two French renegades civilly but with suspicion, especially Radisson, who was regarded, not without reason, as very much of a knave. The ships were making for Hudson's Bay, with trade as their main purpose. Exploration, while not forgotten in their orders, was assigned a secondary rôle. One ketch, in which Radisson sailed, was driven back; the other, with Groseilliers aboard, made the voyage and brought back £1,379 worth of furs and a glowing picture of future prospects. Two years later Hudson's Bay Company was founded and, as a direct consequence of the initiative of the two Frenchmen, was given the royal charter, with proprietorial rights over an immense area of the Canadian North. It was to be, in effect, a monarch, an exploiter and, if it was faithful to its original impulse, an explorer, too. The king's cousin, Prince Rupert, was appointed the first governor. Robert Boyle, the great physicist, a man fascinated by Arctic phenomena, was one of the original shareholders. Thus, two roving French fur traders, annoyed by the obtuseness of their own colonial administration, inspired a historic British enterprise. The notions of conquest, commerce and scientific curiosity were interwoven in varying proportions in a fabric of imperial grandeur, intoxicating alike to monarchs, merchants and learned societies. And lending a special, almost mystical, quality to it all was the conception of which Cartwright overheard a whisper in Boston and mentioned to Arlington, and which about that time messengers from Holland were urging on Colbert, the great minister of Louis XIV – who for the rest was willing enough to be urged – 'Le Chemin des Indes par la mer du Nord!'

On his way to Hudson's Bay in 1664, Captain Zachariah Gillan, a New Englander, master of the *Nonsuch*, was ordered to have in his thoughts the discovery of the Passage, although his main interest was to be the fur trade. That, too, was the main interest of those who had bought shares in the new company with the resounding name and the romantic powers, 'The Governor and Company of Adventurers of England trading into Hudson's Bay'. Fur. Above all, beaver. The skins came out of Canada at the rate of sixty to eighty thousand a year and from them, when properly treated by a technique of which the Russians alone had the secret, although it was soon known to others, the hats were made without which gentlemen could not be seen in society. Groseilliers and Radisson had been right. The skins abounded in the forests round the Bay and were readily brought by the trappers to the Company's trading post on Charlton Island at the 'bottom of the Bay', Captain James's old wintering-place. The French outlet on the St Lawrence suffered. The Jesuits, brave explorers of the wastelands and zealous seekers of Indian souls, complained of the damage done to the work of salvation by those English, Protestant interlopers. But the Company's shares on the London Exchange rose to a premium of 53 per cent. And, for close on half a century, the Company kept its eyes firmly on business – beaver skins, bought from the Indians and brought to London for the annual sales to the furriers. As for China? It was far away and the route to its fabled riches was something that could not be allowed to distract hard-headed man, establishing and managing a vast new commercial empire, and troubled enough by drunken sea-captains, dishonest subordinates and pilfering Indians!

But legend may sleep – it does not readily die.

10

Seventeen Rivers from Churchill

'La géographie est une science de faits; on n'y peut rien donner dans son
cabinet à l'esprit de système, sans risquer les plus grandes erreurs.'

Bougainville

In 1716, Cree Indians from the North brought interesting news to James
Knight, an officer of the Hudson's Bay Company at Churchill on the West
shore of the Bay where, by that time, a trading post had been established.
The Crees reported that at the mouth of a great river, the Coppermine, there
was an alluvial deposit of copper. The story fell on receptive ears. Knight
had begun life as a shipwright at Deptford, on the Thames, and, by energy,
practical ability and strength of character had, through thirty years, risen in
the Company's service until he had become 'Governor in the Bay', that is,
in effect, the Company's Viceroy. In spite of the dangers ('them natives to
the norward are more savage and brutelike and will drink blood') Knight
had established Churchill as his outpost. 'Great quantities of pure copper;
lumps of it so big that three or four men cannot lift it.' This was what the
Indians promised could be found where the Coppermine River ran into
the sea. Could there be news more likely to interest a man like Knight?
Old in years (he was probably over seventy), but young in temperament,
expansionist, optimistic, he had come out of sharp conflicts with the
French, the Indians and the Eskimos, and he believed in holding firmly
what he had won and in pushing further on: 'Loose not the East Main
trade [the trade on the east shore of the Bay] but encourage it all you can.'
Meanwhile, he would seek trade further north. The copper deposits were
not the only prize the Indians dangled before him. They told him that
there were Indians on the seas to the west who used gold as other men used
copper. Those gold-using Indians were separated from Churchill by
seventeen rivers, of which the fifteenth ran into the Western Ocean. At the
mouth of this fifteenth river, the copper mine was to be found. Listening
to what they had to say, Knight concluded that the last river, the seven-

teenth, was probably the route that would lead him to China. It would be the channel which, through the ages, had come to be known as the Strait of Anian. In the existence of that channel Knight believed passionately, as Foxe had done before him.

With the Indian's stories revolving ceaselessly in his head, detailed and enthralling – a sea not so cold as that of eastern America; a sea with ships on it and islands; copper; gold! – Knight came to an important decision. Leaving a subordinate in charge at the post at Churchill, he sailed for England. His plan was simple and sufficiently bold. Having persuaded the ruling committee of the Company of the good sense and expediency of what he meant to do, he would return to look for the North-west Passage. He would sail through it to China and the gold.

In London, Knight's strength of character, the eloquence which he drew from his deeply held convictions, won the day. An expedition was fitted out. In consequence, one day early in June 1719, James Knight set sail from Gravesend in command of a frigate, the *Albany*, and a sloop, the *Discovery*. The plan was that the ships were to meet at Resolution Island at the entrance to Hudson Strait; after that, they were to explore the coast of the Bay and, further north, the coast of Melville Peninsula. They were to sail to the north of the 69th parallel, searching for the Strait of Anian and the gold and copper mines. They were to be careful, above all things, not to allow themselves to be frozen in. And so the old shipwright sailed away, the gleam of an ancient quest rekindled in his eye. And that was the last glimpse men have of James Knight, the *Albany*, the *Discovery*, their captains and crews – twenty-seven men in all.

In the summer of 1722, three years later, a sloop set out from Churchill northwards along the western coast of Hudson's Bay. It returned with the bad news that its crew had found a fragment of a ship's mast, part of a cabin lining and a medicine chest. Of survivors, none were found and nothing certain was known. Except that there was a story current among the Eskimos of a lonely man who had sat day after day on a headland looking to the south. Looking for a sail? Hoping to be rescued? And waiting for death from scurvy or famine or cold?

Alarm deepened into gloom and then into despair as it became certain that Knight's expedition had met with some unknown but total disaster. But forty years passed before the riddle was solved. Then the two ships were found, under five fathoms of water in an inlet of Marble Island, three hundred miles north of Churchill and far to the south of the 65th parallel. Deeply discouraged by the disappearance of the Knight expedition, the

Hudson's Bay Company lost interest in the North-west Passage and in the Indians' stories of gold and copper. There had, nevertheless, been a tincture of truth in these inflammatory tales. The so-called Copper Eskimos live in the region from which came the stories that excited Knight. They work copper by cold hammering, using the pure metal which is found exposed on the surface of the rocks in various places. It is possible, then, that the Crees, from whom Knight picked up the reports which led him to his fatal voyage, had heard something of those extrusions of the metal and had, after the manner of their kind, wildly exaggerated what they had heard. They told the white man what they knew he was eager to hear. As for the gold, the yellow metal which Indians on the Western seas were said to use like copper, it, too, may have had some basis in fact. After all, centuries later, gold was found in the Yukon. But it was not found by Knight in 1719. He died, perhaps in battle with the Eskimos but more probably of starvation, for he was far beyond the point at which Europeans could provide for themselves by hunting and fishing. He was beyond the sub-Arctic front: he was in the tundra. The waters of the Bay closed over his little ships. The Eskimos carried off what could be removed. And Hudson's Bay Company, which had lost £7,000 on the venture, wrote off the amount to experience and put firmly behind them the temptation to explore.

In the early 1730s, the matter of the North-west Passage came to life again. This time the man responsible was a wealthy Ulster landowner, named Arthur Dobbs, High Sheriff of Antrim and member of the Irish Parliament. Dobbs was an energetic, active-minded man, who took an interest in Arctic exploration and the various attempts made throughout the years to find the northern route to the Pacific. He was what would have been called later an imperialist, with a vision far-reaching and ambitious. Dobbs had read about the claim made by the Greek pilot, Juan de Fuca, who had met Michael Lok in Venice one day in 1596 and fascinated him with the story of the great inlet north of California thirty leagues wide. Having brooded over the records of all the explorers of Hudson's Bay, Dobbs came to the conclusion that the North-west Passage existed and could be found. Believing this, he ran headlong into the scepticism of Hudson's Bay Company's officials who were as conservative as officers of a monopoly are apt to be. But Dobbs found supporters as well. 'We may consider Hudson's Bay a kind of labyrinth,' wrote one of the latter. 'The tide is a kind of clue which, if studiously followed, must lead us out.' Dobbs suggested to the Company that it should order its sloops to sail north from Churchill along the west shore of the Bay to Roe's Welcome and measure the tides there. This, he said, would surely show whether the Passage existed or not.

Having studied all the relevant legal documents, Dobbs had no doubt that, by its charter, the Company had the sole right to navigate the Passage if it were found. But along with this privilege went the obligation to *find* the Passage! The Company were soon to hear more about this aspect of the business. By that time, Dobbs was attacking them for what he thought was their sloth, and the Admiralty, not loth to annoy the powerful monopolists of the Company, had sent out two ships on an expedition of discovery under Captain Christopher Middleton, a navigator who had been in the Company's service and was a crony of Dobbs. In addition, he was a Fellow of the Royal Society. It was natural, then, that out in the Bay relations between Middleton and the Company's officials were of the most equivocal kind. To complicate things even more, Middleton proved to be a turncoat. Once he had urged Dobbs to challenge the Company's charter; now he seemed to be mainly anxious to protect the Company's fur trade. Dobbs later said that the Company had offered Middleton a substantial bribe to ensure the failure of the expedition.

Meanwhile, scurvy, frostbite and boredom struck Middleton's crew out in the Bay. He distributed brandy among them with a lavish hand. It made matters worse, as Luke Foxe could have warned him. The death roll in the ships wintering in the frozen Bay was a heavy one. When the ice broke up in the summer of 1742 the exploring season opened; Middleton reported that he had not three seamen fit to man his ships and that most of the crews, who had been press-ganged into the service, were rogues who deserved hanging. Even his officers for the most part, were incompetent. In spite of these disabilities, Middleton sailed up the west coast of the Bay to the 66th parallel. He explored the inlet which he had thought held most promise of being the way to the west. Alas, it turned out to be only an inlet which he named Wager River. When he returned to London he brought discouraging news: there was no hope of finding a way out of the Bay as far north as he had gone; if there was a way further north, it would be blocked by ice for fifty-one weeks in the year. It was, more or less, the verdict that Foxe and James had brought in a century earlier. Middleton read a paper to the Royal Society on 'The extraordinary degrees and surprising effects of Cold in Hudson's Bay', for which he received the Society's gold medal. But one man remained unconvinced by this depressing evidence. Arthur Dobbs.

The Ulsterman accused Middleton of hiding the facts about the west coast of the Bay, of having failed to probe deeply enough into Wager River and, finally, of having been bought by the Company. He was quite sure that the lands round the Bay could be made as comfortable as Sweden. All that was needed was convenient houses with stoves! But there was an obstacle, 'the avarice of the Hudson's Bay Company (not to give it another name)'. By this time, Dobbs had convinced himself that the Company was terrified of having interlopers come into the Bay lest, under the pretext of searching for the North-west Passage, they should break down the fur monopoly. This, he thought, was the grand obstacle to exploration of the Passage. He now determined to destroy the Company's monopoly. In this campaign Middleton was chosen as his first victim. The Admiralty called on Middleton to answer the charge brought against him by Dobbs that he had accepted a bribe. Until that accusation was refuted, the Admiralty proposed to keep Middleton ashore. A bitter controversy broke out. Middleton published a 'Vindication'; Dobbs answered it; Middleton replied to Dobbs, and so on. Finally, the Admiralty held a Court of Enquiry which vindicated Middleton. But in spite of that, his career had been heavily damaged. He was given no new command until 1745, the year of the Jacobite rising and then it was only of a small ship. On the whole, public sympathy in Britain lay with Dobbs in his attack on a well-entrenched monopoly, enormously rich and, therefore, naturally anxious to keep intruders out of its preserves.

At this juncture a useful ally appeared. Joseph la France, a *coureur de bois* who had fallen out with his own people, provided Dobbs with ammunition, in the form of a reasoned argument to use in the controversy. The Company, he said, ought to attack the French trading posts in Quebec, where the Indian canoes were intercepted on their way downstream to the Bay. If this advice was taken, there would be need for an aggressive policy – an economic war with France – for which the Company was not prepared. Looking about for arguments, Dobbs found in a magazine a letter from a Spanish admiral who claimed that in 1640 he had found channels leading far into the interior from the north-west coast of America. The admiral even said that in one of these channels he had met a Boston merchantman! This letter was put to use by Dobbs in his campaign to expose the lethargy of the Company. But better than this testimony was the fact that various respectable authorities supported Dobbs in his argument that the tides in the Bay indicated that it had an outlet somewhere to the north.

John Campbell, a writer on navigation, appealing to a semi-mystical doctrine of 'balance', thought that there must be a stretch of water between Asia and America equal in extent to the Atlantic and that, therefore, the North-west Passage must be short. A body of Dobbs' supporters, known as the North-west Committee, raised £10,000 to fit out an expedition which sailed to the Bay in 1745 under the command of William Moor. Its progress was anxiously watched by the Company. As it turned out, however, Moor had no better luck than Middleton. The Company's servants in the Bay treated him with caution, bordering on incivility. This they could justify by the fact that Britain was, just then, at war with France. It was their national duty to be suspicious of interlopers. In addition, Moor's shipmates quarrelled bitterly among themselves, scurvy broke out, and, worst of all, the chief objective of the expedition, the exploration of Wager Inlet, ended in disappointment. The explorers probed it for 150 miles – 'all our hopes vanished! Our hitherto imagined Strait ended in small unnavigable rivers.' After this, opinion among the explorers was divided, one party among them believing that another expedition would solve the problem of the Passage one way or the other, while the opposition said that they had found nothing which would make anyone believe that the Passage existed at all. But one heart still beat strong and true. Dobbs blamed the failure on 'the timidity, ill-conduct or bad inclinations of some of the commanders'.

With more venom than ever, he renewed his attack on the Hudson's Bay Company. It had not, he alleged, carried out the terms of its Charter, through its failure to seek the Passage. He went further than that. The Charter was, he insisted, in any case, illegal. He appealed to the Privy Council and, when that line of attack failed, to Parliament itself. In doing so, he counted on the support of a Member whom he believed to be the sworn enemy of monopoly. But, once again, Dobbs met with disappointment. The friend whom he had trusted had, he discovered too late, 'a prepossession in favour of the Company'. After all, there was no hope that Parliament would support him against the cautious directors who, as he saw it, were making too much money from their shipments of fur from the Bay to spend money and time seeking the gateway to the East. Yet, he was convinced, it lay open somewhere, beyond the careful reconnaissance of the Company's sloops but visible and dazzling to the eyes of faith.

But this time, at last, Dobbs gave up his battle with the Company. He could still be excited by a reminder of the legendary voyage of Juan da Fuca or some other narrative belonging to the old romantic days when the legend of the Passage first laid its fingers on his imagination. But the excitement could no longer stir him to action. And those who shared it had become fewer. An atmosphere of scepticism about the whole business of North-western exploration was abroad. Hearing a new, marvellous story from the North, John Merry, deputy governor of the Hudson's Bay Company, remarked drily, 'when the sky falls, a great many larks may be catched'. Dobbs was, however, not wholly unrewarded. He was appointed Governor of North Carolina, where he lived – in constant dispute with the local legislature – until his death at Town Creek in 1765.

But, where his persuasions had failed, alarming news came from another quarter which had a more stimulating effect. A Russian expedition led by the Dane, Vitus Bering, had sighted the American continent from Asia. This was an important, perhaps an ominous, development.

Vitus Jonassen Bering, born in Jutland in 1681, had, as a boy, gone to sea where he had fallen in with a Norwegian Admiral, Cornelius Cruys, one of the Scandinavian sailors who helped to found Peter the Great's navy. Through his influence, Bering became a Russian sub-lieutenant. Before long, he was involved in Peter's schemes for exploration in the Siberian Far East. He was to go to Kamchatka and find out whether Asia was joined to America. The Tsar's order ran, 'You are to enquire where the American coast begins and go to some European colony; ask what the coast is, note it down and return.' Bering set off a few days after Peter's death and when he reached Kamchatka overland, built a ship there and, after a two months' voyage, came back with the report that there really did exist a North-east Passage, dividing Asia from America. Not far to the east of Siberia was a large, wooded country. Although he had not seen it himself, he reported that the driftwood on the Siberian beaches had not come from Asiatic trees, and that the birds of passage flew from the East.

But when he returned to the West, Bering found the political atmosphere unsympathetic to his ideas. He was neglected until the Empress Anne came to the throne and there was a reversal of policy. The 'Old Russian' party of conservatives was crushed. The Empress became an enthusiast for Far Eastern discovery and the Great Northern Expedition was prepared. It was on the most extravagant scale. When, eventually, Bering set off from St Petersburg in 1733, he led a convoy of 570 men. In addition, most of the officers were accompanied by their wives and children. Bering's second-in-command was a Dane named Spangberg, who had a varied reputation. Some thought him a general, others an escaped convict. In addition to this main party, the expedition had an academic branch, known as The Professors. It included an astronomer, a physicist, a historian, two landscape painters, a surgeon, an interpreter, an instrument-maker, five surveyors, six scientific assistants and fourteen bodyguards. The astronomer alone was accompanied across Siberia by nine waggonloads of instruments. For the edification of the party, a travelling library of some hundreds of books went along. The Professors were not under Bering's control, but did not cease to rain their complaints upon him.

Something between a military operation and a folk wandering, the Great Northern Expedition moved eastwards three thousand miles across the Siberian forests, amidst frightful sufferings and with a heavy toll of lives. It was incomparably the most ambitious scientific enterprise that had ever been organized. There were, of course, troubles; above all, the failure of local officials to cooperate. Bering had to complain of the enmity of Major-General Pissariev. This officer, for conspiracy against an important official, had been knouted, branded and exiled to Siberia. He was not even allowed to hide his brands. He caused Bering endless trouble. In 1737, Bering reported to the Admiralty in St Petersburg, 'not a pood of provisions was bought for us, not a boat built for transport; we did it all ourselves.' It was an extraordinary feat of logistics and determination accomplished against Russian xenophobia, surly officials and grumbling professors. But meanwhile money was pouring out – 300,000 roubles – and there was nothing to show for it!

Bering was criticized by some for weakness, by others for arrogance. However, he built a town, Okhotsk, and two ships, the *St Peter* and the *St Paul*, then six more. They were rigged with the cordage and sails that he had dragged that vast distance across Siberia. By May 1741, eight years after his departure from St Petersburg, Bering set sail in the *St Peter* to look for a non-existent land, Gamaland, in which the cartographers firmly believed. By that time, his strength was failing. Scurvy, which had brought down a third of the crew, attacked him. However, on 16 July 1741 he sighted the American coast, Kajak Island in the Gulf of Alaska. By then he was no longer capable of controlling events. Bad water, cold, starvation, scurvy – men were dying every day. When at last the ship ran ashore on Bering Island on 8 December 1741, Bering died, worn out. After that, there came a pause in the extraordinary upsurge of national energy which had begun when Peter the Great gave the native dynamism of Russia the impetus of his own brand of furious intellectual effort. The achievement had been impressive. The Swedes had been struck down. St Petersburg had been built. And now, a Russian ship had sighted the American coast! As the news filtered through to the West, men were filled with admiration and alarm. Especially men in Whitehall.

Thus, fourteen years after Dobbs withdrew from the struggle, the wind of British opinion swung round once more in favour of the exploration of the North-west.

In 1764, two naval vessels left Plymouth under Commodore John Byron with orders to reach New Albion, the land that Drake had annexed on the Pacific Coast about two hundred years earlier and which had 'never been examined with the care it deserves notwithstanding the frequent recommendations by the said Sir Francis Drake'. Further than that, the expedition was to seek the Pacific entrance to the North-west Passage, examining the West American coast as far north as the 54th parallel, that is to say, as far as the point where the port of Prince Rupert now stands and not far from where the Alaskan boundary runs into the sea. This intervention by the Admiralty, which was obviously no accident, marked a change in the nature of the problem. Instead of being, as it had been for two centuries and more, a commercial question, the North-west Passage was now a strategic one. The Russians had seen America. Their Danish pioneer, Vitus Bering, was dead, shipwrecked on that island near Kamchatka. But how long would it be before his employer, the Tsar, laid claim to a foothold on American soil? There was, too, another factor. Spain, now the enemy of Britain and the ally of France, had, in her own opinion, altogether special privileges in the Pacific. When the Duke of Richmond, Secretary of State for the Southern Department, asked the Spanish Ambassador, 'Does the whole world belong to Spain?' the answer was polite but emphatic. 'As to that portion, yes.' He pointed to the Pacific. Already, in order to counter the dangers that threatened from Russia and Britain, Spain was pushing northwards along the Californian coast towards San Diego and Monterey. Any effort, whether ostentatious or covert, to look for a short way into the Pacific was therefore liable to cause the profoundest emotion in Madrid. This was the reason why Commodore Byron sailed from Plymouth with secret orders about which the false impression was spread that they instructed him to go to India.

Byron's task was far more interesting than that. He was to look for the continent which, as many theorists believed, lay hidden in the southern stretches of the Pacific. And he was to find the Channel where the North-west Passage ran into the Western sea! In Rio, Byron met another, and even more famous, Englishman. He fell in with Clive, who was in a hurry to reach Bombay and was much dissatisfied with the slow speed of the East Indiaman in which he was travelling. Clive had good reason for his impatience. He had been given a task of great urgency. The civil service in Bengal was corrupt and incompetent. Insubordination was rife in the army in India. A terrible massacre of Europeans had occurred at Patna. The owners of East India stock, in alarm, called for Clive to go out and restore order there. But when, in Rio, Clive tried to obtain a passage from the Navy, on the ground that he was on immediate business of state, Byron was able to argue that he, too, had an important mission to discharge. Clive had to find his own way to India.

Byron sailed on through the Strait of Magellan and began his search. 'Foul-Weather Jack', as he was called, was a tough, intrepid sailor who had already endured extraordinary hardships on a voyage in which his ship was wrecked on the coast of Chile. He had curiosity and narrative power which, in due course, he passed on to his grandson, the poet. But Jack did not, it seems, have the ultimate essential gift of the great explorers: the irresistible need to press on into the unknown when common sense says, Turn back. He left it to someone else to discover the Great South Land. And he did not explore the Pacific coast of North America as thoroughly as he might have done. He returned, reasonably pleased with himself, by way of the Cape of Good Hope. Ten years later, he had the worse of a muddled naval battle with a French fleet in the West Indies. He died in 1786, in rather muted glory, and his grandson turned his account of his shipwreck and sufferings to good use in *Don Juan*. But so far as the search for the North-west Passage is concerned, Foul-Weather Jack's contribution may be dismissed as of little importance.

In London, enthusiasm for Arctic discovery was by that time at a high pitch of fervour. In 1755 an Act of Parliament was passed, offering £5,000 reward to the first ship to reach a point within one degree of the Pole. And at the Royal Society Daines Barrington, a jurist, took up the cause. Barrington was an oddity rather than a figure of the time. As a judge, Bentham, whose standards were high, had an indifferent opinion of him: 'not intentionally a bad judge though he was often a bad one'. But he was a tireless and versatile writer with opinions about such diverse subjects as the Flood, which he thought had been a local occurrence; Dolly Pentreath, the last person to speak Cornish; the antiquity of card-playing ('Barrington is singularly unfortunate in his speculations about cards' – Chatto, *History of Playing Cards*); and Arctic exploration. He believed, as other theorists did, that the North Pole was free from ice. Samuel Engel, with whom he corresponded, shared his views, admitting that ice was found on the seas South of the Pole, but holding that most of it came from rivers. This, he suggested, was shown by the fact that it was thick only near the land.

Barrington gave a good deal of thought to the problem of a voyage due north over the Pole to Asia. Crews might, he thought, be recruited in Orkney and Shetland which were inhabited by a seafaring population inured to the cold. The ships to be used should be modelled on those used in the Greenland whale fisheries. They would need to be well-provisioned since they might have to winter in the ice. As boredom would obviously be a problem during the Arctic winter, Barrington was ready with ingenious counter-measures: dumb-bells would keep the sailors fit and, to the music of a barrel-organ, they would perform country dances. As for the problem of liquor, his solution was simple: 'the stronger the spirits, the less the stowage.' However, Barrington was more than an amiable eccentric. As the son of a viscount and a friend of Lord Sandwich, First Lord of the Admiralty, he had political influence. In consequence of his propaganda, a naval expedition of two vessels was sent to the North in 1773, with Captain Constantine John Phipps, M.P., in command. Phipps's commission instructed him to sail on the same meridian towards the Pole but on no account to sail beyond it. Off the north coast of Spitzbergen, the skipper of a Greenland ship told him that the main icefield was ten leagues ahead. Phipps went forward, cautiously, in foggy weather and brought the ship about a cable's length from the ice-pack. Next day, he reconnoitred the ice and found that it stretched without a break from one horizon to the other. It was, as he reported later, 'one compact, impenetrable body'. After three weeks spent in trying to break into the barrier, Phipps found that far from penetrating the ice, his most pressing need was to save his ships from it. The season, which had been unusually mild, was now nearly over. He had all but reached the 80th parallel, but he had found the ice barrier impenetrable. Now it was time to return to the Thames. However, after this setback one man still remained convinced that a ship could sail over the Pole.

Daines Barrington wrote to the Royal Society, as 'the unworthy proposer of the voyage', urging that a new attempt be made. His arguments were scarcely impressive. A barber, named Andrew Leeke, while shaving Captain Robinson of H.M.S. *Reading*, had heard him say he had sailed to 84½°N. Captain Cheyne had reached 82°. Captain MacCallum, of the Greenland fishery, had reached 83½° one day in 1751 and thought he might have reached the Pole if his mate had been less of a coward. A certain Dr Daly, whom Barrington had not met, had reached the 84th parallel on a Dutch naval vessel, the captain of which, fearing a reprimand, had not kept a journal of the voyage. On tittle-tattle of this kind, Barrington based his case for a new expedition. And at that point there was a turn in events which favoured his propaganda.

For now the most famous English sailor since Elizabethan days appeared on the scene. James Cook, after the voyage of circumnavigation in the course of which he had discovered New Zealand, had come back to England in July 1775. He was not allowed to spend much time at home. In him the government saw the obvious commander of the new expedition they were preparing. But could Cook be asked to go out again so soon after his return? In his dilemma, Lord Sandwich, First Lord of the Admiralty, acted with subtlety. He invited Cook to dinner. The hospitality was lavish, the company shrewdly chosen. The new project of discovery arose in conversation and was discussed by men who knew what was contemplated. Cook's advice was respectfully sought; bit by bit, he was drawn into the talk and became interested. In the end, he volunteered to lead the expedition. The Admiralty wasted no time in giving him his commission. It reached him little more than six months after his arrival in England. He went out again from Deptford in June 1776, destined for the Pacific by way of the Cape of Good Hope, his mission this time being to search the west coast of America, north of 65°N – that is, north of the line where the Alaskan border runs into the sea – for any major inlets which might take his ships through to the east coast; maybe, to Hudson's Bay. In the meantime, in a secondary part of the scheme, Captain Richard Pickersgill in a brig named the *Lion* had set sail for Baffin Bay. The idea was that he would be conveniently stationed to help Cook when he came through from the west. Pickersgill was, however, unlucky off the south tip of Greenland. He ran into ice 'almost beyond belief; what to do, I know not'. From the skipper of a Whitby whaler he received a discouraging message. The skipper wished him luck but, apparently, did not expect to see him again. Pickersgill found an anchorage on the west coast of Greenland, well within the Arctic Circle. The nights were growing longer; fever broke out in the *Lion*. Pickersgill sought consolation in the bottle and left for the Thames not long afterwards. On arrival in London, he was immediately dismissed the service.

Cook's voyage of 1776 was the first serious attempt by the British to tackle the problem from the west side. This approach had several advantages; above all, the sailing season in the west was four months longer than it was in Hudson's Bay. Cook, in the *Resolution* sighted the American coast in March 1778 and turned to the north, surveying it with care but without success. No promising channel opened to the west. One day in August he saw 'the blink', the white light above the horizon to the north, which to the experienced Arctic navigator betokened the presence of a great mass of ice. The promise – or menace – of the blink was soon borne out. As far as the eye could see, there was a barrier of ice, rising ten feet above the level of the water, and stretching from south-west to north-east. What was more alarming, it was moving steadily towards the south. This was different from anything the theorists had led Cook to expect. Where was the ice-free polar sea of which Barrington had spoken so confidently? How was it possible to believe that ice on such a scale came from the petty rivers of north-eastern Asia? Cook turned his ship's bow to the south-west. He made for the Sandwich Islands where, as it chanced, he had an appointment with destiny five months later.

After Cook's failure to find a way through from the west, there was a ten-year hiatus in public or official interest in the enterprise. Then, in 1787, William Barkley in the *Imperial Eagle* announced that he had found the Strait of Juan de Fuca at Cape Flattery, a headland at the entrance to Vancouver Sound. Barkley omitted to explore the Strait which, however, he named. But his report caused a fresh rush of interest in the problem of a route over North America to the Pacific. In the meantime, the riddle had been attacked by land over the Canadian northlands. The British took up the task which the French had begun long before.

The rulers of the Hudson's Bay Company were either troubled in conscience over their sloth in seeking to explore to the north-west, or, as is more likely, they feared the effect on public opinion, which was already cool towards them, of their seeming lethargy in the matter. They were nervous about their monopoly. By 1770, they prepared to send out a new expedition in an endeavour to reach the shore of the Arctic Ocean and investigate the persisting rumours about the great treasure in copper and, possibly, gold which was waiting to be picked up there. In that year, the governor of the Company's trading post at Prince of Wales' Fort was a half-breed named Moses Norton, son of a former governor. Norton had relapsed into native ways. In fact, he had, in the words of his subordinate, Samuel Hearne, 'fallen into all the abominable vices of his countrymen', selfishly keeping five or six of the finest Indian girls for himself, going to ridiculous lengths to prevent any European from having relations with them and even owning a box of poison to be administered to anyone who refused him his wife or daughter.

Norton was asked by his superiors to pick a man to make a journey overland to the shores of the Arctic Ocean. He chose Hearne, a Londoner, son of the Clerk of the Waterworks at London Bridge. He had entered the navy at eleven in 1756 and later became a mate on a Hudson's Bay Company's sloop. Why Hearne was chosen is a matter of conjecture, although it is possible that Norton was glad to be rid of one who, like himself, had an eye for the local girls and no particular respect for Norton's prosy warnings of the jealous nature of Indian men: 'Lectures of this kind,' said Hearne, 'from a man of established virtue might have had some effect but when they came from one who was known to live in open defiance of every law, human and divine, they were always heard with indignation.' As it chanced, however, the selection of Hearne was on other grounds a sound one. He was a keen observer of nature and men and a level-headed explorer.

After Norton had signed the orders for the expedition, Hearne left for the north, taking with him as his guide a tall Indian named Mattanabee, the son of a Northern Indian and a slave woman. Thanks in great measure to Mattanabee the journey, although long and trying, was successful. Hearne reached the Coppermine River, found nuggets of copper – one of them four pounds in weight – and, after seven and a half months of trudging, reached the place where the Coppermine River ran into the sea, after passing through miles of flat country where only stunted pines and dwarf willows grew. He returned by a more indirect route to the fort where he arrived on 30 June 1772, having been eighteen months and twenty-three days on the way. In that time, he had travelled 1,300 miles.

He had suffered for days from what he called foundered feet, the result of long journeying over the cruel stony ground of the North. He had been the unwilling witness of a massacre of defenceless Eskimos, surprised in their little camp by the Indians in his company. 'I am confident that my features must have feelingly expressed how sincerely I was affected. Even to this day, I cannot reflect on the transactions of that horrid day without shedding tears.' This day had, in fact, been not a little 'horrid'. The Indians, in their hatred of the Eskimos, had gone to a great deal of trouble to ensure that their enemies did not die too quickly or too painlessly. They treated Hearne's protests with contempt.

Hearne's journey had achieved something for geographical knowledge. By reaching the shores of the Arctic Ocean without crossing any seaway, he had 'put a final end to all disputes concerning the North-west Passage through Hudson's Bay.' He also reported that, when he was at the westernmost point of his journey, five hundred miles further west than his starting point at Prince of Wales's Fort, his Indian guides could tell him of no end to the land lying still further to the west. It seemed that the North American continent was wider than had been supposed.

Moses Norton, who had sent him on his mission, died in agony a year after Hearne's return. His last reported words were spoken on his favourite subject. When he saw an officer lay hands on one of his wives who did not sufficiently resist, he cried, 'God damn you for a bitch! If I live, I'll knock your brains out.' A few minutes later, he died. As for the tall Indian, Mattanabee, he hanged himself ten years later when war broke out and the French destroyed Prince of Wales's Fort. Hearne, who surrendered the fort, died not long afterwards of dropsy.

Nineteen years passed before there was another serious attempt at exploration northwards over the Canadian tundra. This time, the explorer was a Scotsman from the Island of Lewis named Alexander Mackenzie, who had begun his business career in the Toronto offices of one of the partners in the North-west Fur Company, which had sprung up as a rival of the Hudson's Bay Company. Mackenzie, a young man in his thirties, had shown a good deal of audacity and enterprise in his dealings with American traders in the region of Detroit. Accordingly, when his employers thought of exploring to the north-west, they chose Mackenzie as the likeliest man for the job. He set out on 3 June 1789 from Fort Chipewyan at the head of Lake Athabasca. With him were a dozen Indians and half-breeds.

The party travelled northwards in five canoes on the Slave River and, in six days, had arrived at the Great Slave Lake which was covered with ice but mercifully free from mosquitoes. Mackenzie's Indian guides reported that the plains in the area were teeming with bison and that the woods bordering the lake were the haunt of moose and reindeer.

As they progressed further to the north, it was obvious that summer was coming: clouds were more frequent, weather was changeable, mosquitoes appeared in dense swarms. When they reached the lodges of the Red Knife Indians the Indian guides were unwilling to go any further, although, when they saw the midnight sun, they thought that it was a signal to advance. On the other hand, they were approaching Eskimo country and Eskimos, they said, were treacherous and cruel. In the end, the head man of the Indians, who was known as the English Chief, was bribed by Mackenzie with a mooseskin. On 15 July, after traversing a bleak coastal plain where only dwarf trees grew, Mackenzie reached the mouth of the river on the

Frozen Sea, which the Indians insisted on calling the *Mer d'ouest*. He erected a post to show he had been there. The local fishing was poor. From the Eskimos he heard of white men who had come from the west in big canoes, eight or ten years before. He was not able, however, to find out more about this story. Two months later, he was back at Fort Chipewyan. He had proved, he said, that there was no navigable North-west Passage. He urged the British Government to seek a trade route to the west along the Canadian rivers.

At the End of the Bay

'When, in short, there is neither water nor land to be seen, or when both
are equally undiscriminated, as well by shape as by colour, it is not always
so easy a problem as it might seem on a superficial view, to determine a
fact which appears in words to be extremely simple.'
    Sir John Ross, Narrative of a Second Voyage in search of a North-west Passage, 1834

Captain William Scoresby, a young whaler captain from Whitby, in
Yorkshire, wrote a letter to his friend, Sir Joseph Banks, President of the
Royal Society, one day in October 1817. Scoresby was a sailor whose
opinions must be treated with respect. Already he had an impressive record
of adventure and study. He had made the Greenland voyage with his father
many times. He had served and suffered as an Able Seaman in the navy. He
had studied chemistry and physics at Edinburgh University. He had in-
vented a device for taking deep-sea temperature. Obviously he was a
young man of unusual gifts and experience. And what he told Sir Joseph
now was likely to excite the scientific world. He had just returned, he said,
from a voyage to the Arctic. During that trip, he had found 2,000 square
leagues of the Greenland Sea, between 74 and 80 degrees north, completely
clear of ice! If his task had been exploration and not whaling, he had little
doubt that he would have solved the mystery of the North-west Passage.
He would have been able to explore the east coast of Greenland and, perhaps, clear up the mystery that had, for centuries, shrouded the fate of the
colony established by the Icelanders centuries before. He offered to lead a
new voyage of exploration.

Clearly, if Scoresby was right, the ice barrier between Spitzbergen and
Greenland, which had prevented ships from sailing to the Pole and had
defeated Phipps in 1773, had been dispersed. The ice had drifted further
south into warmer seas. The prospects for exploration to the north or
north-west were better than they had ever been in the memory of man. Sir
Joseph realized at once how important was the change, whatever might be

the reason for it. He passed the news on to the First Lord of the Admiralty, Lord Melville, linking it with other facts, such as the unusual prevalence of icebergs in the Atlantic, the abnormal amount of ice on the north coast of Iceland, the recent flooding in Germany caused by snow melting in the mountains. All this evidence led to one conclusion. 'New sources of warmth had been opened.' The Arctic seas were more accessible than they had been for centuries. In these circumstances, the government should seize the chance to find out more about the geography of the North. The President of the Royal Society was a man whose views had to be taken seriously.

Within three weeks, Melville had ordered four ships to be fitted out – two for a voyage to Davis Strait, two to sail towards the Pole by way of Spitzbergen. To the bitter disappointment of Scoresby, the command of the first expedition was given to Commander John Ross, R.N., a Wigton-shire man, while Commander David Buchan led the second. From the beginning, there was a sharp difference of opinion about the double expedi-tion. Captain Bernard O'Reilly, a Greenland skipper, wrote that while there might well be a way to the Pacific by way of Baffin Bay, the notion of a voyage over the Pole was only a 'closet lucubration'. This was an open attack on John Barrow, the Second Secretary of the Admiralty, who had poured out a stream of polemics urging the cause of Arctic exploration. O'Reilly said that if Barrow chose to amuse himself by writing articles about a Polar voyage, no great harm would be done. But it would be different if he were to mislead the public as he misled himself. Barrow was furious: 'The glaring folly that pervades every page of Mr O'Reilly's book forms a sufficient guarantee against its mischievous tendency.' Thus Barrow, a civil servant in a key position, was emotionally involved in the outcome of the voyages.

Ross, the son of a minister of the Church of Scotland, served in the Navy from the age of ten until thirteen, after which he was an apprentice in the merchant service for four years. After that, serving once more in the Navy, he was wounded fourteen times and was three times in French prisons. Now he sailed to the North in the *Isabella*, a whaler chartered for the pur-pose. With him sailed Lieutenant Parry in the *Alexander*, which had been specially strengthened at Deptford to resist the Arctic ice. Ross's orders were to look for a current which was believed to flow from the north or north-west through Davis Strait. Having found it, he was to follow it. The sea to the north of Davis Strait – Baffin Bay – would probably be free of ice, in which case Ross should stand well to the north before turning westwards, so as to have a good offing in rounding the north-east point of the American continent. After that, he should steer for Bering Strait and the Pacific. On arrival at Kamchatka, he was to hand over a copy of his journal to the Russian governor who would send it on to London. After filling up with stores at Hawaii, Ross was to take his way back to England by the route he had found in the Arctic.

With these instructions, Ross sailed on 25 April 1818. His ship's company consisted of naval officers and ratings and one Greenland Eskimo, named John Sacheuse, who was to act as interpreter at £3 a week. Sacheuse was an extraordinary representative of his people, gifted, energetic, and filled with the inspiration of what could be the future of the Eskimos. His story was simple and touching. Two years before he had stowed away in a Leith whaler, the *Thomas and Ann*, during its stay in Greenland waters. When the skipper had proposed to send him back to Greenland, Sacheuse had begged to be allowed to accompany the ship to Scotland. His plea had been successful. He was a convert to Christianity; his ambition was to carry on missionary work among his own race, 'the wild people' who were still heathen. Now he was eager to go north with Ross.

By the early days of July, the two ships under Ross's command were making their way painfully up the west coast of Greenland. At one point they paused near a community half-Dane and half-Eskimo. Sacheuse presided with aplomb when Eskimo girls and sailors danced reels on the deck.

By August their voyage had become perilous. The pressure of ice floes on the hull of the *Isabella* had become so great that beams in the hold began to bend, and it seemed that they would snap at any moment. The ship was forced upwards and then, by a sudden change in the movement of the ice, she was driven back against her consort, the *Alexander*. There was a collision between the two vessels violent enough to smash a ship's boat which was between the hulls, and the two bower anchors were hooked together until the cable attached to one of them snapped with a loud report, and the ships fell apart. Not long after that, by one of those sudden brief changes characteristic of Arctic weather, a clear channel opened in the ice ahead of them. It seemed for a moment that there was a pool of clear water in which the ships could find refuge. But the snow was falling so heavily just then that nobody could be sure how far the clear water extended. What was more, a gale had sprung up and grew stronger moment by moment.

Ahead, Ross saw an icefield on the move and bearing down on the *Isabella*. He ordered the crew to get to work with nine-foot saws and carve a refuge dock for the ship out of the mass of ice. It was useless. The ice was too thick for the saws to cut through it. A little later, he and his officers recognized that this had been a piece of good fortune for them. The icefield in which they had thought they might find refuge was drifting rapidly towards a reef of grounded icebergs, which would probably have crushed the ships. As it was, they were able to take advantage of an opening in the ice to pass beyond the bergs and reach open water.

Soon after this hair-raising experience, they had an adventure of a different kind. On the ice, they caught sight of men and sledges. At first they thought the strangers might be shipwrecked sailors, but Sacheuse said, 'These are real Eskimos. They are our fathers.' He meant they belonged to his people. They were Eskimos, members of an isolated community who had never seen a white man before and, indeed, had no knowledge of any other living beings in the world. For centuries – how many? – they had dwelt in their remote corner of the Greenland coast. They had lost contact with their own people. They had forgotten the arts with which Eskimos further south had carried on their war against the Arctic. They had forgotten how to make kayaks. They had no fish spears. They were, perhaps, the most isolated community in the world. They were the most northern. And not surprisingly they were shy and frightened. Sacheuse was appointed to open conversations with them. It turned out to be a difficult task. After a little, he found that by drawing out Eskimo words, he could make himself understood. When he told them he came from the south, they said, 'Impossible. There is only ice there.' They themselves came from further north and were on an expedition hunting narwhals.

Ross painted a flag which showed the sun and the moon over a hand holding a sprig of heath. This symbol of friendship he nailed to a pole which was set up in the ice with a sack of presents alongside it with a hand pointing to the ship. After several days, the Eskimos grew somewhat less frightened of the visitors. Sacheuse found that they could count up to ten. They had the simple fears of children. For instance, they thought that, if Sacheuse touched them, they would die. And they were extraordinarily curious about Ross's ships which they believed to be living beings. Had they not seen them move their wings? They addressed the ships directly and with respect: Who are you? What are you? Where do you come from? The sun or the moon? Do you give us light by night or by day?' After days spent in cajoling and present-giving – the two ships had been well supplied with axes, looking-glasses, cloth, guns, brandy and other forms of temptation – the Eskimos plucked up courage to come aboard the ships. They were amazed to see a sailor swarm up the mast and contemptuous of the ship's dog, which was too small to pull a sledge. They were particularly impressed by the wealth of timber around them. For them, wood was a material of infinite rarity and enormous value, found occasionally by lucky prospectors in the form of driftwood on the beaches. Sacheuse painted a picture of the meeting with these Eskimos. 'It has the merit of being at least a good representation of the objects introduced,' Ross thought.

Not long after leaving 'the Arctic Highlanders', as Ross called those Eskimos, the ship came in sight of an extraordinary phenomenon, the 'red snow' on the Crimson Cliffs. These were rocks which were stained by a substance resembling snow but of a brilliant crimson colour. It was ten or twelve feet deep. Was it animal, vegetable or mineral? They took specimens of it back to England where the story of 'red snow' caused some eyebrows to be raised. (Eventually, an expert at Kew Gardens pronounced it to be of vegetable origin, akin to 'smut' in wheat.)

With the wind in their favour, they made their way through loose ice to Smith Sound, and found it blocked with ice. Ross decided that the sound was about forty-five miles in length and, a fog coming down, he hauled to the west. There was, it seemed, no hope of finding a through channel in those waters. Accordingly, he turned south-west and came upon a large inlet which Baffin had found before him and to which he had given the name of Alderman Jones' Sound. Thinking that he saw mountains closing the gulf, he passed on to the south. On 29 August, the two ships entered a wide channel with high, snow-covered mountains to north and south. Ahead, under a yellow sky, there was no sign of land and only a few icebergs. The strait narrowed as the ships went westwards. Fog made it hard to decide the shape of the coastline. Captain Sabine, an artillery officer who came with the expedition as an astronomer, thought that they were off Lancaster Sound and that there was no hope of a passage until they reached Cumberland Strait. There was, he pointed out, no appearance of a current, no driftwood, no swell from the north-west. Crows' nest and masthead were crowded with observers as the ships moved cautiously to the west. By sunset they had come to no conclusion.

At four o'clock in the morning, Ross saw – or thought he saw – land at the bottom of the 'inlet'. It was in his opinion a range of mountains very high in the centre. In that case, the exit to the west was sealed up. But though the prospect of finding a way out seemed poor, he kept sailing westwards through the fog. When the weather cleared, at three o'clock in the afternoon, he went up on deck and distinctly saw land about twenty miles away, in what seemed to be a continuous line of peaks round the end of the 'bay', joining together the mountain ranges to the north and south. He named these heights Croker's Mountains. Deciding, on that evidence, that Lancaster Sound was not a strait but an inlet of the sea, Ross gave the order to return to the east. He sailed southwards down the coast of Baffin Island to Cumberland Sound. After that, he set off for home and arrived at Lerwick on 13 October. From Lerwick he sent a preliminary report to London by the packet.

The fate of one Eskimo should be noted. John Sacheuse died in Leith Hospital soon after his return to Scotland. He succumbed to an epidemic of cholera which broke out in Edinburgh at that time.

Commander Buchan arrived in the Thames nine days after Ross reached Shetland. His two ships had run into a gale of exceptional violence off the east coast of Greenland. They had been for days in deadly peril from a storm that drove them against an ice barrier which they could not penetrate. At last Buchan had given up the attempt to get through and brought his badly damaged ships home. John Barrow, chief inspirer of the two expeditions in the Admiralty therefore suffered, within a matter of days, a double blow to his hopes and his pride. It seemed that O'Reilly had been proved right. But Barrow was not the man to let misfortune pass without a riposte. He selected Ross as the main target of his attack, perhaps because he had expected more from him than from Buchan. He wrote with all the passion of one who had publicly expressed his faith that the North-west Passage would be found through Baffin Bay. Now, as it seemed, Ross's report had proved him wrong and his enemies – with the *Edinburgh Review* as their mouthpiece – were rejoicing. Writing of the total failure of the two expeditions which had so much excited the attention of Europe, Barrow dismissed Buchan's failure as 'one of those accidents to which all sea voyages are liable'. But of Ross's voyage he wrote in a very different tone, 'we hardly know in what terms to speak or how to account for it!' From that beginning, the attack on Ross's honesty and competence was conducted over a wide front and on issues minor as well as important.

In particular, said Barrow, Ross had not been within forty miles of the entrance to Smith Sound, far less at that distance from the bottom of it. And when Ross said that everyone on the ship shared his confidence that Lancaster Sound was an inlet, Ross was lying. At this stage in the controversy, Ross had two strokes of bad luck. Captain Sabine, R.A., whom he had quoted as the leading sceptic about the Sound, now wrote an article of a different tenor in which he spoke of the 'many encouraging coincidences' seen in the Sound. To make matters worse for Ross, an officer on the second ship, the *Alexander*, sent a letter to *Blackwood's Magazine* in which he said that his shipmates had been optimistic about prospects in Lancaster Sound: 'Every breast beat high, and everyone was desirous to mount the crow's nest to look out for the opening which would conduct us into the Polar Sea.' At the moment the ship's prow had turned about, to the surprise of all, there was no land ahead to be seen from the crow's nest of the *Alexander* which was, admittedly, four or five miles astern of Ross's ship, the *Isabella*. There were 650 fathoms of water beneath the *Alexander*. From what they had seen, they could not positively assert that there was no passage from Baffin Bay into the Pacific. This letter was approved by Captain Sabine, who said of Lancaster Sound that 'this magnificent inlet will, no doubt, be fully explored by the expedition' of 1819.

The truth seems to have been that Sabine changed his mind about Lancaster Sound on the homeward voyage, and that other officers, who had doubted at the time, felt their faith grow stronger when they learned, as soon as they did, that John Barrow was organizing a new expedition to explore the Sound. This time, they were certain, Ross would not be in command. In that, they were right. Not only did Ross not get the command but to make the criticism more pointed, it was given to Lieutenant Parry, who had been captain of the *Alexander*. Ross had lost the debate, although he still had his supporters; for instance, although perhaps more out of enmity to Barrow than from belief in Ross, the *Edinburgh Review* was steadfast. However, from that time forward, Ross was not given command of another voyage of exploration backed by the British Government. He demanded a court-martial at which he would have the opportunity of clearing himself. But in this, too, he was disappointed. He had been promoted to Captain and how, asked the First Lord, could it be thought that any shadow rested on the reputation of an officer who had been promoted? Ross might be dissatisfied; he might feel that he had been victimized, but he had to content himself by saying that Barrow, unlike the Lords of the Admiralty, was no gentleman. It was his misfortune that, in a question where the evidence was doubtful, he had collided head-on with a powerful civil servant, who was not only emotionally engaged on one side of the argument but also had considerable gifts as a propagandist. Barrow was one of those men of the study and the map who kept the flame of the North-west Passage burning at a time when the explorers in their ships brought back depressing news from the Frozen Ocean. He was predisposed to find negligence or worse in Ross's survey of Lancaster Sound.

'The Threshold Passed'

'If the weather should prove favourable, you are to remain in the vicinity of the Pole for a few days.'

Admiralty instruction to Lieutenant Parry, 1818

The man chosen by the Admiralty to command the expedition of 1818 was a naval lieutenant of 28, William Edward Parry, son of a Bath doctor. Like so many of the group of Arctic explorers of that period, Parry had served in the Navy during the war against France. At the age of thirteen, he first stepped aboard Admiral Cornwallis's flagship cruising off Brest. From that moment, until peace came after Waterloo, Parry was a fighting sailor. He had spent three years as a young lieutenant watching over the British whalers in Spitzbergen waters, so that he had some experience of the Arctic before his voyage with Ross to Baffin Bay. Now he was going to take two ships back to the same waters. They were the *Hecla*, a bomb vessel of 375 tons, which was to be accompanied by the *Griper*, a gun brig of 180 tons. Both ships were strengthened for the rough usage they were likely to meet in the Arctic; they carried enough provisions for a cruise of two years. As for the officers, they included many men who had served with Ross the year before, among them, Captain Sabine, R.A. Parry's orders were to proceed at once to Lancaster Sound and pass through the strait he ought to find there. Failing that, he was to make for Alderman Jones' Sound and, if that too, proved to be a disappointment, to Smith Sound. In other words, Parry was to pay special attention to the three openings which Ross, in Barrow's opinion, had neglected. At the same time, the Admiralty was organizing a complementary expedition which was to travel overland from Hudson's Bay to the mouth of the Coppermine River, as Hearne had done 48 years earlier. From that point, it was to explore the coastline to the east. As leader of this second expedition, Lieutenant John Franklin was chosen. Already he had some experience of the Arctic, having commanded a ship under Commander Buchan in the expedition which had attempted the Polar voyage in the year of Ross's trip to Baffin Bay.

Parry's ships left Deptford on 4 May 1819, and reached the entrance to Lancaster Sound on 30 July. It was a momentous occasion. Men's convictions were going to be put to the test; men's reputations were at stake. 'We were about to enter and to explore,' wrote Parry in his *Journal*, 'that great sound or inlet which has obtained a degree of celebrity beyond what it might otherwise have been considered to possess from the very opposite opinions which have been held with regard to it.' Progress was slow against a west wind. From the remarkable number of whales that were visible, eighty-two in the day's log, Parry concluded that he had stumbled upon a 'headquarters' of these mammals and the Greenland master who was with him, Mr Allison, reported that a whaler could have obtained a full cargo in a few days. Parry and his officers were concerned with a nobler quest. They had seen a flight of white ducks which they thought might be male eider ducks passing over, flying east. They would sail towards the region in which those birds had begun their flight. They felt that the success or failure of the enterprise depended on whether or not they would find a way through to the west. Leaving behind his slower companion ship, the *Griper*, Parry began to enter the sound. Four days later, however, the *Griper* had been reached by a wind from the east, so that she caught up with the *Hecla*. Together the two vessels were, it seemed, on the immediate approaches to the Polar Sea.

The explorers could see both shores of the Sound – high, jagged snow-covered mountains to the south, while to the north the land, which had been low-lying, now rose in naked cliffs on successive tiers, like fortifications. The *Hecla* thrust ahead in the breeze once more and soon left the *Griper* out of sight. Parry's ship pitched so violently in the swell that once or twice water was hurled into the stern windows. This was thought to be another sign that open sea lay ahead. Excitement was high. The mastheads were crowded by officers and men. Every report from the crow's nest was eagerly greeted on deck. Omens remained good. The sea had turned the usual 'ocean' colour. A long swell was rolling in from the south and east. With the sea as free from ice as the Atlantic, Parry and his comrades thought that they had come through to open water. To the north the coastline seemed to end in a promontory which they named Cape Fellfoot. They had, indeed, reached the point at which Lancaster Sound begins to open out and a vast channel, now called Prince Regent Inlet, leads off to the south. The ship's surgeon, Alexander Fisher, who had accompanied Parry on Ross's voyage, wrote in his diary: 'The momentous question . . . has this day been decided. No land exists on the west side of Lancaster Sound.' Secretary Barrow of the Admiralty had been proved right. However, disappointment awaited the ships: land ahead was reported. Although it turned out to be only a small island, soon the news was worse. Ice was found, very thick, stretching for some miles alongside the ships.

After Parry tried for two hours to find a way between this ice and the northern shore, he was at length forced to recognize that half a mile ahead of him an impenetrable mass of ice filled the whole space between one shore and the other. Somewhere beyond, a 'water sky' gave hope that there was open sea in that quarter, but a bright ice-blink to the west quenched their hopes of finding a way through. Parry turned northwards – no exit in that direction. Then the look-out reported that one was opening in the ice to the south of them. Parry steered that way, passing southwards along Prince Regent Inlet for a hundred miles or so. At length he turned about and resumed his westward course through a wide channel which continued the line of Lancaster Sound. As he went, he named prominent features after distinguished figures of the time: Wellington Channel, after the Duke, Cornwallis Island after his first admiral, while the gauntly impressive channel along which he intended to proceed was named after the official who had been, more than any man, the mainspring of the expedition – Barrow Strait.

As August drew to an end, Parry thought that things were going pretty well. The sea was navigable, if not open, and likely to remain so for another six weeks. There was plenty of food aboard and the crews were in good spirits. When it seemed for a moment that the way to the west was blocked by ice, a lieutenant in the crow's next located a spot at which the barrier was thinner. The *Hecla* struck it with great force and drove a passage through for both ships. Further west, a north wind blew, sign that the land mass in that direction was probably broken up into islands. Ahead there was a stretch of water – Viscount Melville Sound – so wide that Parry, looking out from the crow's nest, fixed a rendezvous with the *Griper* in case the two vessels should become separated. When he reached Byam Martin Island, between Bathurst Island and Melville Island, it seemed that the ways to the west and the south were alike barred by ice at no great distance ahead. For a little, then, the two ships continued to move cautiously to the west, the *Hecla*'s helmsman having orders to keep the *Griper*'s masts always in line.

On 1 September, it was observed that the sun did not rise clear of the horizon at noon. The Arctic winter was beginning. The time was at hand when they should seek a place of refuge where the months of darkness could be spent. While Parry kept that in mind, he postponed the moment of decision. For this there was a good reason. The ships had reached the 105th meridian; if they passed the 110th, they would win a bounty of £5,000 which Parliament had voted to the first ship to reach that point on a westward voyage within the Arctic Circle. When the *Hecla* did so, on 4 September, Parry named the headland they had reached Bounty Point. There were great rejoicings on board the ship. He ordered beer for the crews and a modest addition of meat for the Sunday dinner. In a rousing speech, he told them that, at this rate, they would find the Passage before the end of another year.

At length, after exhausting struggles with the ice, which was closing in at an alarming speed, the ships were brought into an inlet on the south of Melville Island, where they dropped anchor for the first time since leaving the English coast. But powerful currents, working together with the unpredictable movements of the ice, made it hard for them to reach a satisfactory anchorage. At one moment, when the *Hecla* was forty yards from the beach, a main field of ice moving with the current struck a berg projecting from the shore, shattering the ice with terrifying reports and piling up enormous fragments only a hundred yards from the ship. As the pressure of newly-formed ice grew, the *Hecla* was carried slowly but irresistibly towards the shore. The *Griper* was in the same plight, although more liable to heel over than her consort, as floating ice had caught in her anchor cable and was dragging her towards the shore.

Parry held a council of his senior officers who agreed with him that the moment had come to seek a refuge for the winter. They could already look back on a magnificent achievement. As a result of extraordinary daring and skill, they had penetrated unknown channels so that they were about seven hundred miles due west of the entrance to Lancaster Sound. Parry's hope that they would find the North-west Passage did not seem too extravagant. They were, in fact, three hundred miles from the western limits of the Arctic archipelago. No feat of exploration in the North could compare with theirs. Parry decided to run back some distance to the east where he knew a suitable harbour could be found. Meanwhile, a gale blew up from the north. Ropes were stiff with frost. The rudder was choked with ice. And they had enormous difficulty in raising the anchor. At evening, there was a danger that the *Griper*, trying to reach a new anchorage, would be frozen up at sea. Soon after sunset, Parry, noticing the speed with which young ice formed on the surface of the water, had the same fear about the

Hecla. The danger was averted. The *Griper* tied up to some grounded ice; the *Hecla* was able to anchor in nine fathoms of water. All that night, snow fell heavily.

Next morning began three days of strenuous work, first a reconnaissance to decide on the best place for an anchorage, then the sawing of a channel through the ice which was six to twelve inches thick. This proved to be a long and wearisome operation. The line of a channel was marked out in the ice with boarding pikes. The ice was cut by saw at intervals of ten or twenty feet and, in width, a little more than the width of the *Hecla*. The seamen, 'always fond of doing things in their own way', set boats' sails on the pieces of ice to float them out of the channel. At the end of the first day's work, Parry ordered an extra allowance of half a pound of fresh meat to be issued every day to the crew. Next morning, it occurred to somebody that it would be easier to sink the sections of ice rather than to float them away. The officers took turns standing on a corner of each segment of the ice they had cut and so that it could be hauled beneath the surface of the ice that was still fast. Although the fourth day was a Sunday, Parry ordered work to go on. By noon, the sawn channel had been completed, 4082 yards long, through ice of an average thickness of 7 inches.

They had arrived in harbour just in time. That first night, the thermometer fell below zero. Next day, the sea was seen to be frozen over as far as the eye could see. The ships were prepared for winter. The top-masts were lowered, except the *Hecla*'s main-top which was kept in place for the periodic hoisting of an electrometer chain to test the electricity in the atmosphere. The lower yards were lashed fore and aft amidships to support the planks which covered the ships. These were roofed over with cloth (wadding tilt) used for covering waggons. The upper decks were cleared as far as possible so that they could be used for exercise. The frozen sails and ropes were taken ashore and stored under canvas to remain there through the winter. The anchors were carried over the ice to the beach so that, when the ice broke up in the spring, the ships could be held fast. This turned out to be a needless precaution.

Parry now turned to the health and comfort of his ships' companies. The doctor's report was highly satisfactory; not a man had reported sick since they passed the Arctic Circle, apart from one officer who had been attacked by rheumatism soon after leaving England. Not a sign of scurvy so far! But precautions were taken. Once a week the doctors were to examine every man's gums and shins, where the first symptoms of the disease would be most likely to appear. Meanwhile they prepared to entertain themselves in the usual ways. A weekly magazine, the *North Georgia Gazette and Winter Chronicle* was launched with Captain Sabine as its editor and censor. Amateur theatricals were organized in which Parry himself took part, 'considering that an example of cheerfulness was not the least essential part of my duty'. These were amusements for the long winter evenings in England. Parry and his comrades faced a winter evening that would last nine months.

They watched the reindeer (which were probably caribou) assembling for their annual journey over the ice to the mainland. Soon they would be completely isolated. The snow fell so heavily it was necessary to lay a line between one ship and the other for men to find their way. Frostbite stiffened the fingers of unwary men into the shape of the object they had been holding. In the extreme cold, men talked thickly and wildly, as if they were drunk. On fine days before the animals went south, hunting parties set out. Although the thermometer was 15° below zero, the air was pleasant and bracing, and they were anxious to get as much fresh meat as possible for the larder. Bottles containing the ships' precious supply of lemon juice burst with the frost. Beer and vinegar froze in the cask. Smoke from the ships' galley fires hung in the icy air immediately above the roofing.

On 4 November, the sun was visible from deck for the last time. On the following evening the first performance was given in the ship's theatre. The piece chosen was a farce by Garrick entitled *Miss in her Teens*. This was such a success that it was repeated a week later with an additional song entitled *The North-west Passage*, or *The Voyage Finished*. After that, there was a new theatrical performance once a fortnight, sometimes with the temperature on stage below zero. In addition, men danced and sang when off duty, a diversion on which Parry remarks rather primly, 'it is scarcely necessary to add that the evening occupations of the officers were of a more rational kind . . . a game of chess or a tune on the flute or violin.' The permission to dance may have cost Parry a struggle with his conscience. 'As an art,' he wrote,* 'dancing is lawful and commendable, but, if practised in a mixed company, it exposes the dancers to a thousand disorders.' In Arctic conditions, this severe view could be relaxed.

On 2 January 1820 the first case of scurvy appeared. Mr Scallon, the gunner of the *Hecla*, developed the unmistakable symptoms of the disease in his gums and was at once plied with all the usual antidotes – preserved vegetable soup, lemon juice, sugar, pickles, preserved berries and spruce beer. In addition, Parry was growing mustard and cress in shallow boxes in

Universal Magazine, 1853.

his cabin. The crop might be colourless, because the only light in the *Hecla* came from candles, but it had the same taste as if it had been grown in the usual way. Whatever the explanation, Mr Scallon recovered in nine days.

Then weeks passed during which there was little to do except observe how the ships' dogs made friends or enemies among the local wolf pack. Once they saw a white wolf, long and lean, and running like an Eskimo dog with his head very low. Try as they might, however, the hunters could never succeed in killing a wolf. As January came to an end, some of the ports were opened, so that light might come in to help the carpenters at their work. And, bit by bit, the ordinary routine of preparing a ship for sea was resumed. The colours which the sky wore at noon – orange and crimson – were more beautiful than anything of the kind they had seen before. It was, however, not a moment for relaxing any precautions, for the coldest part of the year had still to come.

On 24 February a new crisis broke out. The little hut they had built ashore to house scientific instruments took fire. Officers and men rushed out to fight the flames, a battle that lasted three-quarters of an hour. After five minutes in the open air, every one's face was white with frostbite. John Smith, of the artillery, was worse off still. He saved the dipping-needle without having time to put on his gloves. The outcome was disastrous. When the surgeon plunged Smith's hands into a basin of cold water, the water was immediately covered with ice. Smith lost seven of his fingers by amputation.

During the last days of January, men were sent up to the masthead for ten minutes before and after noon to catch the first glimpse of the sun. On 3 February it was seen, after being absent for 84 days. Soon after this occurred the first serious breach of discipline came when two of the *Hecla*'s marines were sentenced to 36 lashes for drunkenness. To have gone without crime for thirteen months was a record which Parry thought was extremely creditable to the crew.

On 1 June, he set out on an expedition northwards across the ice of Melville Island. He had eleven men with him and food for three weeks. They carried, on a light, home-made cart, two tents improvised out of boarding pikes and blankets. After a time, the sailors rigged up a blanket on the cart as a sail, which made matters easier on their way across fields of blinding snow, over narrow ravines and through dense fogs. Nor did they forget their patriotic duty. On 4 June, the King's birthday, officers and men alike drank to His Majesty's health, 'unaware that our venerable Monarch had many months before, paid the debt of nature'. They reached the north shore of the island after six days' trek and found it desolate and devoid of life except for half-a-dozen duck. From the top of a hill, looking seawards, Parry could see nothing but great masses of ice piled up. Beneath the ice was salt water. Nine days later, the travellers were back at the ships, in better health than when they had left.

By this time there was only one thing to do; wait for the ice to break up and release the ships for sailing. Meanwhile, there was good hunting; the weather was mild and the symptoms of scurvy were disappearing. On 1 August, Parry saw clear water offshore and gave the word to sail further to the west. Fifty miles further on, he turned to the south, but, once more, the ships were caught in the ice. Parry examined the food situation. He found that enough remained to last, at the present rate of consumption, until November of the following year. Plainly, they would be well advised to leave the Arctic before the end of the 1821 season. With bitter reluctance, Parry decided there was no hope that year of reaching Icy Cape where the Arctic coast begins to turn south towards the Pacific. Navigation was already too dangerous and, to the west, he could see an unbroken surface of impenetrable ice. What should be done? When he asked his officers their opinion, they agreed to a man that it was time to give up the attempts to sail further to the west. It was time to turn the ships' prows towards home. Six days later, they had reached the entrance to Lancaster Sound, and within thirteen weeks they sighted the Scottish coast. With the exception of one man who had died of an illness which was already active in him at the time of sailing from England, the ninety-four men who set out in the *Hecla* and the *Griper*, returned in good health. It was, in its way, a remarkable tribute to Parry's leadership and to British naval discipline.

As for the outcome of the voyage regarded as a contribution to geographical knowledge, the North-west Passage had once more eluded the seekers. But on the other hand, the ships had sailed more than six hundred miles further west through Lancaster Sound than had any ship before them. Ross's belief that the Sound ended in a range of mountains, which he imprudently showed on a map he drew, was exploded. The North-west Passage existed – Parry was certain of that – but he had gone looking for it in the wrong place, into seas where the ice was too thick and the cold too severe. The next explorer who looked for it should, he thought, hold closer to the mainland coast where there would be the best hope of finding openings between ice and shore. Much further south than the route he had followed, further south than the west shore of Baffin Bay – there on some stretch of coast still unexplored, the opening to the west should be sought.

'Cumberland Strait, the passage called Sir Thomas Roe's Welcome, lying between Southampton Island and the coast of America, and Repulse Bay, appear to be the points most worthy of attention.' Parry, in short, was suggesting a new search in that ancient breeding-ground of delusions, Hudson's Bay. In the meantime Parry wrote to the rector of St Mary-le-Strand, London, asking for a service of thanksgiving – 'I have solicited this favour in perfect ignorance whether it is proper or not and with a sincere desire to give glory where alone the glory is due.'

One man, however, was not prepared to see the glory go unshared. Secretary John Barrow regarded the fruits of Parry's voyage as a complete vindication of himself and his opinions. The Passage might not yet be found but, he told the readers of the *Quarterly Review*, in the course of an article in which he delivered a few sly digs at Ross, 'the ice is broken, the door opened, the threshold passed and the first stage of the journey accomplished!'

To the Hyperborean Sea

'If you want a good Polar traveller, get a man without much muscle, with good physical tone and let his mind be on wires of steel.'
Apsley Cherry-Gerrard, *The Worst Journey in the World*, 1922

Nineteen days after Parry sailed from Deptford, Lieutenant John Franklin, R.N., left Gravesend in a Hudson's Bay Company's ship, the *Prince of Wales*. Franklin was the son of a Lincolnshire shopkeeper. As a boy, he had distressed his father by a fixed, irrational resolve to become a sailor. After a struggle, the shopkeeper had capitulated and John, aged fourteen, joined H.M.S. *Polyphemus* as a 'first-class volunteer'. Into the next few years the boy crammed enough adventure to satisfy most men for a lifetime. He was present at the Battle of Copenhagen, sailed with Captain Flinders to Australia, returned in time to take part in the blockade of Brest and, finally, was in the thick of the fighting at Trafalgar. His ship, the *Bellerophon*, lost three hundred dead that day. Franklin, who escaped unhurt, was slightly deaf for the rest of his life. The end of the naval war against France closed one avenue of adventure to the young man and, what was worse, appeared to end all hope of advancement. The First Lord of the Admiralty, Lord Melville, left Franklin in no doubt of the position: 'As the Navy is now placed on a peace establishment, all promotion must in consequence cease.' This was not a prospect Franklin relished or could afford. He was a typical product of the harsh ordeal of the war at sea, with an additional vehemence of character all his own. The shopkeeper's self-willed son had grown up into a self-reliant young man, hard on himself and exacting to others; devout, determined, fiercely ambitious. Franklin was going to hew out a career for himself. If the Navy, now settling down to a hundred years of peace, did not look like a favourable sphere to do it, he would still find one, somehow. But where? The opportunity came when the Admiralty rediscovered its interest in the Arctic. Exploration!

When Commander Buchan was sent on his voyage to the Pole, Franklin went with him in command of the *Trent*. It was a turning-point in his career. When the Admiralty planned an expedition over the Canadian Northern Territories to the shore of the Arctic Ocean, as a complement to Parry's voyage, they looked for a man to lead it. Franklin, just back from the North with a high reputation for courage and skill, was an obvious choice. He had the experience, the temperament; he was the right age – thirty-three. To accompany him, the Admiralty selected a tough Scots naval surgeon named John Richardson, a year younger than Franklin; two midshipmen, George Back and Robert Hood, and an able seaman, John Hepburn. Like their leader, both Richardson and Back had seen active service in the war, which for Back began when he was twelve years old. Back and Hood were to help Franklin with his survey of the Arctic coast; Richardson was to serve as naturalist. Hepburn was to be the handyman. The plan of the expedition was simple. Franklin was instructed to reach the mouth of the Coppermine River and then to explore along the coast to the east of its estuary; alternatively, he could travel due north from Hudson's Bay and then westwards along the coast to the river mouth. With this wide commission Franklin set out, and, after a slow voyage lasting three months against 'a determined wind', he and his party arrived at York Factory on the west coast of Hudson's Bay.

There now began one of the grimmest, most extraordinary of all the chapters in the Arctic story. By the time, two years later, when Franklin and the survivors of his party returned to their base, they had covered 5,550 miles, six hundred and fifty miles of which had been in the Arctic Ocean itself, while most of the rest was by boat or canoe on the rivers of the territory. Their sufferings had been appalling. Franklin's journey took place in an area which lies, roughly speaking, eight hundred or a thousand miles due south of the harbour at Melville Island where, at the same time, Parry's two ships were wintering. The two expeditions were, however, closely linked in purpose. They were a part of a great design which the strategists in the Admiralty had laid out.

Franklin's task was to determine the configuration of the Arctic coastland of Canada, to note any useful harbours and, if possible, to set up cairns on its main headlands for the benefit of ships that might, later on, pass that way to the Pacific. Franklin left York Factory on 9 September 1829, in a boat which the Hudson's Bay Company had provided, with a steersman who was reckoned to know the way and a crew of boatmen from Orkney. These, with some difficulty, were recruited in Stromness by

the customary method, a notice on the church door, 'as the lower classes in
these islands invariably attend divine service every Sunday'. After listening
to the advice of Hudson's Bay Company officials who knew the country,
he struck off south-west into the wilderness by way of Hayes River. The
party's rate of progress was hardly impressive – two miles an hour, rowing
and sailing, or towing the boat when the current was unusually rapid. In a
month's time, they pitched their tents on the nearby northern shore of
Lake Winnipeg. They observed as they went the customs of the Cree
Indians – their passion for gambling; their practice of seducing each other's
wives, 'the most fertile source of their quarrels'; their tolerance of their
wives' behaviour; even their drunkenness; their excessive indulgence to
their children. So far as their religion went, Franklin noted that they believed
in the Flood, caused by the fish in an attempt to drown a demi-god with
whom they had quarrelled. The Crees worshipped a being they called
Kepoochikawn but whom, however, they treated with contemptuous
familiarity. In due course, the explorers entered the great Saskatchewan
River and made their way upstream, past an endless series of cataracts, to
Cumberland House, a trading post of the North-west Company on Pine
Island Lake. They had covered close on 700 miles. The ice was forming on
the lake. Winter was not far off.

At Cumberland House, the new arrivals noted approvingly that the
half-breed children of the Orkney men at the fort behaved much better
than those of the Canadian *voyageurs*. The Orkney men had taken some
trouble to educate their children. After staying some months at Cumberland House, Franklin decided to push on to Lake Athabasca, five hundred
miles to the north-west. By this time, it was mid-January. Snow covered
the ground. Supplies were brought along in sledges drawn by dogs. The
travellers used snow shoes which Franklin for one found agonizing to walk
with. In twelve days they had reached Carlton House in the country of the
Stone Indians, a handsome, treacherous people and, after a few days' rest,
set out for Ile à la Crosse and thence due north to Fort Chipewyan on
the north shore of Lake Athabasca. They had walked 850 miles since leaving Cumberland House. At the fort they paused a while.

They had met very few white men on the way but now they were overtaken by Mr Isbister and another Orkney man who were in search of an
Indian band who, probably, had some furs to sell. In the snow the Indians
had left no tracks and Isbister, four days without food, was thinking of
killing one of his dogs when, in time, he stumbled on some Indian lodges.
After that, Franklin met a famous traveller, named John Stuart, who had

twice reached the Pacific by travelling down the Columbia River. Stuart's assistance in obtaining guides for a journey to the Arctic would be of great value because, at this point, Franklin met a difficulty which was to plague him often in the months to come. No French Canadian would willingly enter Eskimo territory. However, he had some good fortune. One day a half-breed was tracing the line of the Coppermine River on the floor, when an Indian took a piece of charcoal and drew in the outline of the Arctic coast which he said was free from ice in July. Then another problem arose. Franklin could get help from neither the North-west Company nor the Hudson's Bay Company, both of which were engaged in fierce commercial rivalry. But about this time, a message came from the chief of the Copper Indians at Great Slave Lake. The chief said that he would be waiting at the lake to greet Franklin. After that, the French Canadians volunteered to accompany Franklin on his march to the sea.

On 13 July, Richardson and Hood, whom Franklin had left at Cumberland House, arrived with a company of Canadian voyageurs. Their journey had been marked by hardships and dangers. They had suffered from the mosquito, the plague of that season. It 'chases the buffalo to the plains, irritating him to madness, and the reindeer to the seashore from which they do not return till the scourge has passed'. No sooner were they free from the mosquito than the horsefly attacked. While the voyageurs paddled in time to their songs, they had descended the Athabasca River, watched by eagles from the summits of pines, and had come into the smaller river which the French called L'Embarras. On either bank were gigantic pines, two hundred feet high, as they guessed. And so, at length, they joined Franklin at Fort Chipewyan.

Five days later, the reunited expedition set out to the north in three canoes – five British explorers, sixteen voyageurs, two Indian interpreters and two Indian women. When they reached Fort Providence, a post of the Hudson's Bay Company, they were on the borders of the Copper Indian country and were glad of the services of a Hudson's Bay official, Mr Wentzel, who could speak the Indian language. A tribal chief named Akaitcho said he was ready to guide them on their way to the coast, although he could not understand why there was all this urgency to travel through a country which, he said, was not only a hunting ground of ferocious grizzly bears but was also inhabited by Eskimos, a notoriously treacherous race. As it turned out, there were no grizzlies in the region, only brown bears which turned out to be much less alarming. And the Eskimos gave less trouble than the Indians.

By 20 August, they were 553 miles north of Chipewyan and began to look about them for a place to spend the winter. The usual signs of a change of seasons had appeared. One morning the small pools were covered with ice and flocks of geese were seen flying to the south. Then fog came and the ice vanished. But they had been warned. While Franklin was reluctant to halt the march to the Frozen Sea, trouble arose with Akaitcho, who refused to go any further. After some argument, the Indian agreed that some of his young men might continue with the explorers so that it could not be said he had allowed the Englishmen to perish alone. But from the moment the young Indians left, he would mourn them as dead. In the end, Franklin decided to remain where he was until winter had passed. He contented himself by sending Back and Hood on a reconnaissance by boat as far as the Coppermine River. With them went nine half-breeds and one Indian. If they found that the river water was warmer than 40°, Back was allowed to go further on. If the water was colder, he must return at once. The water was much colder.

One day towards the end of August, Akaitcho, who had heard Franklin talk about an approaching eclipse of the sun, asked a series of intelligent questions about it: what caused it; what effect would it have; above all, how did Franklin know it was going to happen? As well as Franklin could, he explained it to the Indian. Deeply impressed by the white man's wisdom, Akaitcho promised to do all he could to keep the explorers supplied. Unfortunately, on the day of the eclipse there was a heavy snowstorm making observation impossible. The Copper Indians had another disappointment when they heard that Dr Richardson, although a distinguished medical man, could not bring the dead to life. While Back and Hood were on their trek to the north, Franklin and Richardson journeyed to the Coppermine on foot, sleeping at night on fir brush under a single blanket, fording icy streams which wet them to the skin and shooting reindeer for food. Raw marrow from the hind legs of the animal turned out to be a great delicacy. By the time they set off on the return journey to Fort Enterprise, the weather had worsened. The ground was covered with snow, and the small lakes were frozen. They were glad to be back at the Fort, some miles to the west of the Great Slave Lake, where Back and Hood had already arrived and where Mr Wentzel had built excellent winter quarters for them. The lake itself they found to be a vast sheet of water (it is bigger than Lake Erie) set in wild and desolate surroundings.

The main party now settled down with the carcasses of a hundred deer in the storehouse to see them through the winter, plus another eighty cached under heaps of snow at varying distances from the house. Meanwhile, Back and Wentzel set off for Fort Providence to arrange that the stores they expected from Cumberland House should be sent on to them. By this time, the summer birds had flown off to the south, leaving only the raven, the crow, the ptarmigan and the snow bird. On 5 October they gave up fishing for the season. One necessity was in very short supply – musket balls. In this emergency, pewter cups were melted down, enough for five rounds to each hunter. But only Akaitcho had any luck with this improvised ammunition.

Meanwhile, they waited with some anxiety for news that Back and Wentzel had arrived safely. The Indians, who had calculated how long the double journey should take, were very soon pessimistic. They were sure that the whole party had fallen through the ice, if they had not been slaughtered by Dog-rib Indians. 'The ice at this season is deceitful and the Dog-rib, although unwarlike, are treacherous.' Gloom quickly spread. At last, a voyageur named Bélanger staggered into the hut, encrusted with ice from head to foot, his hair matted with snow. He had walked alone for thirty-six hours over the barren country through a storm which his Indian companions dared not face. Among other things, he brought letters which had been posted in England in the previous April. From the newspapers, Franklin learned of the 'demise of our revered and lamented sovereign, George III' – and prudently kept the news from the Indians 'lest the death of their great Father might lead them to suppose we should be unable to fulfil our promises to them'. Relations with the Indians were more than usually delicate just then. Those of them who had followed Bélanger back from Fort Providence brought a report, attributed to the official in charge of the Fort, that Franklin and his companions were not, as they pretended to be, officers of a great king, but wretches whose only object was to live comfortably among the Copper Indians whom they could not possibly reward for their services. Behind all this there lay some hostility among the fur traders to Franklin's expedition. This was probably the reason why only five of the ten cases of stores sent from York Factory reached them. Their supplies of ammunition and tobacco had been dumped on the beach at Grand Rapids on the Saskatchewan River by a Hudson's Bay officer. These stores were not forwarded, deliberately it seems.

Meanwhile the cold grew more severe. Axes were broken in trying to cut down trees frozen as hard as stone. Chronometers, kept by Hood and Richardson under their pillows, stopped when they got up to dress. Before the fire was lit in the morning, the temperature in the house was as low as

40° below zero. Outside, during these spells of intense cold, the air was still and men went about their usual occupations without any need to take exceptional precautions. The Indians continued to hear unpleasant rumours about Franklin and his party. Influenced by these stories, Akaitcho complained that they had not given him enough ammunition. Were they trying to degrade him in the eyes of his tribe? Franklin sent him a keg of spirits to restore his confidence. Two Eskimo interpreters joined the party and were named Augustus and Junius. Augustus, who understood English, had no difficulty in reading a map which Franklin spread out before him. He pointed out Marble Island, where Knight's ships had been wrecked exactly a hundred years earlier. Franklin spent a great deal of time that winter reading a book he had brought out with him, Law's *Serious Call to a Holy Life*.

On 5 March Back returned, after an absence of five months, and without Wentzel, who had stayed to arrange supplies. He had travelled 1,104 miles on snowshoes and with no covering at night but a blanket and a deerskin, in temperatures which, at times, were 57° below zero. He had gone for two or three days at a stretch without eating. The Indian women with him insisted that he should eat while they went without: 'We are used to starving.' In an old deer's skin they pounded meat, fat and deers' hair, which seemed a great luxury after three days of starvation. At other times, Back was not so fortunate and was glad to eat a variety of lichen called *tripe de roche*. This he scraped from the rocks where it grew. The time had not yet come when this lichen became the staple diet of the explorers. While preparations for the final stage of the journey to the sea were going forward, Franklin was worried about signs of disaffection among the Indians. Saint-Germain, a voyageur and a born agitator, tried to persuade Akaitcho that he was not being treated with the dignity owing to a chief. Worse, he spread alarming reports about the dangers of the journey before them. Franklin told him that, if the expedition failed because of him, he would be taken to England and tried. 'It does not matter,' said Saint-Germain, 'where I lose my life, whether in England, or accompanying you to the sea, for the whole party will perish.'

After this, there were weeks of tedious haggling with Akaitcho about the presents he should be given. His position as a chief was suitably recognized on his arrival at the camp by the hoisting of a flag and firing a salvo. He approached at a slow, majestic pace, accompanied by braves who had a daub of vermilion on their cheeks. He opened the negotiations with a speech full of complaints. His aim was evidently to grab as much as possible for himself so that nothing would be left for the Eskimos. However, in the end, he overplayed his hand, saying indignantly, 'There are too few goods for me to distribute; those that mean to follow the white people to the sea may take them.' At that, most of the guides and the hunters stepped forward to claim their share of the goods and Akaitcho retired in dignified disgust. However, he returned next day as cheerfully as if nothing had happened and, in fact, put on his best clothes for the final meeting.

In May, the bilberries and cranberries that had spent the winter under the snow appeared in abundance, the sap thawed in the pines and the gulls and arctic divers were seen on the river.

And, at last, on 4 June, the departure for the north began. An advance party set out under the command of Dr Richardson – fifteen voyageurs and eight Indians with their children, most of them dragging their belongings on sledges. Each of the Indians took with him, in his medicine bag, a small packet of medicines which the doctor had prepared for him. Ten days later Franklin followed with the main party, leaving behind in one of the rooms a box containing his journal and charts. On the door someone drew the picture of a man holding a dagger. This, it was thought, would deter any Indian who might try to break in.

From the beginning the journey put a severe strain on their endurance. The temperature varied within forty degrees. When it was hot, mosquitoes abounded. The few dwarf birches they could collect were not enough to make an adequate fire. Meat which had been cached on the route by the hunters had been eaten by wolverines. First Franklin, and then Back, fell through the ice into a lake. The day after, it was even worse, with a gale blowing and a blizzard beating and no fuel for the fire but some twigs of stunted green willow. On 28 June, after living for days on the deer the hunters killed, and after they had dragged their canoes over the ground, they reached rapids where, as they thought, a lake emptied into the Coppermine River.

On the last day of June, they started to descend the river which, in the meantime, had widened into a lake so choked with melting ice that, although they kept well apart from one another, they were in danger every minute of breaking through it. That day they covered six miles and rested at the lakeside under pine trees, where they lit a fire to let the hunters know where they were. Next morning they spent hours looking for the place where the Coppermine River left the lake on its way to the north. The guide, who had been so confident that he knew where the river could be found, now confessed that he was not sure where to go. At four o'clock that afternoon the river was seen, flowing at the base of a commanding rock called by the Indians the Rock-nest. The river was two hundred yards across, flowing fast between wooded banks over a rocky bottom. Next morning they shot a series of dangerous rapids, emerging at length on a gentler stretch of water. Here the channel was blocked by drift ice, covered with snow. With hatchets and poles, they drove a way forward for a time until they were compelled to carry the canoes and their baggage across the barrier. At this point the guide was seized with doubts. Was this a reach of the river, he wondered, or was it a lake? If it was a lake, would it be the last between them and the sea? He went ahead to scout and came back that evening with the news. The lake he had mentioned lay below them and it was navigable.

By this time, leaves were appearing on the trees, flowers were blossoming and the smaller summer birds had begun to return from the south. On the explorers' way northwards they were kept in meat by the hunters who, on one day, killed eight musk-oxen, dangerous animals when wounded and having a musky flavour when killed and cooked. The rapids stopped after they had passed a tributary stream called by the Indians Fairy Lake River,* and the pace of their journey increased to fifty miles in a day. They were now not far from the Arctic Circle – they had reached 66°45′N and they were about to begin the last stage of their journey. When two of the guides were told that they need come no further each insisted on completing the trek to the sea. To one of the hunters, however, the call to glory was less insistent. Summer was at hand. He stayed behind to court an Indian girl, called Greenstockings, regarded as a great beauty. Greenstockings, less than fifteen years old, had already been married twice.

The course of the Coppermine River, which had been running northwest for thirty miles, now turned towards the north and broke through a high mountain barrier. The river became narrower and deeper; rapids were steep and frequent. Anxious about the shortage of food, the explorers fell in with a party of three old Copper Indians who had supported themselves and their families all through the winter with the bow and arrow. They had seventy pounds of dried meat to spare and six moose skins for making shoes. Continuing on their way downstream, Franklin and his companions came to an obstacle of which they had heard – a furious rapid foaming between vertical walls of rock towering as high as a hundred and fifty feet above the water. From this defile they emerged on sandy plains on

*Indian fairies are six inches high; they are excellent hunters and very hospitable.

which the hunters went to work on a grazing herd of musk-oxen. They were now on the borderlands of Eskimo country. The French Canadians and the Indians advised them to be careful about betraying themselves by lighting fires or crossing the ridges of hills without suitable precautions.

After prolonged debate the two interpreters, Augustus and Junius, a cheerful and popular pair, volunteered to make contact with the Eskimos who, after all, were men of their own race. They went forward, carrying beads, looking-glasses and other articles likely to be useful in diplomacy. Each carried a concealed pistol. Diplomacy might not be enough. By nightfall, they had not returned. When there was no sign of them next morning, Franklin and the other Englishmen went out to investigate. Gloomy as usual, Akaitcho predicted that the Eskimos were lying in wait for them. In spite of this warning, Franklin and his party went northward expecting that, when they reached the crest of a mountain range some miles away, they would be within sight of the sea. Alas, what they saw was a grassy plain, with a glimpse of blue mountain peaks beyond it! On the banks of the river grew a few stunted pine trees. But out of the north, as evening fell, Junius, the younger Eskimo, appeared. He brought this story. He and his companion had come upon an Eskimo encampment. A wary exchange had taken place, but Augustus had not been allowed to land on the distant bank of the river on which the encampment stood. Nor had he obtained any food from the Eskimos. The first need, then, was to send provisions to Augustus without alarming the Eskimos.

At this moment, Akaitcho and his Indians appeared. They had promised to stay behind until they were sent for. Now their presence was likely to rouse the worst suspicions among their deadly enemies, the Eskimos. Franklin persuaded them to remain behind when, next morning, the other members of the party went forward, some in canoes, the rest on foot. They arrived at the moment when Augustus was about to persuade one of the Eskimos to land on his side of the river. But the abrupt arrival of the main party caused an instant panic. The Eskimos fled and, during the night, retreated to an island further down the river. At the same time, they razed their old lodges to the ground as a warning to others of their tribe that enemies were about.

Days passed before contact was once more made with them, for the Indians were terrified of the Eskimos, who were equally terrified of the white man and their companions. When a party was sent out to look for dry wood to be used as floats for salmon nets, they caught sight of the Eskimos, who danced in a circle to show that they meant no harm. The

English replied by politely lifting their hats. But neither side would approach any nearer to the other. Indeed, the Eskimos disappeared. At last an old Eskimo, named White Fox, too infirm to run away, gave Franklin some useful information about the country to the north: Reindeer came down to the coast in summer; fish abounded at the mouths of the rivers. There were seals but no whales, and musk-oxen were not far away, up the rivers. As proof of his friendly intentions, he gave each of Franklin's party a piece of dried meat. It was tainted, but good manners compelled them to eat it. He was shown his face in a mirror and remarked cryptically, 'I shall never kill deer any more.' However, in spite of this promising start, good relations could not be established between the Indians and the Eskimos. Indeed, the Indians in Franklin's party were so alarmed at their position, far from home and surrounded by enemies, that they insisted on leaving at once. Franklin and a party which included the English and the half-breed hunters, passed down the shoreward reaches of the Coppermine River, through a plain on which only a few stunted willows were growing, along a channel of bright green water. At last, on 19 July 1821, they reached the bleak shores of the Polar Sea. They had travelled 334 miles since leaving Fort Enterprise and for more than a third of they way had dragged their canoes over snow and ice. They had reached the first of their main objectives.

The French Canadians, who did not like what they saw, wanted to go back without further ado, but Franklin was adamant that they should stay. He kept a close watch on them lest they should bolt. 'And the manner in which our faithful Hepburn viewed the element that he had been so long accustomed to contributed not a little to make them ashamed of their fear.'

'Dieu, que nous sommes maigres!'

'The Barren Lands must be seen in Spring.'
Eskimo, by Edmund Carpenter, Frederick Varley and Robert Flaherty, 1959

'Carrying food to the Arctic is carrying coals to Newcastle.'
Vilhalmur Stefansson

Franklin was now embarking on the second and more important phase of his journey, the exploration of the coast to the east of the river mouth which might establish whether or not there was a waterway between the Arctic Ocean and the Atlantic. He and his party set out in two canoes. They had many disappointments. Fishing was a failure, yet the voyageurs would not dream of saving food for a future emergency. Worse, they were guilty of pilfering stores. An Eskimo tribe that Franklin had counted on for food and shelter could not be found. Where Bathurst Inlet opened up to the south, the explorers thought that they had chanced upon an outlet to the Atlantic. It came to a dead end. The season was by this time getting late. The seas were liable to run high. And the voyageurs were restive and were, more and more, alarmed by what they saw of the open sea. It was too rough for comfort and safety. Worse, the reserve of food was low. Their only luxury was a little salt and a drink smelling like rhubarb. This they made by boiling the Indian tea plant which they found growing abundantly on the seashore. The English, less dainty than the voyageurs, boiled the paws of a brown bear they had killed and ate them with a good appetite.

After pausing for a day on the shore above the Hyperborean Sea, as he called it, Franklin set off by canoe eastwards. The weather was stormy; the wind drove the ice floes against the rocky, barren coast. It was no voyage for two frail bark canoes intended to be paddled in Canadian rivers. The food situation continued to worry them. Two of the bags of pemmican turned mouldy; the beef had been so badly cured that it was scarcely eatable. For a time they did reasonably well, hunting and fishing, but the time came when the hunters reported, truthfully or not, that they could see no animals to kill for food, except seals which kept out of range, and, occasionally, a deer which had come down to the shore. However, the explorers paddled resolutely on, keeping their fears to themselves and helped by a current running to the east at two miles an hour.

And what of the North-west Passage, the search for which was, after all, the impulse of the whole adventure? At that point in his journey, Franklin gave thought to the question. His provisional judgement was that the Passage existed and could be navigated. Probably the coast ran roughly west to east between the mouth of the Mackenzie River and Repulse Bay, on the north-west of Hudson's Bay. Many things pointed that way, for instance, the similarity between the kinds of fish they had found on the coasts they explored and those caught to the north of the Churchill River in the Bay. He had found a sea navigable for ships of any size, and ice that would not have held up a strong ship. He was, indeed, very optimistic that Captain Parry would soon solve the problem. If Parry kept close to the American mainland, as he had intended to do, he would find herds of deer flocking to the coast in spring before the ice broke up. There were shoals of salmon. Driftwood could be gathered on the shore, and if he won the trust of the Eskimos, he would be able to get supplies from them. He noted, for Parry's benefit, that the mouth of the Coppermine River was not where it was shown on the charts, but at the supposed place Parry would find a post which Franklin had put up to catch his eye. Below the post was a letter containing useful information.

On 18 August, after having been 28 days on this coastwise voyage, Franklin thought it was time to turn back. He, Richardson and Back made a final reconnaissance on foot. But where they had hoped the coast would turn eastwards, it trended to the north. They named the place Point Turnagain and went back to join their comrades. The party had travelled 555 miles eastwards from the mouth of the Coppermine River. Winter was at hand. Flocks of geese, flying to the south, passed over the tents. Hepburn killed a white fox, which they found good eating when boiled.

Now Franklin turned his back on the Arctic Ocean, and, at the south of Bathurst Inlet, set off up the Hood River, towards the Great Slave Lake. Sometimes the explorers travelled by canoe, sometimes on foot, through deep snow, battling against winds that often brought down the men who were carrying the canoes. Rations were short. And the prospect of finding food on the way was remote. They were about to cross the Barren Lands, the most unfriendly region in the Canadian North. They lived on half a partridge each, roasted over a few willows from under the snow and eaten with lichens scraped off the rocks. After five days, they broke up the canoes and built two smaller canoes from their timbers. Baggage was cut down to a minimum. Even so, each man carried a load of ninety pounds and progress was at the rate of a mile an hour. On 1 September, they ate the last of the pemmican at the end of a day in which they had walked for twelve miles. Then disaster struck: one canoe was so badly damaged against the rocks that they had to cut it up for firewood. It made a fire over which they cooked what was left of the 'portable soup' they had brought with them.

By 10 September, when they had been more than three months on the journey, the food shortage was acute. On that day they shot a cow, one of a herd of musk-oxen. The contents of the beast's stomach were eaten at once, and the raw intestines were thought to be excellent. After six days without a good meal, famine had reached that point. The rest of the animal was cooked for supper. That night they slept in their damp clothes, keeping their socks and shoes underneath their bodies so that they would not freeze.

Two days later – two days of semi-starvation – men were complaining bitterly of weakness. They found themselves on the shores of a lake stretching across their path as far as they could see. Later, they found out the Indians called it Rum Lake. There they camped for the night, cold, hungry and miserable, all the more so when they discovered that their companions, the voyageurs, had thrown away three fishing nets and burnt the floats. The truth was that these Canadian trappers were in country that was as unknown to them as it was to the Englishmen. Their morale began to give way. They would not believe that Franklin knew his way through the wilderness. They were lost, lost, lost – and ready to down their packs in despair! The English, who were physically less robust than the voyageurs, had a steadier courage.

In this emergency, Franklin gave orders for the heavier equipment to be jettisoned. He promised his gun to anyone among the half-breed hunters who might kill animals. At the same time, Hood lent his gun to Michel, an Iroquois, who was an enthusiastic hunter. It turned out to be a mistake. A voyageur named Perrault at this point came to the officers gathered miserably round a small fire. He presented each of them with a small piece of meat which he had saved from his ration. Such self-denial, such kindness from a voyageur! The starving English wept with gratitude.

In crossing the river, three hundred yards wide and running fast through a rocky defile, Franklin was tipped into the water, but scrambled ashore, dripping, while one of the voyageurs, Bélanger, was caught waist-deep in the current. When, at last, he was rescued, it was hours before he recovered his power of movement. In the accident Franklin lost his journal containing all his astronomical and meteorological observations. Next day Perrault shot a stag and they were all in good spirits. But hunger soon returned. The ground grew rougher and the trudging men grew weaker. Dr Richardson dropped his plant and mineral specimens, unable to carry them further. For this strong, determined man and devoted naturalist to admit defeat in this way showed how desperate the situation had become. More serious still, the last canoe was left behind by the voyageurs who had been entrusted with it. They said it was beyond repair. Franklin heard the news with 'indescribable anguish'.

Not long after, there was an emergency in which the canoe would have been invaluable. Continuing on their way south-west, they reached the Coppermine River on 26 September. How were they to cross it? Make a raft, said Franklin. The voyageurs dismissed the idea as preposterous but had nothing better to suggest. While they were looking for trees big enough to build the raft, they came upon the decomposing carcass of a deer and fell on it with a furious appetite. As no logs big enough for use could be found, they constructed a floating platform of willows which would support one man at a time in crossing the stream. It would be pulled to and fro by rope. Somehow, therefore, it was necessary to get a line across for the first trip. Dr Richardson volunteered to swim the river. When he stripped, the voyageurs raised their hands in horror: 'Dieu, que nous sommes maigres!' The water was so cold that, a little way out, Richardson's arms became numb. When he tried to finish the crossing by swimming on his back, he reached a few yards from the further shore. Then he found that he could move his legs no more. With great difficulty, he was saved from drowning by his comrades. Hours passed before he could talk. Richardson said later that he had often swum in water colder than 38° Fahrenheit but, on that occasion, he was weakened by famine and exhaustion. It was obvious that a fresh attempt at a crossing must be made by another method. Franklin offered a reward of 300 livres to the first person to carry a line to the far bank. While the explorers starved on the river bank for several days, the voyageur Saint-Germain put together a canoe from willows and canvas sheets.

While they waited to see if a crossing was possible, they had the good fortune to come upon the antlers and backbone of a deer that had been killed months before. Wolves and birds of prey had picked the carcass clean. But some of the spinal marrow was left: it was putrid but it was eaten – and the bones were burnt and eaten too. Life in the navy of Nelson's time – on weevilly biscuit and the product of the occasional rat-hunt – was an excellent preparation for the rigours of the Arctic. On the next day (2 October) snow fell and the voyageurs, in despair, refused to look for any more *tripe de roche*. But Saint-Germain went on with his canoe-building while Back kept an eye on him to see that the acute depression to which he was a prey did not slow up the work too much. When Franklin went next morning to see how things were progressing, the snow was so deep and his body so weak that it took him three hours to cover three-quarters of a mile. Back was too feeble to walk without a stick. Dr Richardson was lame as well as weak. Hood suffered from dysentery as a result of eating *tripe de roche*. The French Canadian cook, Samandré, gave up any pretence of working. In this crisis, Hepburn, the seaman from the lower deck, was a tower of strength. As Franklin put it, he was 'animated by a firm reliance on the beneficence of the Supreme Being' and gathered all the *tripe de roche* for the officers' mess. For Hood, a partridge was reserved but somebody stole it. Meanwhile, Saint-Germain had put together his canoe from willows and canvas sheets and on this craft the river was crossed at last. Franklin then sent Back and Saint-Germain along with two other voyageurs to Fort Enterprise to seek help. Everybody felt more cheerful, not knowing that they faced the worst part of their ordeal.

By 4 October their advance through the snow was barely perceptible. They breakfasted at noon on lichen. Hood was, by this time, so feeble that Dr Richardson as a precaution walked with him at the rear of the file. When it was time to pitch tents for the night, Crédit, a voyageur, who had carried the men's tent that day, was too exhausted to stand. Next day, his burden was lightened so that he had only to carry his personal baggage. Before starting on the day's march, they ate their old shoes and any scraps of leather they could find. The scenery did nothing to make them feel happier. Ahead, the route lay over a range of desolate hills. A cold gale was blowing, sharp as a knife. The drift of the snow made it hard to follow the leaders. At noon, the cook told Franklin that two of the voyageurs, Crédit and Vaillant, could go no further. A fire was lit and Dr Richardson went back to look for them. Vaillant struggled forward, falling at every step and was eventually rescued by Bélanger, who had been told of his plight by Dr Richardson and found him lying on his back, numb with cold and incapable of being roused. Crédit was lost.

In this extremity, Hood and Richardson proposed that they should stay behind with one of the voyageurs at the first place where a store of wood and *tripe de roche* could be found likely to last ten days. Franklin, they proposed, should press on to Fort Enterprise with all speed. This, with some reluctance and after prayers, he agreed to do, while the staunch Hepburn remained behind. After a few miles' journey through the snow, two of the voyageurs in Franklin's party, Michel and Bélanger, begged with tears to be allowed to return to Richardson and Hood. Finally Franklin agreed, only insisting that Michel should divide his ammunition with the others, leaving him with only ten rounds for himself.

Two other voyageurs, Perrault and Antonio Fontana (an Italian and an ex-soldier) were now taken with giddy fits but, after drinking some tea and eating a few scraps of burnt leather, they were willing to go on. By this time, despair had spread among their comrades. Franklin had no sooner talked them out of it, and they had walked a bare two hundred yards further on, than Perrault burst into tears and swore he could not go on. There seemed to be only one thing to do: send him back to the camp where Michel and Bélanger had been left. While this was being arranged, Franklin and his companions had lost sight of the Eskimo they called Augustus. Losing patience, he had gone ahead.

Very soon the march through deep snow became too exhausting for the travellers and they took the direct way over the ice of a small lake. But the ice was slippery. The wind was strong. At almost every step they fell. When the far side of the lake was reached, Fontana gave up. What was to be done, for they were far too feeble to carry him? By this time they had travelled two miles from the camp where the three other voyageurs had been left. The track through the snow was plain. He should be able to make his way back and find a fire and, with luck, some *tripe de roche* when he got there. Franklin watched him go and thought that he was keeping on his feet better than before. There were now five men left in Franklin's party. After another hour, they pitched their tent and made a meal of ice and leather.

Next morning they came to the shores of Martin Lake. It was frozen, so they walked directly across it and encamped among frozen willows and alders at the side of a rapid on Winter River. They had no food, and the fire they made was not enough to warm their shoes. But spirits were high for now the voyageurs were back in country they knew. They set off again early next morning and, although they had nothing to eat but *tripe de roche* and the relics of their old shoes, they pressed on silently until they saw Fort Enterprise. Franklin rushed forward and flung open the door. But bitter was the disappointment that awaited them. The Fort was deserted. They wept, English, French and Indians, for themselves and for the friends they had left behind.

All that they found was a note from Back, two days old, to say that he was going off to look for Indians in the neighbourhood and, if that led to nothing, he would go on, if he had enough strength, to Fort Providence. He did not expect to have enough strength. Franklin decided to wait for two or three days to see if his companions would recover their strength and, in the meantime, to look for any signs that Back had fallen in with the Indians. In the meantime, they hoped to live on deerskins left from their former stay at that place, bones which they gathered from the cold ashes of their fire and *tripe de roche* which they could find growing in the neighbourhood. On this fare they should do well enough. There was also, however, the question of shelter.

The parchment which had covered the windows of the hut had been torn out. They found loose floorboards and used them to fill up the gaps. Floorboards of the rooms they were not occupying were used as fuel. Melted snow was their water for cooking. Cooking what? Deerskins. On 12 October Franklin went out but could walk only a yard or two. Others collected bones which they boiled to make soup. It burnt the mouth but was palatable enough when boiled with *tripe de roche*. Next day, Bélanger came in, speechless and covered with ice.

Bringing him back to life with hot soup and massage, the voyageurs quite recovered their cheerfulness. They even forgot to swear, which pleased Franklin greatly. He sent word to Back, asking him for a rendezvous at Reindeer Lake, about thirty miles away. With this message, Bélanger set out on 18 October, rejecting all attempts to delay him. The reason, as Franklin discovered later on, was that he was afraid the whole party would descend on Back's camp together and eat all the meat Saint-Germain might kill. At this stage Adam, a hunter, who was left with Franklin, reported that he had swellings of the body which prevented him from going on. Franklin left Samandré and Peltier with the sick man and pressed on with Benoit and Augustus. Going was slow – six miles in four hours – then, a lakeside camp and an unsuccessful attempt to fish. They ate skins and drank tea. Next morning, Franklin broke his snowshoes by falling between two rocks. He sent the other two on to find Back at the rendezvous and returned to where he had left Adam, Samandré and Peltier, whom he found in a state of deep depression. Franklin urged them to eat but he was himself too weak to pound bones to make soup. Next day there was a blizzard and neither Adam nor Samandré would get up. However, Samandré was well enough on the following morning to gather *tripe de roche*, on which they lived, apart from Adam, who could only digest bone soup.

From day to day during this period of waiting, their strength grew less. When they saw a herd of reindeer at a distance of half a mile, none of them had the energy to go off in pursuit. Nor could they have aimed a gun without resting it. On the evening of 29 October, Peltier, who had been so weak that he could not carry wood from the adjacent buildings of the fort, which he was pulling down, suddenly recovered. He called out joyfully, 'Ah, le monde!' It was Richardson and Hepburn, whom they had left behind. They brought shocking news. Hood and Michel were dead. Perrault and Fontana were lost.

Each party was horrified by the change that days of starvation had wrought on the other. Richardson begged Franklin to speak in a less sepulchral voice if he possibly could. At this moment there was a piece of good luck. Hepburn shot a partridge which, after they had taken off the feathers, they divided into seven equal parts. It was the first flesh any of them had tasted for thirty-one days, apart from the small gristly particles they had sometimes found in the pounded bones they had been eating. After prayers, read from Richardson's prayer-book, they retired to bed. Next day Richardson and Hepburn went out after deer, but could not hold their guns steady. Franklin spent the time hunting under the snow for skins, and brought in two. These would be eatable enough provided that they were not putrid. After supper – singed skin and bone soup – Richardson told how Hood and Michel had died.

Michel, the Iroquois, had been in the company of Bélanger when he left Franklin. When he arrived at Richardson's camp, he was alone, and explained that Bélanger had wandered off and failed to return. Michel brought a hare and a partridge that he had killed that morning. Hood, who was too weak to get up, shared his buffalo robe with him. Next day Michel, who had borrowed a hatchet, was separated all day from the others and, when he turned up, reported that he had found the body of a wolf killed by the stroke of a deer's horn. He brought back a portion of the body. 'How I shall love this man,' exclaimed Hepburn, 'if he does not tell lies like the others!' Later on, Richardson thought that the meat was probably part of Bélanger's body. Days passed in which they waited in vain for some word from Franklin, and lived miserably on *tripe de roche* which Hood could not digest. They gave Bélanger up as lost, and assumed that their own chances of survival were small. Hood could hardly sit up at the fireside but lay shivering in his rime-covered blankets. Meanwhile, Michel was sulking and, when urged to go out hunting, replied angrily, 'It is no use hunting. There are no animals. You had better kill and eat me.' This, later, was thought to be a revealing remark. On Sunday morning (20 October) after the morning service, Richardson went out to look for lichen, without success, however, for the snow that had drifted the day before was frozen on the surface of the rocks. At that time, Hepburn was cutting down a tree for firewood at some distance from the tent. Michel, the Iroquois, stayed beside the fire, cleaning his gun. After a time, Richardson and Hepburn went to the tent. They had heard a shot. They found Hood dead.

He had been shot in the back of the head by a long gun which, when it was fired, had set Hood's nightcap alight behind. It would have been impossible for him with that gun to inflict the wound on himself. Beside his body was lying a copy of Bickersteth's *Scripture Help.* Michel's story was that the gun had gone off in his absence. Hepburn explained that he had not gone immediately to the tent when the shot was fired because he thought that Michel was cleaning the gun. Richardson and Hepburn carried the body to a clump of willows and read the burial service over it. An uneasy day followed during which the Scottish doctor thought that Michel's behaviour was increasingly threatening. The Iroquois urged Richardson to go further south, into the woods, where they would find plenty of game. Richardson, at last, told him to go southwards if he wanted to do so. Michel muttered obscure hints that next day he would free him-self from all restraints. He confessed how much he hated the whites (whom he called the French) who had, he said, killed and eaten three of his relatives. Counting up the weapons, Richardson found that he and Hepburn were vastly inferior in armament to the Iroquois; they had a firearm each while Michel had a gun and two pistols, an Indian bayonet and a knife. He decided that the Indian meant to kill them and had not done so before be-cause they knew – and he did not – the way back to Fort Enterprise. What must be done called for stealth and surprise. It also required some ruthless-ness. They were in the wilderness with a fully armed Indian who had greater physical strength than they had, a man of uncertain temper and secretive ways. They had no doubt at all that he had murdered Hood. Perhaps he had killed and eaten Bélanger, too. Richardson thought it highly probable. By this time, everything that Michel did or said strengthened their suspicions of him. Freezing and famished, none of the trio was likely to see things rationally.

At one point in the march, when Michel had fallen behind them, Richardson and Hepburn debated what should be done. It was the first time they had been left alone together since Hood's death. Richardson was sure that the Indian had halted for the purpose of putting his gun in order. Hepburn offered to kill the Iroquois but Richardson decided that the responsibility fell on him. It was his duty, he felt, to protect Hepburn as well as himself. When Michel overtook the two, the doctor drew his pistol and shot the Indian through the head, reflecting that, although the Iroquois were, generally speaking, Christians, this one was totally ignorant of the duties inculcated by Christianity. Dr Richardson had no difficulty in deciding that he had done the right thing. The two men went on, too weak to shoot the reindeer that passed, too weak to get up, unaided, when they sank in the snow under their load of blankets. Once they came on the spine of a deer, killed the season before. They pulled out the spinal marrow and ate it, although it burned their lips.

After a week they had arrived, as night was falling, at Fort Enterprise and saw the smoke rising from the chimney. They were shocked by the filth and misery of the place, the ghastly faces, the dilated eyeballs and the sepulchral voices of Franklin and his companions. All that they found unbearable. But their own plight was hardly better. Hepburn was unable to hold his gun firmly enough to shoot a caribou. The day after they arrived, two of the most loyal of the voyageurs died. Peltier, a favourite with all, slid from his stool; there was a sinister rattling in his throat. He died during the night. Samandré, plunged into gloom by his comrade's death, lay down and was dead before daybreak. The third voyageur, Adam, was so depressed by these deaths, that Franklin, too weak to gather firewood, devoted himself to sitting beside him in an effort to prevent him from brooding over the deaths of his friends. Hepburn and Richardson grew weaker as the days passed. By this time, they were living mainly on deer-skins, but the task of separating the hair from the skins was becoming too wearisome. Hepburn suffering from swellings of the legs; Adam, in a worse state from the same affliction, was often incoherent in his talk. In their feeble state, they became childishly ill-tempered and sensitive. 'If we are spared to return,' Hepburn wondered, 'will we ever recover our understanding?' They slept well enough although the floor was unconscionably hard on the bones. They dreamt mainly about food.

In the morning of 7 November, when Adam's death seemed likely at any moment, a shot was heard not far off. Richardson, who had gone out to cut wood, staggered in with the news that relief had arrived! Adam tried to rise to his feet but collapsed. It was the Indians, whom Back had sent to rescue them. They brought with them some food – dried deer's meat, fat and a few tongues. The famished men devoured it and suffered terribly afterwards. Richardson, who knew the danger they were running, could restrain himself no better than the others. Adam, too weak to rise when the rescue party arrived, and too weak to feed himself, suffered less. The relief party of Indians seemed, to the men they rescued, to be of super-human strength and stature. For their part, they were horrified by the long beards of the white men and insisted that they should wash and shave. They refused to live in the same house with the corpses of the dead, lying un-buried where they had died. So Richardson and Hepburn dragged the bodies out and covered them with snow while the Indians cleared the house of its accumulation of filth and pounded bones. A day later, the Indians vanished, without warning and without leaving any food.

Once more, Franklin and his comrades were plunged into anxiety and driven back on a diet of singed deerskin. In two days, however, the Indians returned. The house was swept clear of any vestige of deerskin, which the Indians thought would bring them bad luck in hunting. The ordeal was over. Franklin decided that in a few days, they would leave for Fort Providence, a journey which, in their weak state, took ten days. On the way, Franklin was told, by a letter from England which reached him by dog-train, that Parry's voyage had ended well and that he, Back and the dead man, Hood, had been promoted in the Navy List. When, at last, the party reached Fort Providence by following the course of the Yellowknife River, one of their first visitors was the Indian chief, Akaitcho, to whom it was necessary to explain why the supplies which had been promised to him by way of reward, had not arrived.

After smoking a pipe, Akaitcho made a dignified speech. 'The world goes badly,' he said. 'All are poor. You are poor. I and my party are poor likewise. Since the goods have not come, we cannot have them. I do not regret having supplied you, for a Copper Indian can never permit white men to suffer from want of food on his land. I hope we shall receive what is our due next autumn and' – his face broadened into a smile – 'at all events it is the first time the white people have been indebted to the Copper Indians.' The time had come to distribute the prizes – the Indians were paid for the provisions they had supplied by a deduction made from their debts in the Hudson's Bay Company's books; each man who had come to their relief at Fort Enterprise was awarded sixteen beaver skins. After the accounts were settled, the Indians were given a keg of diluted spirits and several fathoms of tobacco. Then Franklin and Richardson set off by sledge to join Back who was three days' march distant at Moose-deer Island.

The tale Back had to tell when they met him was almost as dreadful as Franklin's: extreme cold, freezing winds, hunger, a diet of *tripe de roche* and swamp 'tea', relieved by a lucky find of deers' heads buried in the snow without eyes or tongues. Crows perched on the top of pines had given the clue to this treasure. 'Oh, merciful God, we are saved!' the travellers cried. With extraordinary difficulty, they carried the heads thirty paces to their fire. One of the voyageurs was lost and was at last found lying on his back frozen to death on a sandbank beside a lake seventeen days' march from the nearest Hudson's Bay fort. Reduced now to two – Back and Saint-Germain – the party were at this point joined by Bélanger whom they found, barely able to move. So after all, he had not been killed and eaten by Michel! When they had still fourteen miles to travel in order to reach Fort Providence, they calculated that they would be six days without food unless they killed a deer. Just then they saw wolves and crows in the middle of a frozen lake and guessed that there was some carrion nearby. They were right. It was the remains of a deer's carcass. They made off with what was left of the wolves' dinner. The aurora was exceptionally brilliant that night. By its light they saw eight wolves which, with difficulty, they frightened away from the carcass. Some days later, Bélanger, who was in the lead, pointed to the snow and called out, 'Footsteps of Indians.' Saint-Germain was sent on ahead. And so, at last, contact with Akaitcho's tribe was made.

It was a time for the closing of accounts. Akaitcho and his tribe were in the direst want, having, as was their custom, destroyed all their goods when Akaitcho's mother died. Happily, Franklin had enough ammunition to pay all that was due, with enough left over to requite everyone who had been with the expedition. Mr Wentzel was able to explain his failure – which had nearly caused the deaths of the whole expedition – to leave food for Franklin's party at Fort Enterprise. Wentzel's party had lived for eleven days on nothing but *tripe de roche*. An Indian, and his wife and child, had perished from starvation. When Wentzel met Akaitcho, the Indian denounced him in violent terms for having led him and his people into danger but, he would see to it that Franklin and his friends would be supplied. Another Indian hunting party lost three men who were drowned crossing a lake and were capable of nothing except mourning their loss. Franklin accused Wentzel of breaking his promise to leave a letter at Fort Enterprise. 'But you forgot to leave me paper when we parted,' said Wentzel. 'I wrote the news in pencil on a plank and placed it on top of your bedstead . . . Some Indians must have broken into the house and destroyed it.' With that report, Franklin had to be satisfied . . .

On 14 July, after five months' rest, Franklin and his companions were able to go on, health restored, limbs no longer swollen, appetite back to normal. Their tragic round trip of 5,550 miles in the Arctic was at an end. Three months later, they arrived in England. Franklin was promoted to the rank of post-captain and was made an F.R.S. Richardson was appointed surgeon of the Chatham division of the Royal Marines. Back, now a lieutenant, was sent to the West Indies station as a change from the Arctic. Franklin wrote an account of their journey. In August 1823, he married a girl named Eleanor Anne Porden who had won some fame as a poet ('*Coeur de Lion*, an epic poem in 16 cantos'). She undertook, however, that in no circumstances would she try to turn her husband aside from the duty he owed to his country and profession. And already Franklin was planning a new expedition to the North. This time, if the Admiralty approved, he would explore the coast from the mouth of the Coppermine River westward to the Bering Strait. And, once again, it was his aim to work in cooperation with a naval expedition of Parry's.

The fruits of the first two expeditions of Franklin and Parry were quite substantial. Franklin had found a navigable seaway along the coast of the American continent. Parry, further north, had explored Lancaster Sound and the channels that continued its course further west. Neither had found the North-west Passage, but each had added to what was known of the geography of the Arctic. Franklin was eager to set off on a new journey of exploration; he found on his return that, eighteen months before, Parry had sailed on his second voyage to the North-west.

Good-bye to the Search

'Such enterprises, so disinterested as well as so useful in their object, do
honour to the country which undertakes them, even when they fail.'
William Edward Parry

When Parry came back from his voyage through Lancaster Sound believing that, after all, Hudson's Bay held the secret of the Passage, he found in Whitehall men with the same faith. When Parry left on his second voyage, his instructions from the Admiralty conformed to that opinion. He was to sail to the west through Hudson's Strait until he reached the western shore of Hudson's Bay. Then, steering northwards, he was to proceed along this coast, looking into every inlet which seemed likely to lead to the west. His main object was, of course, to find his way from the Atlantic to the Pacific. To this, every other purpose was to be subordinated. If he were unable to reach the Pacific earlier than the autumn of 1824 – two and a half years after the time that the officials in Whitehall were drafting the instructions, Parry would find provisions waiting for him at an inlet on the Arctic Coast, not far from the Bering Strait. The Commander-in-Chief on the South American station would send a supply ship there and raise a flagstaff which Parry would be sure to see. In short, Parry was to look for the North-west Passage some hundreds of miles further south than on his previous voyage. The old idea that the way to the Pacific would be found close to the American coast still had powerful supporters in the Admiralty. Rejecting Samuel Hearne's opinion that the way to the west did not lie through Hudson's Bay, their belief was that the Bay had not yet given up its secrets.

While Franklin's return from his journey was still awaited, Parry left the Thames in May 1821, in command of the bomb ketch *Fury*. His old ship, the *Hecla*, of similar size, sailed too, under Commander Lyon, an officer twenty-six years old who had served in the Navy for thirteen years. The flotilla was completed by a transport ship, the *Nautilus*, which was to carry stores to the margin of the ice and then leave for home.

Parry had no difficulty in finding men for the ships. There was, in fact, a rush of volunteers from his previous expedition. Parry was mobbed by seamen clamouring to go with him. He was a popular commander who had conducted an adventurous but highly successful voyage in the Arctic. He was the kind of leader who finds plenty of followers. There were, in all, 118 men in the expedition. On 1 July, when the flotilla had reached the southern end of Davis Strait, the *Nautilus* transferred her cargo to the other two ships and turned back to England. It was a carefully selected cargo, the result of Parry's experience of what would travel best and occupy least space. Instead of biscuit, kiln-dried flour was carried, taking up a third of the space. In all, there was enough food aboard to last three years. Spirits were carried, 35 per cent above proof, to be watered down later to the regulation naval strength. The comfort of the ships was improved by cork lining. Hammocks were used instead of bedsteads, which had been found to impede ventilation and, therefore to encourage the formation of damp and ice.

When Parry reached the south end of Fox Channel, his first objective was to investigate the Frozen Strait lying to the west between Southampton Island and the Melville Peninsula. It had borne that name from the time of its discovery in 1742 by Captain Middleton, who had reported that the strait ended in a bay which he called Repulse Bay. The optimistic desk-explorers at the Admiralty believed, however, that it was probably not a bay at all, but was, on the contrary, a channel which led through to the Arctic coast. Obviously, then, Repulse Bay must be investigated. The immediate problem which Parry faced was complicated by the choice of his route to the Bay. Should he go through the Frozen Strait which Middleton had seen long ago, or should he accept the opinion of that eloquent home-staying propagandist, Arthur Dobbs, who had dismissed the Frozen Strait as a figment of Middleton's imagination? Parry decided that, on the whole, Middleton was more reliable than Dobbs. He stumbled on the Frozen Strait after a false move which led him into a larger land-locked bay. Passing through the Strait, he entered Repulse Bay. But, alas, after all, it was only a bay. There was no channel to the west that way. In that case was there an opening to be found on the north shores of the Frozen Strait? At first, it seemed likely enough.

A reconnaissance party, sent out in boats, brought back news of a ground-swell from the west, which seemed to mean that some major body of water was near. But once more there was disappointment. After this, Parry worked his way north for a time, along the coast of Melville Peninsula, diligently probing the likely inlets to the west. At last, he saw an ice barrier stretching across his path. Fog came down. And then a wind from the north sprang up, driving the two ships back to the point they had reached a month before at the entrance to the Frozen Strait. It was early September and the end of the sailing season was near. There was only one thing to do. Parry dropped anchor in a small cove on the south coast of Melville Peninsula. From there, he set out on voyages of investigation by boat – once, at least, the rowers thought that they were on their way to the Polar Sea. In the end, they gave up and the ships settled down at Winter Island, off the coast of the Peninsula. Young ice was forming, sure sign, as Parry knew, that the ships would soon be unable to move.

During that winter Parry and his crews became friendly with a neighbouring community of Eskimos, about sixty all told, who lived in igloos not far from the ships. One group soon learned from the other. The Englishmen were, in particular, impressed by the speed and skill with which the Eskimos built their dome-shaped houses of snow, each with a circular piece of ice inserted in the roof as a window. Inside, the house was comfortable. The light was pleasantly soft. The ice floor was a magnificent blue colour. There were other surprising examples of technical skill. For example, the Eskimos set traps for wolves which closely resembled those used by the Kabloona (Europeans), the only difference being that the Eskimos' traps were made of ice. One made a dog-sledge of ice which was perfectly serviceable.

The Eskimos, to Parry, were like children, good-natured, callous – especially to their old people – unlikely to keep a promise, perhaps because they had the short memories of children. Although thieves by instinct, they were capable of making the effort to be honest in order to meet this prejudice of their visitors. Their manners were excellent. An Eskimo who spent a night aboard one of the ships even learnt to throw the bugs he caught into the fire instead of into his mouth. Some of them were talented artists and Parry set them to work drawing maps of the neighbouring country, the distances being measured in the 'sleeps' – the day's journeys – a man remembered he had needed in making a journey from one point to another. Having only, it seemed, one song of their own, they were sent into raptures by European music as played on a hand-organ. They danced with enthusiasm.

The Eskimo maps were, however, particularly interesting to Parry, especially those drawn by a woman named Iligliuk. They seemed to show – and there was a general agreement among them – that the ships were wintering off the coast of a large peninsula, and that they were not far from the Polar Sea. Before the arrival of winter, Parry had seen from the top of a nearby hill something in the western sky which had the appearance of an ice-blink. He had at that time decided that it probably indicated the presence of a lake. Now, with the Eskimo maps before him, he changed his mind. He decided that he had seen the ocean. By sailing round the north coast of the peninsula, along a channel which Iligliuk had shown in her map, the ships would probably reach the Polar Sea.

One day in March 1822 the task of probing began. Commander Lyon led a party northward into the blizzard, to look at the narrow channel which divided Winter Island from the mainland. They had travelled only six miles when the cold drove them to make a shelter for themselves in the snow. After a wretched night, they set off next morning to return to the ships. Blinded by snow, numbed by cold, unable to find the track they had made the previous day, they wandered aimlessly about and would probably have perished had not one of the officers found a trail which, by chance, led them back to their base. The first reconnaissance had not been a success. In the meantime, the ships were held fast in the ice and it was June before the task could begin of sawing out a channel to release them. The ice was four feet thick and, in places, as much as ten feet thick. After thirteen days of strenuous toil, working from six in the morning till eight at night in beautiful weather, they rested for half a day. Another six days and it seemed that the ships would be free to sail. But not yet! The Arctic was more capricious than they thought. The tide brought in ice from the open sea which closed the channel they had cut, while opening a new channel so as to release one of the ships but not the other. After that, a new canal was cut. Once more, the ice moved, closing the channel which the tide had opened.

A month passed before, at last, a gale from the north opened a way through the ice along which the *Fury* and the *Hecla* could reach the open sea. They headed north-east, keeping clear of the icefield that ran parallel to the coast. After a day and a half they had reached Cape Wilson, the most easterly point of the Melville Peninsula. There the sailors spied a string of tiny figures moving north over the ice. Eskimos with dog-sledges. Not just any Eskimos – but the same Eskimo community who had become their friends! And, most fortunate of all, among them was a map-maker whose work had excited Parry. Standing at the bow of the *Fury*, Ewerat, as he was called, pointed to an island further to the north. That, he said, appeared in the chart which the woman, Iligliuk, had drawn. Ten days' journey further on was Iligliuk's birthplace. Ten days? In terms of distance, it might mean anything. That depended on the time of year, the state of the weather, the memory of those who had travelled. In addition, it was notorious that Eskimos had difficulty in counting to ten. As for fifteen – it was almost impossible!

For days after this, the ships were engaged in a struggle against powerful tides which hurled great masses of ice violently against them. The *Hecla* was squeezed between a floe to which she clung with seven hawsers, and tide-thrust ice which snapped the hawsers and unshipped the vessel's rudder. At last, under the pressure of the sea-borne ice, the floe was shattered but the ship survived. At the same time, the *Fury* was threatened when a huge floe advanced menacingly towards her. But, when only a few hundred yards distant, the floe struck a mass of ice that was fast to the land. The shock of the collision was so great that blocks of ice were hurled sixty feet high in the air. After that, the floe drifted away from the ship. The *Fury* was saved. But it was a time of extraordinary danger.

The two ships made painful, spasmodic progress to the north for some days, often forced to seek anchorage close to the shore, unable to hold their own against the tremendous surge of flood water pouring down from the north. Then the wind changed, the ice opened; and twenty-four hours later, they reached the island which the Eskimos had called Igloolik and which, according to the charts which they had drawn, lay in the gateway to the Polar Sea.

As it was still too early in the season to attempt to sail through the strait, Parry sent out a series of reconnaissance parties. On one of these, he saw the Strait, loaded with ice from shore to shore, ice that was very salt to taste as ice made from seawater was apt to be. He raised a cairn of stones on the desolate shore, where scarcely a tuft of moss was showing, although in places that were exceptionally sheltered and moist, sorrel could be seen. There were many small lakes bearing a ten-inch covering of ice. He named the channel the Strait of Fury and Hecla and returned to the ships to wait for the day when the ice should have decayed sufficiently to justify an attempt on the strait by sea. In a few days it seemed that the moment had come when patience would be rewarded. A wind from the west had sprung up and swept the approaches to the strait free from ice. The two vessels moved in. In mid-channel, they sighted a small island in the middle of the fairway and chose the passage to the south of it. But, at a time when all was hope and anticipation, bad news was called down to the deck from the crow's nest. Ahead was another ice barrier, a continuing and impenetrable field stretching across the strait from shore to shore. There was just a chance that they might force a way through it, for the ice was decaying. Under full sail, then, the two ships charged the ice in the hope of smashing a way through to the west. But after they had advanced a few hundred yards, they were brought to a standstill. It was a bitter blow. In the hope of finding an alternative route to the west, Parry sent out several expeditions to explore overland. None of them was fruitful. The *Fury* and the *Hecla* now settled down to spend their second Arctic winter, this time near Igloolik. Soon spirits were beginning to drop and health to fail.

One day in April 1823, Parry announced to the assembled crews that he meant to send the *Hecla* home and go on alone in the *Fury* when the ice made sailing possible. Supplies were moved from one ship to the other. Volunteers for a third season in the North were invited to come forward. But summer was late in coming to the Arctic that year, and before the ice had released the ships, the first signs of scurvy had appeared. This was hardly surprising after twenty-seven months of restrictions to the food that was carried in the storage chambers of the ships. Then one day that August, Parry climbed to the masthead of the *Fury* at sundown. He saw – daunting sight – one vast expanse of ice to the west with no sign of a break in it. His hope of finding a passage through the strait must be given up. Meanwhile, the doctor reported that the health of the crews was deteriorating. Discouragement as well as poor diet was at work. In these conditions, Parry resolved to make sail for home with both ships. On 9 October the *Fury* and the *Hecla* approached the Orkneys: 'It can scarcely be imagined by those who have not been similarly situated, with what eager interest one or two vessels were this day descried, being the first trace of civilization we had seen for 7 and 20 months.' They were sighted in the bay at Lerwick, in Shetland. Bells pealed. The town was illuminated. And in the parish church the Rev. Mr Menzies gave eloquent thanks to the Almighty. So ended Parry's second voyage. It had added something to man's knowledge of the geography of the Arctic. It had not advanced the quest for the North-west Passage.

When he reached London on 14 October, Parry read Franklin's account of his journey to the Frozen Sea. In the light of that, he decided that the problem was how to reach from the Atlantic side the coast east of the Coppermine River which Franklin had surveyed and found navigable.

When that had been accomplished it ought to be possible to make the voyage further to the west through open sea. But the Strait of Fury and Hecla should not be relied on. Twice it had been found beset by ice, probably because the strong eastward current flowing through it would tend to pile up ice at its western entrance. He put little faith in a new thrust through that channel. Better it would be to make the next attempt to sail to the west from the southern part of the Prince Regent's Inlet from which it was only 450 miles to Point Turnagain. In conclusion, Parry said that he had found where *not* to find the Passage which, however, he remained sanguine would be found.

Sailing due west from Disco Island, about half-way up the west coast of Greenland, Edward Parry met the main ice pack about seventy miles further on. It was towards the end of July 1824, and the explorer was making his third attempt to find a way to the Pacific. He had with him the same two ships as on the previous voyages, the *Hecla* and the *Fury*. This time, however, he flew his flag on the former. Captain Hoppner commanded the *Fury*.

Parry's instructions were the result of profound reflection in the Admiralty on the conclusions Parry had drawn from his previous voyage and those Franklin had brought back from his overland journey. Franklin thought that there would be open water along the coast, eastwards of Point Turnagain. Parry thought that he had seen the southern stretch of Prince Regent Inlet during a reconnaissance along the coast of Fury and Hecla Sound. Now, perhaps, he could reach those waters by sea from the north. His orders, therefore, were to pass through Lancaster Sound and try to reach the American mainland by way of Prince Regent Inlet, a broad channel leading southwards from the Sound. In other words, his new search was to be through channels further north than those he had examined on his last voyage. But first of all he had to reach Lancaster Sound, and this proved to be harder than he had expected. It seemed that he had a chance of breaking through the ice where he met it in Baffin Bay, west of Disco. But after a fortnight's struggle he abandoned the attempt. The ice barrier was a hundred and fifty miles wider than it had been the last time Parry saw it. He sailed further north until, at the 74th parallel, he found that he was clear of the pack. Then he sailed due west into Lancaster Sound. By that time, it was the second week of September; young ice was forming; winter was at hand and Parry's instructions from the Admiralty forbade him to winter in the Arctic if he had not passed a point which he could expect to reach on a fresh voyage from England in the following year. Parry, however, had no intention of going home just then. He argued that, owing to his struggle with the ice in Baffin Bay, he had not really begun the task of westward exploration, and that, therefore, the Admiralty would not wish him to return. It was a splendid example of casuistry in a good cause. In the last few days of September after a long, wearisome battle with head-winds, hostile currents and capricious ice, an easterly gale broke up the young ice and enabled the two ships to pass through Lancaster Sound and, at last, to turn south into Prince Regent Inlet.

By that time it was necessary to find – on the east shore of the inlet – a harbour for the winter. This was duly accomplished at Port Bowen on the east side of the inlet, just north of the 73rd parallel. After that, until the following July there was little to do, apart from the customary diversions to ward off boredom, to which the officers added courses for the crew in reading, writing and scriptural knowledge. The neighbourhood was explored without any discovery of importance being made. When, at last, the ships put to sea again, they sailed southwards, as near as possible to the western side of the Inlet, until after eight miles they were brought to a halt by ice. Parry then thought that by reversing course to the north, he would find a way to come closer to the west coast and work his way south between shore and ice. In this he was helped by a gale which broke up the hummocky shoreward ice and opened a way past limestone cliffs, seven hundred feet high, rising sheer out of the sea in a majestic and alarming panorama with the 'appearance of some huge and impregnable fortress, with immense buttresses of masonry supporting the walls'. On 28 July, after the ships, reversing their direction, had made spasmodic progress to the south, they were halted by ice which compelled Parry to make them as fast as was possible along the shore while waiting for conditions to improve. He had great confidence, for the snow had already vanished from the land; modest green shoots were showing here and there. The early summer was full of hope. Alas! A north gale swooped down suddenly on them, driving a mass of ice against the *Fury*. The vessel was grounded. She was manhandled into deeper water by a team of men from her consort. A day later, however, both ships were caught in a turmoil of shifting winds and driving ice in which neither ship could be managed. The *Hecla* was forced aground in sixteen feet of water – one less than she needed to keep afloat and free. The *Fury*, helpless in the grip of the storm, was driven violently past her, only a foot or two separating the two, and, at last, shuddered to a standstill against a huge ice-floe lying on the shore. Captain Hoppner sent a signal to Parry reporting that his ship had been severely 'nipped' and was making four inches of water every hour.

By high tide, the *Hecla* was floated off again and was made fast to a floe. The *Fury* followed. But Parry was sent the news by signal that the water was gaining fast in the *Fury*'s hold. Already part of the ship's double bottom had floated up within her. 'Find the nearest place inshore that you can,' Parry signalled and, himself, went to look for a shelter for the *Hecla*. The prospects were not good. The coast was now lined with huge icebergs and the water was shallow far out from the shore. While he was still engaged in the search, Parry rowed to the *Fury* where he found four pumps hard at work, and Hoppner and his men almost exhausted by their labours. In spite of everything, the ship was still making three feet of water every hour. By that time, it was obvious that the *Fury* needed major repairs. The problem was to find a place where this could be done. It was a problem to which the ice, closing in violently once more, found its own answer. The *Fury* was grounded in water two and a half feet deep at low tide and, it was clear that she would have to be heaved over on one side so that her hull could be repaired. Meanwhile, four pumps were kept at work and stores were taken to the *Hecla* or put ashore on the beach so as to lighten the grounded ship. The wind was still blowing and the ice was pressing against both vessels. Then, on 5 August, Parry mounted an iceberg from which he saw, half a mile to the south, a little bay. But when he rowed to it, he found that it had a depth of only six feet of water.

Returning to the ships, Parry decided that it was impossible to float the ice out of the basin he had intended the vessels to occupy. The only thing to do was to defend the ships, as well as could be, against any new inrushes of the ice. Anchors were fastened to the shore; cables ran from them round masses of grounded ice; thus a small expanse of water was enclosed in which the ships could find refuge. By nightfall, the task was finished and the tents were put up on the beach to house the *Fury*'s stores. After days of exhausting labour, a gale sprang up which destroyed the grounded icebergs on which they depended to secure them from the ice that surged in with the flood water. Plainly there was now a danger that both ships might be driven on shore. Parry and Hoppner decided to make the *Hecla* ready for sea so that she, at least, might be saved. As for the *Fury*, it was found that her sternport had been broken, her rudder damaged, and part of her false keel torn away.

Working all through the day, the task of repairing the *Hecla* was finished by midnight. Next day, the wind lightened and the work of re-loading the

Fury began. At the same time, invalids and officers were put to work preparing a sail so that it could be passed under the ship's keel to lighten the burden of the men, a dozen in all, who were constantly at work on the pumps. The main mass of ice had, at this time, retreated to a distance of five miles. They kept a distrustful eye on it. With reason! Scarcely had the exhausted crew been sent to rest than a new inrush of the ice began; the wind rose; the swell increased. There was a danger that the main cable holding the ships fast to a grounded iceberg would part. More cables were run out. The acutest danger seemed to have passed when, in the midst of the crew's dinner, great masses of ice were seen driving along the shore. Two of them smashed against the *Hecla*. Parry saw that the moment had come when it was necessary that the *Hecla* should be got under sail. Five minutes after the *Hecla* had cast off, news of disaster came by signal. The *Fury* had gone aground. Two bergs, grounded between her and the sea, had been torn loose by the wind and current. Parry, who could not leave the *Hecla*, which had only ten men on board to navigate her, signalled to Hoppner to return with all hands until the wind changed. At that moment it was the only hope he saw of the *Fury* clearing the shore. When Hoppner arrived, he reported that by sawing up some of the ice under his ship's stern, she could, perhaps, be released. There was no other hope of saving her.

For the moment, he left an officer and some men on the ship to work the pumps but, in a little, Parry decided that they, too, must be withdrawn. Half an hour later, a barrier of closely packed ice, half a mile wide, had been driven between the *Fury* and the open sea. Through the night, this barrier grew wider. Two days later, on 25 August, Parry and Hoppner were able to reach the trapped vessel by boat. They found that she was heeling over so much that her main channels were within a foot of the water. Only a large floe alongside her prevented her from falling over still more. She had been driven further up the beach than when they had seen her last and had nine feet of water in her bilge. The damage to her keel and sternport was worse than before. In fact, Parry decided, she could not be moved from the stony beach on which she was grounded, and, that in any case, she was beyond repair. He consulted his officers and the ship's carpenter. The carpenter estimated that it would take five days to free her of water, after which her pumps could not keep her free. Three weeks' work would be needed to make her seaworthy, in the unlikely event that she could be careened. Sorrowfully, but unanimously, it was agreed that the *Fury* must be abandoned. Even more bitter was the corollary: there was now no hope that the *Hecla* – carrying a double complement of men and stores – would be able to complete her mission. The *Hecla* must go back to England.

So, as soon as the boats were hoisted up and the anchor stowed, the ship's head was put to the north-east. A light air off the land gave her the offing she needed to get clear before the ice set inshore again. Parry consoled himself with pious reflections suitable to the occasion. A ship, like any other work of man, sank into insignificance when measured against the stupendous works of Nature; she was little better than a nutshell when caught between the shore and a moving body of ice. And so forth. What made it more galling was the fact that the ice at the time of the disaster had been lighter than any Parry could remember for seven years at least. Of snow, fog, rain, they had seen little. The vegetation, where there was any soil, had been extremely forward. It was, perhaps, for these very reasons that the ice had been incessantly in turmoil. From his terrifying, and it must be acknowledged, unsuccessful trip, Parry returned to England with a new respect for the navigation of men like Davis, Baffin and Hudson who, in twenty-five ton ships, ill-prepared for the problems of wintering, had sailed the same seas as he sailed, two hundred years before him. 'How little, with all our advantages, we have succeeded in going beyond them!'

As for the vexing, baffling, eternally fascinating problem which was the basic impulse of all these enterprises – the search for the North-west Passage – Parry noted 'the favourable appearances of a navigable sea near the south-western extremity of Prince Regent's Inlet'. He recommended that any future attempt should be directed there. For he was quite sure that the problem would one day be solved. Not, he thought, in a single summer; even one winter in the ice would probably not allow enough time to finish the business. But this need not be regarded as discouraging. With a stout ship and fresh provisions, with warm, well-ventilated quarters and a high standard of moral discipline, men could winter in the ice in health and comfort. This, at least, his voyages had demonstrated.

The original motive of the search – commerce – had long since been given up. What Parry now urged on his country was that she should take the lead in enterprises likely to contribute to the advancement of science and the welfare of mankind at large. For his own part, he said goodbye to the search. He made one more trip to the Arctic, in 1827, this time in an attempt to reach the Pole using sledge-boats. It failed, although he reached further north, 82°45′, than anyone was known to have done until then. Indeed, half a century went by before 'Parry's furthest' was passed. In 1829 he was knighted. After holding various posts, he became Lieutenant-governor of Greenwich Hospital. He died in 1855. Hoppner was tried by court-martial for the loss of the *Fury*. It was a solemn, necessary formality from which he emerged without blame. He, Parry and both the ships' companies were praised for 'their very distinguished exertions'.

Interviews with the Savages

'What can be the reason that you are so particular and anxious in your
enquiries of us respecting a knowledge of this country? Do not you white
people know everything in the world?'

An Indian to Alexander Mackenzie, 1793

The North-west Passage was hard to find by sea. Could its existence, then,
be proved – or otherwise – by searches conducted overland? Faced by the
fact that the problem was much more difficult than they had at first supposed, the officials at the Admiralty, who had dispatched Parry on his third
voyage in 1824, decided at the same time to send out three ancillary expeditions. Commander Lyon would sail to Repulse Bay at the south of the
Melville Peninsula and set out northward on land in search of the body of
water of which the Eskimos had told Parry such exciting stories. Captain
Franklin was to make a canoe expedition northwards from Fort Chipewyan.
But this time he was to follow the course of the Mackenzie River and not
the Coppermine. When he reached the shore of the Arctic Sea, he was to
explore to east and west. And Captain Beechey was sent to Kotzebue
Sound by way of Cape Horn and the Bering Strait. Then, in the Arctic
Ocean, he would meet Franklin – and perhaps Parry – at the end of their
journeys. It was a complex, ambitious and well-devised programme at the
end of which, it was certain, a great deal of the mystery would be torn
from the geography of Arctic America.

The first prong of the attack was that of Lyon, who had commanded the
Hecla on Parry's second voyage, and now sailed from Yarmouth in June
1824 in that clumsy boat, the *Griper*, a gun brig of 180 tons which had been
with Parry on the memorable expedition of 1819 to Melville Island. The
Griper was accompanied by a tender, the *Snap*, which helped the clumsy
old craft as she battled against the Northern seas. From the entrance to
Hudson's Bay, the *Griper* plodded on alone until she reached Southampton
Island towards the end of August. On the south-west coast of the island, the

ship ran into thick weather and a furious sea in a bay where the water was growing more shallow every minute. At high tide, Lyon let the anchors go and the *Griper* was brought to a standstill with heavy waves breaking over her decks. Her future was precarious, her life likely to be short. Soon the tide would fall fifteen feet and, when that happened, the *Griper* had small hope of surviving. She would be ground to fragments on the shore. Swift preparations were made to abandon ship. Five of the ship's boats were filled with arms and provisions. Officers were chosen by lot to command each boat; they picked their crews. When the weather cleared, more light came but no more hope. The *Griper*, swept by an unending procession of giant waves, was wallowing off a sandy beach on which a tremendous surf thundered. Every now and again came a shudder and an ominous sound, a mixture of thud and scrape, as her keel struck the bottom.

At three o'clock in the afternoon, when there was no more than six feet of water between the keel and the shore, the ship was lifted by a tremendous sea and brought down violently with an impact that shuddered through her whole length. Assuming that this was the end, they stood ready to take to the boats. Again and again, at intervals of a few minutes, the ship crashed against the shore and the waves, as they passed over the vessel, flooded the decks. At this desperate moment, Lyon did what he could for the comfort of the crew. It was not much. But the crew bore it all with extraordinary fortitude. Finally, he bade his men make their peace with their Maker – 'enter His presence as men resigned to their fate'. All were calm, talking quietly together or even – where they could find shelter from the water – sleeping. 'Never,' wrote Lyon afterwards, 'was witnessed a finer scene than on the deck of my little ship. Noble as the character of the British sailor is allowed to be in cases of danger yet I did not believe it to be possible that among forty-one persons not one repining word should have been uttered.' The danger passed more swiftly than it had come. The tide rose so that the *Griper* floated free. Rain fell in torrents and with it the wind died away. The *Griper* staggered into a bay and Lyon, calling the hands aft, offered thanks to God 'for the mercy He had shewn to us'. All hands turned in and the ship lay quiet for the night. Next morning, *Griper* sailed out of the harbour which, not without reason, Lyon named the Bay of God's Mercy.

After this, he tried to make headway northwards along the west coast of Southampton Island to his objective, Repulse Bay. But the ship, slow at any time, was quickly brought to a standstill by a head-wind which had sprung up. She anchored precariously. A gale blew. Sleet fell. The decks were coated with ice on top of which lay frozen snow a foot deep. Lyon called the hands up on the deck, and told them that all the bower anchors had gone out, the starboard waist boat had been swept away along with her davits. The compasses were useless. The gale was sweeping down to the south off a shore of which they knew nothing. When he could, he meant to make to the south so as to clear the narrows of Roe's Welcome. But while the storm blew all through a night as black as ink, the *Griper* pitched so violently that it was impossible for men to stand on her deck without holding on to a rope. Helpless, they waited for the end, knowing that the gale was blowing them towards a shore they could not see. The officer of the watch and his men sat shivering by the mainmast, under a tarpaulin, encased in snow. The sole light visible on deck came from a small horn lantern which hung from the mizzen stay and showed where the watch was on duty. In the early morning, before dawn came, the cables parted and the ship lay broadside to the gale. Then the wind shifted, edging the *Griper* away from the shore. By this time, she had lost much of her stores.

When Lyon called his officers together to ask them what they thought should be done, all were in agreement. Battered, stripped of half her equipment, with a crew utterly worn out, the *Griper* was in no shape to continue the expedition. She had tempted God's mercy enough. Her crew agreed. The time had come to go home. On 15 September, Lyon set course for England. His ship entered Portsmouth Harbour on 10 November 1824, having been five months at sea.

The second part of the great design was Franklin's. Although he was aware that the Admiralty might reasonably be concerned about the casualties and sufferings which had marked his last expedition, he wrote a paper putting forward a plan for an advance down the Mackenzie River to its mouth. After that, he proposed the exploring party should go westwards by sea to the Icy Cape, the north-west point of the American continent. He convinced the authorities that, this time, there was no reason to expect that the miseries of the Coppermine River expedition would be repeated. Lord Bathurst, the Colonial Secretary, directed him to prepare a new foray which he would lead. Franklin wasted no time.

He recruited his old comrade, Richardson, to act as surgeon and naturalist with the special task of surveying the Arctic coast between the Mackenzie and the Coppermine. Lieutenant Back, another survivor of the first, calamitous Franklin trip, had just returned from a spell of duty in the West Indies, and was offered the post of second-in-command. He accepted with enthusiasm. Franklin, having harrowing recollections of what the North could mean in terms of starvation, looked for an expert in Canadian fisheries and in the control of Indians and half-breed hunters. He found the man he wanted: Peter Dease, chief trader of the Hudson's Bay Company, which was willing to lend him to the expedition. For, this time, there was going to be full cooperation from the Company. Pemmican and other provisions were sent on in advance to reach Dease at Athabasca Lake before the winter of 1824–5 set in. Dease was expected to live through that winter by fishing in Great Slave Lake; then, in the spring of 1825, he was to move on to Great Bear Lake, three hundred miles to the north-west, and build a base for Franklin and his party. One of Franklin's main concerns was the construction of boats light enough to be carried over the numerous portages on the way and strong enough to stand rough weather on the open sea. He had three boats built in Woolwich Yard, of mahogany and ash to his specifications. One was twenty-six feet long; the other two, twenty-four feet. In addition, Colonel Pasley, R.E., designed a little vessel, nine feet by four-and-a-half and called from its shape the *Walnut Shell*. It weighed 85 lb. and could be taken apart and carried in five or six packages. In less than twenty minutes it could be put together again. Equipped with this novel craft, Franklin would be able to cross any rivers impeding his progress, such as had so nearly caused complete disaster to his first expedition. And so, with two suits each of waterproof clothing prepared by Mr Mackintosh of Glasgow, with guns, bayonets and any amount of goods likely to tempt the Indians into friendly cooperation, Franklin set out. He and his companions, Back, Richardson, Kendall, an Admiralty mate, and Drummond, a naturalist, left Liverpool on 16 February 1825 on the American packet *Columbia*. On departure, they were honoured by a salute of three animating cheers from a crowd of the principal inhabitants.

By mid-July, the party had reached Fort Chipewyan on Athabasca Lake and pushed on northwards to Fort Resolution on Great Slave Lake. Franklin was back in the territory where his disastrous journey had begun. He was back among the Copper Indians. Akaitcho was not there, for he had gone off hunting to bring food for the expedition, but two of his brothers turned up at the Fort, having waited for two months to see Franklin. They confirmed a report which Franklin had already heard – that most of the Indian hunters who had helped him with food on his last expedition had been treacherously killed by their enemies, the Dog-rib Indians. After that, a savage tribal war had raged between the Coppers and the Dog-ribs, which was only brought to an end by the good offices of

Dease and another Hudson's Bay Company officer, MacVicar. The knowledge that Franklin was coming back had been the decisive argument in favour of peace. Akaitcho declared that they had too much esteem for Franklin and his task to impede its success by their wars: 'Therefore, they shall cease.' But he would not go to the places where the bones of their murdered brothers lay for fear that bad passions be aroused. Such sentiments, thought Franklin, showed that the most refined feelings could animate the most untutored people. To encourage him in the ways of refinement, Akaitcho was awarded a silver medal.

On 31 July the explorers set out along the shore of Slave Lake on their way to the Mackenzie River and, sixteen days later, came to the sea, free from ice, and with any number of seals and whales visible in it. A flagstaff was planted and a silk Union Jack was unfurled. A ration of spirits was issued to the men who, with three fervent cheers, drank to the health of their beloved monarch. Franklin and Kendall had planned to do the same in brandy but, by some mistake, seawater was mixed with it. After that reconnaissance they returned up-river to their winter quarters at Great Bear Lake. In all, fifty people lived there, 24 British, 9 French Canadians, 2 Eskimos, 5 Indian hunters, the residue being made up of Indian women, children and cripples. Fish nets set in the river caught three to eight hundred fish a day that autumn. The hunters were much less successful. The Scottish Highlanders, who were a powerful element in the community, were furious when they were described as *Montagnards* to the French Canadians. For *Montagnards* was the name usually applied by voyageurs to Dog-rib Indians. In consequence of this affront, a fight broke out between the French and the Highlanders and one unfortunate Dog-rib, who became involved in it, was badly beaten. He fled, carrying the news to his tribe that the white people were bent on massacring the Indians. It was some time before distrust between the two communities died down. By Christmas, however, harmony was restored. English, Gaelic, French, Eskimo and several Indian dialects were spoken in the little settlement and men and women danced to the bagpipes and the violin. On 16 January 1826 a parcel of letters and newspapers from England arrived. 'The *Quarterly Review*, the *Edinburgh Philosophical Journal* and the *Mechanics' Magazine* were spread upon the table and afforded us the most agreeable amusement.' By the first week of May, swans were seen, then a goose. The snow began to dwindle on the lake. The Northern spring had arrived. Canada geese flew over to the north, white geese and two flocks of laughing geese. Swallows came, and large numbers of small water-birds that lived along the shores of the lake. Mosquitoes arrived, in all their virulence. And the wild flowers appeared in profusion.

By this time, the carpenters had finished building a new boat of fir, fastened together with iron nails which they improvised by cutting up the spare axes, ice-chisels and other iron equipment. On 15 June, two expeditions set out; fourteen men with with Franklin and Back, ten with Richardson and Kendall. A week later they entered the Mackenzie River, greatly troubled by mosquitoes and fatigued by an adverse current. However, they knew that they were following in illustrious footsteps. They ate supper at a point where Sir Alexander Mackenzie had seen flame issuing from a rocky riverbank thirty-six years earlier. They found that the precipice was still on fire.

On 2 July each man was issued with a gun, dagger and ammunition, for they were now on the borders of Eskimo country and, although they had no reason to expect a hostile reception, 'vigilance and precaution', as Franklin put it, 'are never to be omitted in intercourse with strange tribes.' After a jovial farewell party, the two groups, Franklin's and Richardson's, separated. A couple of days later, Franklin's party came upon a large Eskimo settlement at the mouth of the Mackenzie River. At once, preparations were made to open friendly talks. Goods that were likely to appeal to the Eskimos were looked out and every man was ordered to keep his gun ready. For who could say when peaceful commerce would, at a flash, turn into something less agreeable? But readiness was one thing, provocation another. Franklin's opinion was that many lives had been lost 'in interviews with savages' through sheer misunderstanding; he gave orders, therefore, that, when he went forward to parley to the Eskimos, nobody was to fire until ordered. Through Augustus, the Eskimo interpreter who had been with him on his previous expedition, Franklin explained that he was looking for a channel navigable by large ships. The Eskimos received the news with rapture.

After that, barter went on busily until one of these unfortunate accidents occurred to which barter is liable. An Eskimo kayak was upset by one of the boat's oars and its occupant was rescued with difficulty. However, during the process of rescue, he had kept his eyes open. Now he took back to his friends the most inflammatory accounts of the incredible riches which the white men's boat contained. The older Eskimos held a council of war at which it was decided to massacre all the white men. But a difficult question remained: what should they do with Augustus, who could be regarded as a renegade? After debate they came to the conclusion that his life was to be spared. The decision was nothing if not rational. If Augustus were killed, there would be no more white visitors to these shores and no more chance of plunder. If he were spared on the other hand, he could be sent back with a story calculated to induce other white men to visit the neighbourhood. After this decision, the attack on the boats began. One of them had already run aground. The other was dragged towards the shore. While women howled and men shouted, two powerful Eskimos seized Franklin by the wrists and forced him to sit between them. Stripped to the waist, Eskimos pillaged one of the boats, passing the goods from hand to hand and so to a chain of women ashore. In all this scene of confusion and plunder, the boats' crews used only the butts of their muskets with as much good humour as possible. However, it was obvious that matters were getting worse. Tempers were rising. Eskimo knives were out. Franklin struggled with an Eskimo who tried to wrest his gun from him. At that moment, Lieutenant Back ordered his crew to level their muskets. Immediately, in a panic, the Eskimos fled. The battle was over. No blood had been shed. And, as it turned out, few articles of any value had been taken.

In this lull, Augustus went ashore. There he stood alone among forty armed Eskimos and persuaded his fellow-countrymen to abandon their attack. The conference ended as amiably as could be. The Eskimos returned some of the looted property and Augustus sang and danced with them for upwards of an hour. But, in fact, matters were not quite so rosy as they seemed to be. The Eskimos secretly returned to their original plan. The white men should be massacred and Augustus with them! He had gone over to the white men. He must be treated as one of them. Next morning, Back spied the whole body of Eskimos paddling towards the boats which had been beached for the night. At once the alarm was raised. When the Eskimos shouted that they were returning some stolen articles, Franklin refused to allow them to come any closer and fired a shot ahead of the leading canoe to make his meaning clear.

This warning was enough. But clearly it was time to move on. They set sail and, at eleven o'clock that evening, came to a low island covered with driftwood where Franklin proposed to stay and make the boats ready for a sea voyage. For the time had come when the next phase of the journey was to begin – the coastwise voyage towards the west. In this, as it turned out, progress was desperately slow. On the first day they had covered only a few miles when they were halted by a stretch of ice ahead, extending from the shore to some point beyond their seaward vision. They landed and, from a high point, looked out to sea: it seemed to be as firmly frozen as in winter. Close to their encampment on the shore, ice had been piled by tide or wind in masses thirty feet high. Scouting Eskimos, on the point of loosing their arrows at the white intruders, were bought off with presents while Augustus told them alarming stories of the power of the white man's guns.

Franklin explained to them, through Augustus, what was the object of his journey: the quest for a seaway leading to the west. The Eskimos replied that ice, clinging to the shore or driven to and fro by the winds, would make the way ahead dangerous for boats: 'Why are you not provided with sledges and dogs as other men are? . . . Above all, don't stay in the west after the stars can be seen, for then the winds blow strongly off the sea and pile up the ice on the shore.' Franklin decided that these warnings could be ignored, coming as they did from a tribe that spent the summer fishing for whales and seals near the Mackenzie River and did not travel more than a few days' journey farther west.

The men of this tribe, he observed, were tall and healthy, with less prominent cheekbones than those of their kind living farther east. The eyes of most of the adults suffered from ice glare, but some of the younger women were pretty. They lived in a country where there were no walruses and few polar bears but where the seal and the reindeer are often seen. Augustus, who could make himself understood by them, told them of the attack by other Eskimos on the boat. They were duly shocked: 'Those are bad men and never fail to quarrel with us or steal from us. If you come back this way, we'll send our young men to help you to beat off any attack.' The following morning the way to the west was still barred by ice but the Eskimos had vanished by canoe towards the Mackenzie River in order to set their fishing nets and hunt for whales. The Englishmen examined the winter houses of these people, built of driftwood with the roots of the trees uppermost. When they had been covered with snow and had a lamp burning inside, they would probably be extremely warm. Next day, while rain fell incessantly, Augustus went back to catch up with the Eskimos. He wanted to recover Back's protractor from an Eskimo woman who had been seen to pick it up. When the boats set off again to the west they were about to round a cape when a dense and persistent fog descended. Closely packed ice prevented them making any headway and only with the greatest difficulty did they make their way to the shore. In this, they were lucky, as they realized when, having at last found room for boats and tents on the shore, they looked further to the west. Ice completely barred the way.

After this, progress to the west was spasmodic because ice, driving towards the shore, left only a little open water for the boats. Eskimos, who were seen hunting reindeer on the beach, changed their arrowheads at the first sight of the Europeans, so as to be ready for battle. However, warlike preparations did not lead to war and after friendly relations had been established, these Eskimos told of another tribe further west who spoke a dialect they could hardly understand, and of Indians who came down a river from the interior every year to trade. One man drew on the sand a map of the coastline further west. The boats went further on and, on 21 July, Franklin, with two companions, marched inland twelve miles to climb Mount Conybeare, which they estimated rose 800 feet above sea level. It was time for a reconnaissance.

From the top of the hill, they looked seawards in the hope of seeing open water. In vain. Gazing inland, they saw mountain ranges running parallel to one another; the highest was on the distant horizon to the south, its peaks covered with snow. After this, the wearisome task of making further headway to the west went on: every day a few miles were covered and every day clouds of mosquitoes plagued them. On 27 July, they reached a wide river which they knew must be the most westerly in British territory in North America. It was named, with due ceremony, after the Duke of Clarence, and a tin box, containing a silver medal, was left on the nearest high point under a heap of driftwood. Three days later, Franklin realized gloomily that the season for exploration would soon be over. On the same day an imprudence almost cost Augustus his life. He had shot a reindeer which plunged into a lake as it died. Augustus had impulsively rushed into the nearly freezing water to pull his quarry out. Not surprisingly, he was seized with a shivering fit. However, he recovered with remarkable speed and, next morning, was in his usual health and high spirits. Meanwhile, the explorers tried to fend off the ice from their boats with boathooks, but after hours of work and having gained only a couple of miles, they gave up the task. The ice ahead was closely packed and piled twenty feet high. A day of fog was followed by some sunshine and a day of gale. The crew found brilliantly coloured pyrites in the bed of a stream and thought, as Frobisher had done 250 years before, that they had found precious metal. The broken weather continued. The gale blew and the fog clung, killing the few flowers that had appeared on the low, swampy ground along the coast. Several times the hunters went out in the darkness after what they thought were deer, which took wing, being geese.

On 16 August they passed a cape they called Point Anxiety and pitched their tents on a patch of gravel, about five hundred yards round, with no water and only enough driftwood to make one fire. It was time for

Franklin to think of turning back. He was half-way between the Mackenzie River and Icy Cape. The best of summer was past. The coast ahead was unknown. A month of incredible toil and hardship had been needed to take him from Herschel Island to the point he had reached. The temperature was falling fast. The geese had already begun their autumn flight. If the boats should be damaged, there were no Eskimos in the neighbourhood who could give them supplies. The deer would vanish with the first snow. Franklin gave the order to turn the boats to the east again.

He did so at a time when a boat party from Captain Beechey's ship, the *Blossom*, had made its way eastwards from Icy Cape and was only a hundred and sixty miles away. When he returned to England, Franklin said that, had he known what the situation was, nothing in the world would have prevented him from going on to the west. But, in fact, had he done so, he would probably not have overtaken the *Blossom*'s boat. Franklin turned back on 18 August; the *Blossom*'s boat reversed course on 28 August and, after surviving many dangers from ice, returned to the mother ship. In the ten days' interval, Franklin would probably not have covered half the distance between the two boats. Setting off on the return trip, Franklin's boats bore eastwards between the ice and the shallow water, against the wind, with sails double-reefed. At Foggy Island, where they had been held up so long on the outward passage, the crews built a square heap of driftwood on the highest point facing the sea. Above it, they flew a red flag; below it, they left a tin case containing a letter for Captain Parry should he chance to pass that way. There was also a letter wrapped in bark addressed, hopefully, to the Russian fur traders who, as they knew, were busy on that coast.

By this time it was clear that the season was changing fast. The signs were everywhere: weather, birds, insects and humans. A steady stream of geese were flying to the west. The mosquitoes had vanished. Of the Eskimos, only a few were left. Sometimes obstructed by fog, at others by ice, the party made slow headway along the coast. On 26 August they ran into a storm in which the boats almost foundered. When, by good navigation, they at last reached a beach, the boats were filled with surf but the provisions were undamaged. Next morning they set about cleaning the guns and drying the bedding. Some Eskimo women from a local camp were recruited to sew sealskin soles to their worn-out moccasins.

From other Eskimos came alarming rumours of Indian plots to massacre them. Friendly Eskimos begged them not to linger in the neighbourhood and, if they should pull up for a night, to do so on an island out of gunshot of the shore, at least until they reached the western outlet of the Mackenzie. It seemed that the Mountain Indians had been excited by stories spread by the Eskimos of the immense wealth of the white men and that they planned to attack and pillage them. For this purpose they had moved to the mouth of the Mackenzie, where they meant to spend their time fishing and hunting until Franklin and his two boats returned. Then, the attack would be launched on the model of the Eskimo onslaught during the outward trip. They would pretend to help the boats; then they would stave the boats in while, on a signal, hidden Indian reinforcements would rush to the attack. While the Indians were planning the ambush, they spoke of their intentions to an old Eskimo who, without delay, sent two young men of his tribe to warn Augustus of the danger.

Franklin and his party reached the mouth of the Mackenzie on 30 August, having followed the coastline to the west for 374 miles without finding a single harbour in which a ship could shelter. A month later, he arrived at the advanced base of the expedition on Great Bear Lake. He had been absent for three months and had covered 2,048 miles. Six hundred miles of the journey had been through unknown country. Now he sat down to read Dr Richardson's report on what he had accomplished on his voyage to the east of the Mackenzie.

Richardson, like Franklin, proposed to carry out his task with two boats and their crews. Kendall went with him. They were going to survey the coast between the mouths of the Mackenzie and the Coppermine. On approaching the sea, Richardson fell in with Eskimos who told him of a vast lake not far to the east, which he never saw, but which he named Eskimo Lake. It seems likely that the Eskimos were speaking of a long arm of the sea which runs south-westwards into the land not far east of Lake Dalhousie. For a century afterwards, it appeared on maps in the vague, dotted outline which is a sign that a cartographer is in a state of embarrassed ignorance and has no longer the confidence to trust to his power of invention.

At the mouth of the Mackenzie, the explorers came upon an island which was seemingly used by the Eskimos as a burial place. Countless bodies were seen, wrapped in skins, with the heads to the west. Richardson named this eerie spot Sacred Island and hurried on. There followed one of those uncomfortable encounters with Eskimos with which explorers were familiar at that time. Near a group of Eskimo huts, Richardson leapt ashore with the interpreter, Ooligbuck. Meanwhile, Kendall kept the boats clear of the land. The Eskimos came out, alarmed and ready to fight, until a show of presents calmed them down and trade began. As often happened, however, the Eskimos in due course became more confident and demanding. Soon their behaviour was so threatening that Richardson and Ooligbuck retired to the boats, which made off at a speed along the coast. The Eskimos followed in kayaks. As they passed other Eskimo settlements along the coast, more and more kayaks put to sea. All the time the Eskimos were trying to obtain exorbitant prices for their wares. When they could not get what they wanted by barter, they paddled close to the boats and stole anything within reach. However, being Eskimos, possessed of that odd, unpredictable temperament in which dishonesty, violence and good nature were mingled, they handed back, with roars of laughter, anything that they had been caught stealing. The situation was, however, a tense one. The slightest false move might have detonated a catastrophe.

Richardson had the wit to put a ban on all forms of barter, with one exception: he would accept only bows from the Eskimos in exchange for his goods. Unwilling at first to do business on these terms, the Eskimos at length gave up a number of their weapons. Examined, these were found to be made of spruce, strengthened along the back with cords made of reindeer sinews. They were far superior to Indian bows and, indeed, Richardson considered that they were better than the traditional yew bows of England.

However, it seemed that an explosion was not to be avoided. When Kendall's boat ran aground in shallow water, it was at once seized by half-a-dozen Eskimos, while others with drawn knives rushed forward. In this crisis, Richardson gave permission to open fire. Kendall levelled his fowling piece at the foremost assailants. His crew were in the water, struggling to push the boat off while a crowd of Eskimos were trying to drag it further up the beach. Now, on an order, the seamen jumped on board the boat and took up their muskets. The crew of Richardson's boat simultaneously produced their firearms. At once, the Eskimos fled. The crisis which had blown up so quickly was over. The Eskimos had apparently thought that the British crews rowing the boats were women. By Eskimo custom, rowing is a woman's job, and, puzzled by what they saw, they had asked Ooligbuck if all white women had beards.

Later, Richardson's party was overtaken by ten kayaks paddled by peaceful Eskimos who called themselves 'Inhabitants of the land near the mountains'. They were on their way to a place where they were likely to find white whales. It was many day's march distant but, at this time of the year, with so much ice about, it was hopeless to think of hunting the black whale. When Richardson asked questions about the Eskimos who lived at the mouth of the Mackenzie, he was told that these Eskimos would have no dealings with them and that all Eskimos living on the coast farther east were bad men.

The wind freshened and at nightfall a storm blew up. By nine o'clock it was pitch-black with a drizzle of rain, so they made for shore at a small island where they anchored the boats to poles stuck in the mud. After supper, they lay down in their wet clothes, hoping to sleep. But the wind changed, blowing with such violence that they were forced to seek shelter in a small cove. There they made the boats fast and pitched a tent on shore. Again they were unlucky. One of the boats, on which Kendall and a crewman were sleeping, broke loose from her moorings and began to drive across the cove to the lee-shore on which a heavy surf was breaking. With a great deal of trouble, it was brought safely back to the beach. Not long afterwards, the storm uprooted the tent-pegs and the tent, drenched with rain, collapsed on the crews. After that, all hope of getting any sleep was given up. At four o'clock in the morning, the rain ceased and they lit a fire of driftwood to dry their clothes.

After they had travelled like this for six days, Richardson decided that they had at last arrived at the sea, and ordered an issue of rum. For three days the wind blew so strongly that they remained at this mooring-place. When they resumed their course, they found Cape Dalhousie in five days and, to their joy, found that the coastline was trending to the south-east. Soon, however, it turned to the north again, but they pressed on.

Beyond Cape Bathurst, which they believed wrongly to be the most northerly point of the American mainland, except Icy Cape,* the boats entered clear green water, in which they saw many whales, both white and black. They were coming into a wide bay – Franklin Bay – which they crossed in pleasant if at times foggy weather. Sometimes, they put in to the shore and the hunters bagged a deer. Richardson took careful note of the geological structure, the birds and the plants. Kendall kept an eye on the tides. They noted that the sand on the beaches had been piled up by the tides in parti-coloured layers to a height of a hundred feet. They passed no harbours suitable for ships; they saw great heaps of driftwood, high on the beaches, proof that there were times of the year when the tides ran strongly. Richardson predicted that, if ever a steamship could enter these waters, it would have no difficulty in finding enough fuel every day to feed its boilers.

On 9 August the boats arrived at the mouth of the Coppermine, sails

*Cape Barrow is further north and the Boothia Peninsula further north still.

filled with a spanking breeze, oars plied vigorously. They were in fine physical trim after their 900 miles voyage along the Arctic coast, ready for the journey south-west over the Barren Lands to Great Bear Lake and the Mackenzie. Near the river mouth at Bloody Fall they encamped. There they had only one visitor, a starving Eskimo dog. It was hardly a cheerful presage of what lay ahead of them on the next stage of the journey. They abandoned their boats but kept Colonel Pasley's portable craft, the *Walnut-shell*. Every man was allotted twenty pounds of pemmican and the other provisions and stores were equally divided so that each carried a load of seventy-two pounds. At six o'clock in the morning of 10 August, the party set off at a brisk pace. The *Walnut-shell* was assembled and loaded. But now disappointment came. The *Walnut-shell* had been designed to cross rivers; it was not meant to be towed along them through strong rapids. It was therefore left behind, with some reluctance, along with half a bag of arrowroot and five muskets. On a hot, sultry day, the marchers set off again, each lighter by fifteen pounds of burden. The weather was fine, a pleasantly cool breeze sprang up from the north; they observed the grey Arctic marmots playing round their burrows. The whisky john (*corvus Canadiensis*, as Richardson noted) visited them in the evenings. When they climbed out of the river valley, the bog whortleberry was found growing in profusion.

At the end of a day's march, while the men settled down to rest behind a shelter of sandstone rocks, Kendall, sweeping the horizon with his telescope, saw Indians approaching. He and Richardson set out to meet them, unarmed. Fortunately, the Indians, who wore deerskin fillets round their heads and wrists, were friendly; they belonged to a tribe that had supplied Port Franklin with furs and provisions during the winter. During the night, Ooligbuck, who had vanished, returned to the camp. He had gone out hunting and had fallen in with an Indian who, in terror at the sight of an Eskimo armed with a gun, had handed over a piece of venison and fled. In spite of fog, they steered a straight compass course to Great Bear Lake, to the amazement of the Highlanders in the party, old Hudson's Bay hands who knew how hard it was to find a way through the country without guides. Supplied by Indians, they ate well until they came to the Lake where they had a rendezvous with a voyageur named Boileau. He had been ordered to leave Fort Franklin a fortnight earlier and set up a supply dump for them. However, there was no sign of Boileau. But the travellers did not fare badly on whortleberries of exceptional quality, on fish from the lake and the meat which the Indians brought in. And six days after their arrival, Boileau turned up with a party of thirty companions and lavish apologies for his lateness; the weather had been bad, the wind adverse, etc. After that, it was only a three-day journey by canoe across Lake Franklin where they awaited the arrival of the leader of the expedition. In 71 days they had travelled 1,980 miles.

Three weeks after Richardson's return, Franklin and his party appeared. Together, the two groups of explorers had covered 1,600 miles of country which had never been explored by white men before. They had accomplished what they set out to do. Now the northern coastline of the Canadian mainland was surveyed between Beechey Point and Point Turnabout – a distance of eleven hundred miles as the crow flies. But if the task was done, the troubles remained. They were now in acute danger of starvation. Winter was at hand and the hunters, Canadian or Dog-rib Indians, had accumulated no surpluses of food at the fort. There was no meat, no dried fish. The people at the fort were living from day to day on the fish they caught in the nets. The Dog-ribs, in explanation of their failure, said that they were frightened to go hunting too far from the fort lest they should meet Copper Indians who might attack them. Franklin had no doubt what was the true explanation. Indolence, he said, and apathy, vices for which the Dog-ribs were notorious. He set to work with vigour to remedy the situation. Dried meat came in. Useless hunters, who would have spent the winter eating in idleness, were 'allowed' to leave. While Franklin waited for ice conditions to make it possible for him to attempt the journey south to Fort Chipewyan on Lake Athabasca, there was a crime of passion among the Dog-ribs. One of the hunters murdered a fellow-tribesman who had carried off his wife and child. The wronged husband would have murdered the woman, too, but at the critical moment she pushed away the gun. Her husband then struck her senseless and would have beaten her to death had it not been for the cries of the child. Franklin, having heard this melancholy tale of passion in the wilds, dismissed the Indian from his service. What happened to the murderer, his wife and child is not recorded.

At that time, it seemed that something resembling mass hysteria was disturbing the Northern Indians. Perhaps it was caused by the increasing incursions of white men but, in any case, it was a source of potential danger to white travellers like Franklin and Richardson. The Indians believed that a change was about to take place in the natural order. This wave of almost religious belief seems to have begun with a woman, the wife of a half-breed employee of a fur-trading company on the Columbia River. She had, on a sudden impulse, decided to become a warrior and, in man's clothing, with arms, had set out on the warpath with the men of her tribe. She was so brave and so successful in fighting that, in time, she became the chief leader of the tribe. She was known as 'The Woman like a Man', and had taken another woman as her wife. It was she, for reasons of her own, who had spread the story of the coming great change. And then, after remarkable adventures, the Man-Woman had been killed in battle. When that happened the flame of irrational hope she had kindled died out, but the psychological disturbance it caused left its effects. The Man-Woman remains a strange figure on the margin of history, recorded because, by chance, her legend reached the ears of a British explorer whose main interest was of a different kind.

Franklin had not found the North-west Passage. What he and Richardson had done was to solve part of the riddle of Arctic geography. He returned to England as confident as ever that a ship could sail from east to west, although as he decided, the route was more likely to be found on a voyage from west to east. This was contrary to Parry's opinion. But, as Franklin reported, when the ice was in the state in which navigation was easiest, the prevailing wind in those regions was in the north-west. Make the attempt from Alaska and not from the Atlantic! This was Franklin's advice.

As a result of Parry's explorations and those of Franklin and Richardson, the riddle of the North-west Passage had been greatly reduced in scale. More than a thousand miles of the northern coast of the Canadian mainland had been surveyed and found to be navigable. The western approach six hundred miles further north on the line Lancaster Sound–Barrow Strait–Viscount Melville Sound had turned out to end in an impassable ice barrier. There remained a central area of land and water, unexplored and intricate, to which Prince Regent Inlet seemed to offer the most promising entrance. There, if anywhere, the junction between East and West would be found.

Part Three

A Glimpse of the Goal

'If we should allow the completion [of these Arctic expeditions] to be snatched from us by any other power, we shall sustain a humiliating defeat.'

Sir John Barrow, Royal Geographical Society Journal

While during nine years, Parry, Franklin and their associates had enjoyed a monopoly of the search for the North-west Passage, one explorer had been forced to pass his time in idleness. Pursued by the disappointment and distrust of Secretary Barrow, Captain John Ross was, in effect, barred from the command of any expedition under the aegis of the British Admiralty. Ross did not accept his exclusion passively. He felt he had been unfairly treated. He felt that he still had a rôle to play. In 1827, he suggested to the Admiralty that a steamship would be more likely than a sailing vessel to succeed in a voyage of exploration in Prince Regent's Inlet, which he considered to be the most likely place to find the seaway to the west. When the proposal was turned down – the Admiralty had lost interest in the problem – Ross did not despair. He put it before a friend of his, Felix Booth, a wealthy gin distiller. But Booth, too, rejected the scheme on the ground that, as a parliamentary award of £20,000 to the discoverer of the Passage still held good, it might be thought that he was simply interested in the money. Barrow, quick to think the worst of anything that Ross was connected with, suspected just that.

In 1829, when the offer of a reward had been withdrawn, Ross put the scheme once more before Booth. This time Booth accepted. Ross then hastened to Liverpool, where he bought the *Victory*, a small sailing vessel with a steam engine and paddles. The *Victory*, which had formerly plied between Liverpool and the Isle of Man, was brought to London so that she could be strengthened for work among the ice. By raising her sides by two and a half feet, her tonnage was increased from eighty-five to a hundred and fifty. An engine of new design was installed and the paddles were so constructed that they could be lifted out of the water in a minute. Although the main burden of cost was borne by Booth, Ross contributed £3,000 of his own money. He had no difficulty in recruiting all the officers and crew he needed. His nephew, Commander James Clarke Ross, was appointed second-in-command; William Thom, who had been purser in the *Isabella* on Ross's previous voyage, served again. All three were unpaid. In all, the *Victory* was to carry a complement of twenty-five. She carried stores for a voyage of a thousand days, and was accompanied when she left the Thames on 23 May 1829, by a decked vessel of 16 tons named the *Krusenstern*.

From the first day, there was trouble with the *Victory*'s engine, on which such high hopes had been built. At Gravesend its makers, Messrs. Braithwaite and Erickson, left the ship. From their point of view, it was just as well that they did so. Before the *Victory* had reached Margate (at about 3½ knots with a favouring wind) Ross's early suspicions about the engine were surpassed by the discovery of manifold imperfections. Its boilers leaked; fresh water to make up the loss could not be spared; the engine became so hot that men fainted. In addition, the ship was leaking badly. Soon after passing the Lizard it was found that one of the guide-wheels for the starboard piston rod was almost worn through. And so on ran the catalogue of daily disasters, and the attempts more or less unsuccessful, 'to remedy the evil inflicted on us by the discreditable conduct of our engine manufacturers'. After sixteen days, the *Victory* reached Port Logan in the Mull of Galloway which was in Ross's home county.

There they met the whaler which Ross had bought to act as a storeship. With it came a new source of trouble. Mr Thom, who was acting as its captain, announced that his officers and men were on the verge of mutiny. They objected to a long stay in the Arctic from which they could not expect to gain their customary profit from whaling. Ross visited the ship and, from one look at the men, saw that Thom had not exaggerated. When he had tried, and failed, to talk the crew into a better frame of mind, he gave them a direct order. Not only did they refuse to obey it, but they tried to persuade the crew of the *Victory* to 'stand up for seamen's rights'. This propaganda was rejected with contempt and, to three cheers from all aboard, Ross announced that the *Victory* would go on alone. The mutineers – two-thirds of the whaler's crew – went ashore, and began to sell their clothes, to get drunk and to fight. The end of the whaler was as bad as might have been expected. Next year, with the same master and crew, she sailed to Baffin Bay. There a mutiny broke out, the master was killed, the mate and the boat's crew were expelled and lost on the ice. After that, the ship was wrecked and most of the crew were drowned. When Ross heard of these melancholy events months later, he was not surprised (nor was he, it must be confessed, entirely displeased).

The *Victory* cast off on 14 June and went quickly on her way, helped by a fresh wind from the south-west which, however, soon blew up into a storm in which the top of the foremast was broken off. At sunset on 29 June they saw an ice blink and two days later they had their first glimpse of Greenland. From Loch Swilly to Cape Farewell, it had needed just a fortnight to complete a run of 1,300 miles. On 5 July the first icebergs were seen. A month later, 6 August, the ship entered Lancaster Sound. Ross was now on the scene of his celebrated mistake eleven years before. Then he had seen an appearance of land ahead and had turned tail, thus earning the undying contempt of Secretary Barrow. Ross was unable to let the occasion pass without a little outburst. Sir Edward Parry had written something quite innocent about 'the very opposite opinions' which had been held about the Sound. This 'ambiguous language', said Ross, had been taken by some to mean that Parry, who had been with him on the first expedition, had differed from him at the time. This, said Ross, could not be so, for Parry, as the junior officer, would have been in duty bound to tell him that he disagreed with his commanding officer. After awarding himself a few words of praise for his prolonged reticence – 'but the spot recalls a lovely recollection of the various trying emotions of which it has been parent' – Ross choked back his indignation and went on with his account of the voyage.

The ship made her way in mild weather along Lancaster Sound at a speed of one and a quarter knots, which was as much as Ross could coax out of his engine. About 12 August, when the ship had reached the entrance to the great channel known as Prince Regent Inlet, the compasses ceased to be of any use and, from that time forward, navigation had to be carried out by astronomical bearings. Fog beset them, thick enough to conceal a pack of ice until it was no farther off than three cables' length. Tremendous seas were breaking over the ice, and the *Victory* could not escape from taking a heavy blow. The coast which they were skirting consisted of steep beaches and, later, of impressive limestone cliffs rising sheer out of the sea to a height of two or three hundred feet. But unfortunately there was no sign of a suitable anchorage. However, James Ross went off on a reconnaissance in the whale boat and brought back news of a likely bay. Meanwhile, the landscape was all the time grander as they passed southwards – ever-higher cliffs, which in some places formed horizontal shelves, in others soared into turretted shapes reminding Ross of castles in some medieval fantasy.

All this time, one trouble persisted and grew worse; in spite of the labour of the engineers and the curses of the crew, the engine remained ineffective. Ross found that if he allowed the pressure of steam in the boilers to build up for fifteen minutes, the engine would keep going for another fifteen minutes. For fifteen minutes, the *Victory* was held to a warp two cables length ahead; then, for the next fifteen minutes, the paddles would drive her forward until the engine, once more, gave up. It was slow work. At length they found a place to anchor in a natural harbour between one large iceberg and two small ones. It was not far from the place where Parry had abandoned the *Fury* four years before. There on the beach were the remains of the tents he had left; the poles were still standing, although most of the canvas had gone. Ross went to inspect it and found that the bears had visited it before him. But the tins of preserved meat and vegetable had survived intact. The taste had not suffered. The wine and the spirits, the sugar, bread and cocoa were in excellent condition, although it was agreed that the lime juice was not as good as it had once been. All told, it was a most satisfactory find to men who knew that, without it, they would probably not be able to carry out their project in the Arctic. They were surprised, however, that no trace of the *Fury* was to be seen. It appeared that she had been ground into shreds by the restless power of the ice. Ross was elated by the discovery of the stores. He had gambled on the provisions left by the *Fury* to make up his stores to the amount he would need for the unprecedented stay in the Arctic which he contemplated. The gamble had come off.

Several days passed before the crew had loaded on the *Victory* all the stores the ship could carry. A great deal was left. Gunpowder in the magazine was found, dry under its tarpaulin cover. They took what they wanted, and blew up the rest for fear that Eskimos should find it and, in consequence, come to some harm. On 15 August Ross cast off from the ice and made sail for Cape Garry, some fifty miles to the south-west across Cresswell Bay. Here and there vegetation appeared on the rocks – even some flowers which they picked for their collection. Old Eskimo graves were seen and one bird like a sand-lark. By 17 August, they had run into fog again and shaped their course by the wind, an uncertain guide. They were struck many heavy blows by floating ice and on the following afternoon they were so beset by ice and fog that they were forced to make fast to a floe. After that, they resumed their way cautiously to the south along a low coast hollowed out in a succession of little bays with a range of blue hills behind. In a day or two, they freed the ship from the ice to which it had been moored. It was done just in time, for now the whole pack of ice began to move northwards, fast. The engine was given another trial – no use! – seven revolutions a minute; a speed of one mile an hour!

On 26 August, James Ross, on reconnaissance, found a good harbour which they named Port Logan. There they were safe behind a barrier of icebergs, while, day after day, a gale blew from the north-east. On the last day of August, snow appeared on the hills. Although it seemed that the Arctic summer was at an end, there were still days ahead so warm that their dogs were panting in the heat and looking for fluid in the ice. On 6 September, still sailing down the east coast of what he called Boothia, after his friend, the distiller, Ross entered an inlet about a quarter of a mile across and found, to his joy, that it opened into a spacious natural harbour, twenty fathoms deep in the middle, and clear of ice except at the edges. It was a superb anchorage, a shelter for ships surpassed by no harbour in the world, as Ross thought. Indeed, he said in his enthusiasm that the whole British Navy could ride at anchor in it. But although he was tempted to loiter there and hunt the reindeer and the hares that he could see ashore, there was a powerful argument in favour of quitting Elizabeth Harbour, as it had been named: the ice was drifting down on the ship at an alarming speed. But to leave the harbour turned out to be no easy matter. There was only one exit and the wind, which was in the south-east, prevented them from using it under sail. They made what preparations they could, making fast to an iceberg in the throat of the exit channel. On the ebb tide, they might be able to work their way out.

Next day they prepared for a change in the wind that might favour them. The bay ice that was troubling them melted and, as the afternoon wore on, the weather was like an English summer's day. But they were compelled to stay where they were. The wind had not changed. Worse, the deer, shot only three days earlier, was fit only for the dogs. Next day, they set all sail and stood out southward among the ice but, after eight miles, the wind turned against them and they were glad to warp their way into an anchorage for the night. Through a narrow channel they made some progress next day, but in the end were glad to settle in beside an iceberg where all the time the water was moving violently to and fro. Keeping close to the mainland, which was naked of vegetation, they were in growing danger from the current which forced them towards the land where the piled-up ice might destroy them. In the end the wind swung round to the west and ship, icebergs and all were carried with alarming force against a reef. There would be no question of steering the ship or controlling their destiny. They were in the grip of the Arctic sea! Over and over again, the ship was bodily lifted. Once its tender was thrown up on the ice. No sooner had they escaped from this danger than they ran into a whirlpool in which the ship spun round for more than an hour before it was released. Once more, they attached themselves to an iceberg which, moving with the tide, carried them for miles against a strong wind. When, at last, they reached clear water, they knew that still the danger was not over; the next tide might carry them back into it and now the wind was against them. At last, in a sudden calm, they warped into a harbour and found shelter behind a reef of rocks. Their peril was for the present at an end.

Ross – whose powers of narration are not to be despised – despaired of conveying the tumult and the drama that the *Victory* and her crew had survived. He did his best – 'Ice,' he says, 'is stone, a floating rock in a stream, a promontory or an island when aground . . . Then let [readers] imagine these mountains of crystal hurried through a narrow channel by a rapid tide; meeting, as mountains in motion must meet, with the noise of thunder, breaking from each other's precipices huge fragments or rending each other asunder, till losing their former equilibrium, they fall over headlong, lifting the sea around in breakers, or whirling it in eddies, while the flatter fields of ice, forced against these masses by the wind and the stream, rise out of the sea till they fall back on themselves, adding to the indescribable commotion and noise . . . '

Ross had no doubt that if the *Victory* had not been of exceptionally light draught, if she had not been specially strengthened, so that she was stouter than the ships on the earlier expeditions, she would certainly have perished, and all her company with her. After this experience, they ran into more open sea and stormier weather. Squalls and snow struck them when at one point they nosed their way out of shelter, making it hard for them to get back to it. One night – it was 16 September – the wind swung round to the north-west and blew more violently; the seas were furious as they washed over the deck. In two days' time, the gale was more savage than anything they had known up to that point. The icebergs began to move, threatening to sever the cables by which they were made fast to the shore. The danger passed. But for days afterwards, the *Victory* was at the mercy of wind, tide and ice, sometimes protected by ice from the fury of the sea, sometimes within a few inches of destruction from granite reefs which lay a foot or less below the keel. On the last day of September, off a low-lying coast of red granite from which the wind had blown all the snow and with a huge barrier of icebergs ahead, Ross decided that it was time to halt for the season. He estimated that he had gone 300 miles further on that course than anyone before him and that the ship was not further than 280 miles from the coast which Franklin had seen. He did not know that he was sailing more and more deeply into a bay from which there was no way out to the west. At any moment, the ship would be frozen in. Ross found a harbour where he and his companions could spend the winter in reasonable comfort and safety. He called it Felix Harbour.

They were more than half way down the Gulf of Boothia at 69°59' latitude, 92°01' longitude. Comfort or, at any rate, tolerable living conditions were the only virtues they could expect to find on that grim coast: 'Amid all its brilliancy,' said Ross, 'this land has ever been a dull, dreary, monotonous waste, under the influence of which the very mind is paralysed . . . It is but the view of uniformity and silence and death.' A solitary raven, flying round the ship, was held to be an ill omen. Weeks later, the raven was shot.

There, while Ross waited on the ice to imprison them, he unrigged the ship, roofed in the deck and put the guns and the gunpowder ashore. After that was done, the engine was taken to pieces and carried ashore. In future, the *Victory* was going to be a sailing ship and nothing else. A routine of work was established. For instance, tea and cocoa were drunk, but no spirits, although an exception was made for Christmas Day. Every morning, there were prayers and a sermon and, 'to occupy the remainder of the day, there was a collection of tracts, presented by Mrs Enderby of Blackheath, a judicious as well as a useful gift,' as Ross believed. He noticed, with satisfaction, that the crew did not swear any more.

It was 9 January before a break occurred in the monotony of the Arctic winter. On that day one of the seamen saw four living figures near a small iceberg about a mile from the ship. They were Eskimos, from a village of twelve igloos some distance away, who spoke a dialect which differed considerably from the Eskimo speech in their dictionary. With this community, friendly relations were quickly established, especially after one Eskimo, who had lost a leg at the knee, was fitted out with a wooden leg by the carpenter. The leg was ingeniously adapted to walking in the snow and was inscribed with the name of the ship. It was some weeks before the customary outbreak of thieving by the Eskimos made its appearance. But in one respect, Ross was disappointed with his new friends. He had hoped they would give him information about the lie of the land in these parts and, with luck, prove to him that he was on the right track. He showed them sketch maps which they seemed to understand, but he gathered that, if there was any opening to the west, it was at most a very narrow one.

By 21 January, the sun was brilliant at noon and everyone felt that, as Ross put it, 'there was the certainty of a better tomorrow, the assurance that summer was to come'. It was slow in arriving. By the end of March, Ross had heard of a passage to the west. He built up a team of ten good dogs so that it could be explored. He ordered a lane of gravel to be laid out on the ice in the hope that the sun would act on it and thaw a channel for the *Victory*. On 5 April, James Ross, with the Chief Mate and two Eskimos, set out on a long reconnaissance to the west by dog sleigh. There was trouble from snow which froze inside their clothes. There was a mutiny among the dogs which had been kept so hungry that they wanted to eat one of the Eskimos' sledges which was constructed of frozen fish.

After a journey of five days the party returned to the ship; they had not found much of interest. All that seemed certain was that the ship was held fast in the ice on the east coast of a peninsula and that, not far away, was the western ocean. Perhaps they could find a channel which would lead them to a place where the Eskimos had spoken of a strong current running from the west through a narrow channel. But when they were questioned the Eskimos shook their heads: the coast, they said, was continuous from north to south. There was no passage to the west. On 21 April, Commander Ross went out once more to find out what the truth of the matter was. Next day he returned after a terrible journey through drifting snow, having come upon a channel two hundred feet wide and a mile long. But it did not open into the 'western sea'. The current which rushed through the channel from the west came from melting snow. By this time it was clear to Ross that there was no way through to that sea south of the 70th parallel. The search must be switched.

Almost immediately, therefore, Commander Ross set out on a third journey, this time to the north, where the Eskimos reported that the coast turned towards the west. He left on a day when there had been a sudden and ominous change among the Eskimos. The women had disappeared; the men had drawn their knives, they were silent and sullen. One old man was particularly menacing. He was about to throw his hunting knife at Commander Ross when his sons pinioned him. The reason for this crisis was that a young Eskimo boy had been killed by a falling stone. Witchcraft! It was a clear case. And the Europeans, known to have magical powers, were obviously responsible for it. After a long discussion, Ross convinced them that this was not so. Smiles returned; knives were put away; Ross went on his way, accompanied by two of the Eskimos. But when he reached the place at which he had hoped to find an opening to the west, nothing of the kind could be seen. He came to the conclusion that the Eskimos must have been speaking of Barrow Strait, three hundred miles farther north.

In the course of the journey, James Ross killed a musk-ox, to the amazement of the Eskimos, who were even more impressed by the white man's magic when he brought down a brace of grouse with a left and right. After this the two Eskimos, who had built a snow house for all of them, spent a day eating the meat, which they tore off the musk-ox in long strips, cramming it into their mouths and cutting the strip off at the end of their nose. They gave up when they could not force any more down their throats. James Ross was shocked but impressed by their performance. He acknowledged, too, that, while the Arctic wind moaned outside and the snow drifted against their house with a hissing noise, inside all was warmth and comfort. Early next morning they resumed their journey to the ship. On this final stage, they were plagued by a strong north wind and flurries of snow. When they arrived exhausted at a hut which they had built on the outward journey, they found that a wolf had torn off the door. The hut was filled with snow, through which they had to burrow before they could settle down for the night in their sleeping bag. They resumed the journey next day and when they were a few miles from the ship, were met by one of the Eskimos from the local community. He approached them cautiously. The explorers were equally wary. But they saw that his knife was still in its sheath. All was well.

When the first anniversary of their leaving England came round Captain Ross congratulated himself on a successful year. Admittedly, he had not found the North-west Passage, far less passed through it. But he had added something to human knowledge of Arctic geography. Now he decided, quite wrongly, that the channel joining the eastern and western seas was somewhat to the north of Elizabeth Harbour (70°40') near an inlet which his nephew had reached. That problem was for future examination. In the meantime, he recorded that the crew had been healthy during the voyage, apart from one man who had died of tuberculosis. But, it seemed, that he poor man, had been suffering from it at the time they left England.

On 17 May, in the course of a new sledge journey to the west, James Ross and his comrades caught sight of their goal – the sea to the west which they could not reach by ship, the sea that led to the Pacific. 'It was a solemn moment, never to be forgotten,' he said, 'and never was the cheering of a seaman so impressive, breaking as it did on the stillness of the night, amid this dreary waste of ice and snow.' But, alas, the sea was frozen over. At that moment, Ross was standing on a cliff which rose five hundred feet above sea level. The coastline stretched westwards, while opposite him the shore inclined to the south. Travelling on, ten miles further to the west, he came upon a vast bay. Was it the channel leading to the Polar Sea?

Climbing to a height of a thousand feet above sea level, he caught sight, to the north-east, of a river which drained through one lake after another into the bay at his feet. Further along the coast, he arrived at a stretch of sea covered with ice. This surely, was a strait that would lead him to the Polar Sea – if only he could follow its course. Pushing on to the West, he crossed a belt of ice to an island which he named Matty Island and then, south-wards, reached the mainland, as he thought. He turned southwards, and then to the north-west. By this time his companions were quite exhausted. Some days later, after passing headlands which might, for all he knew, have been islands, he reached a promontory he called Cape Felix. He thought, then, that if he were to follow the line of the coast to the west, he would reach Point Turnagain which had been the limit of Franklin's probe east-wards from the Coppermine. But food was running short. The men were worn out. And although he did not know it, the coast did not run in a straight line to the west. While the men rested for a day, Ross and the mate pushed on a little way further west. They built a cairn beneath which they buried a chronicle of the journey. Then Ross turned back. He reckoned that he was 220 miles from Point Turnagain.

It was the last day of May. The party arrived back at the *Victory* on 13 June. But, although by that time the ship might reasonably have been able to move, July came and – what was worse! – the mosquitoes came, and still they could not free the ship from the ice. Nor could they travel overland on the melting snow. The crew passed their time agreeably enough by fishing and shooting until, with September, the snow returned.

On 17 September, the ice in the harbour at last gave way and the *Victory*, all sails set, began to move to the north. She did not go far. After three miles of confident advance, the thermometer fell and ice closed in on the ship once more. A little way north of the anchorage they had left, Ross settled in for another winter: 'Our winter prison was before us.' But the task of moving the ship into harbour through the ice was long and trying. The ice was sawn into large blocks and the *Victory* was hauled slowly for-ward – to pull it 850 feet needed the whole month of October. There was some despondency among the crew, which Ross tried in vain to dispel by speaking of the comfort of the ship, the ample food supply, etc. In fact, they had enough provisions to keep them alive until the day came, sometime in 1832, when they would have returned to what was left of the *Fury*'s stores, or would have abandoned the ship.

Philosophically or resentfully, they faced the boredom and discomfort of a second Arctic winter with what stoicism they could muster. When spring came, the two Rosses, uncle and nephew, each with a party of six men and sledge, went out to cross the Boothia Peninsula westwards to the sea beyond. In eleven days they reached the further shore. There, John Ross decided to make his way back to the ship along a valley only thirteen feet above sea-level, which the Eskimos called Shag-a-Voke. James Ross set out northwards to reach the Magnetic Pole which, from the eccentric behaviour of the compass, he knew could not be far off. A bitter wind blew from the north. The thermometer stood at zero. Snow blindness troubled the travellers but, although progress was slow, James Ross in the early morning of 1 June, pitched his tent at a place where the dipping needle of the compass was within one minute of the vertical. He was at the Magnetic Pole. The spot was low-lying, desolate and unremarkable (70° 5′ 17″ latitude, 96° 46′ 44″ longitude). But there it was, that patch on the earth's surface at which the forces attracting the magnetic needle converge. To have reached it at last was a feat worth noting. Ross raised the Union Jack and buried under a heap of stones a can containing a record. Then he formally took possession of the Magnetic Pole in the name of H.M. King William IV. (Incidentally, the Pole is not a stationary feature. It is at present some distance to the north and east of the location in which Ross found it, although it is still in Canada!) When James Ross and party returned to the ship they found everything in a state of bustle. The *Victory* was being made ready to leave for home. But, once more, luck was against the explorers. Their sentence was to be extended.

Summer passed and the ice held fast. Loneliness and the utter monotony of the Arctic scene lay like lead on their spirits. There were fewer than thirty of them – few enough for small irritations to become intolerable. 'Is it wonderful,' asks Ross, 'that even the visits of barbarians were welcome? Can anything more strongly show the nature of our pleasures than the confession that these were delightful?' Once it seemed that they were about to escape after all. A wind blew from the west making an opening through the ice through which open sea beckoned to them. Alas, the wind changed and the *Victory* was pinned down again. She had been able to make only four miles of headway. After that, the day-long Arctic night returned. Ross resolved that when spring came, at the end of their fourth winter in the ice, he would abandon the *Victory*. A lucky season had brought her into her harbour but it was unlikely that the luck would be repeated to let her out again. Leaving her, he and the crew would set off by sledge and boat to Baffin Bay where, with luck, they would fall in with ships of the whaling fleet. On the way, he would pick up some badly needed supplies from the cache at Fury Beach, two hundred miles to the north. He and his comrades had endured all they could of the sublime beauties of the Arctic.

'To see, to have seen, ice and snow, to have felt snow and ice for ever, and nothing for ever but snow and ice, during all those months of a year . . . during all the months of four years, this it is that has made the sight of those most chilling and wearisome objects an evil that is still one in recollection as if the remembrance would never cease.'

Whatever the dangers of escape, it was time to make an attempt to break out when the spring came. The ship must be left in the ice. The crew must try to save themselves without her. It would be a wild gamble – a journey of 500 miles over ice and sea, with, at the end of it – what? The chance that they might be spotted by a whaling boat which might be hunting in that part of Baffin Bay! Towards the end of April 1832 the advance guard set out, carrying their boats one by one over the rough shoreward ice and the smoother ice covering the sea. By the time they returned, they had established a supply-base 18 miles from the ship, but to do so had required 110 miles of travel. Five weeks later, on 29 May 1832, the moment had come to leave the ship. The colours were nailed to the mast and the *Victory* was saluted in a final glass of grog. Ross made a last sketch of the ship, the first he had abandoned of the thirty-six he had served in.

On the way north, through frightful conditions, there was a near-mutiny when the crew wanted to abandon boats and provisions and make a dash for Fury Beach. A few days later, however, finding that they could not go by water, Ross was obliged to leave the boats behind. James Ross now went ahead to report on the state of things at the beach while his uncle, with the main body, advanced at a more leisurely pace. James Ross brought back bad news – a high tide had carried off three of the *Fury*'s boats and one of them was seriously damaged. As soon as the two parties reached Fury Beach, the carpenters went to work making a shelter on shore for the whole company and strengthening the boats for a sea voyage. Sails were cut and, by the beginning of August, all was ready for the voyage to the north. But progress was painfully slow. Four weeks after starting, they had covered no more than a few miles, terribly battered by a gale. When it subsided

(28 August) things went better for a little. But after a month, faced by an unbroken expanse of ice stretching as far as Ross could see – and he was looking out from a hilltop – they turned miserably back to spend the winter, their fourth, at Fury Beach in the shelter which the carpenters had rigged up for them and which they named Somerset House. It was a shattering blow.

They were now in the depths of despondency, inadequately clad, reduced to half rations and soon in acute danger. For by this time ice made the sea impassable to their boats, which were drawn up on the beach where the tide was unlikely to reach them. Sledges were improvised out of odd pieces of wood and, dragging these behind them over the ice, they reached Somerset House at last. They had food enough to last them until spring. Their huts were made fit to serve as winter quarters. Against the terrible mental and physical strain of yet another winter in the ice – with the uncertainties of yet another spring at the end of it – they mobilized as well as they could the resources of mind and spirit. At Christmas they made a meal of half-a-dozen fox carcasses which seemed excellent eating. By that time the spirits and wine were finished and, when the carpenter took scurvy, lime juice proved to be no help. He died in February on a day when it was too cold ($-24°F$) to read the burial service out of doors and the ground was so hard that they had great difficulty in digging the shallowest of graves. As for the rest of them, their physical survival was a miracle; the survival of their reason almost more so. When April came, James Ross was sent out to find the two boats they had abandoned in the autumn. He found them and, in four separate journeys, provisioned them for a voyage which would be made when, at last, sailing became possible.

One day in July, they began the journey northwards, and, after eight days, reached the boats. But more than a month passed before they could launch them. At four in the morning of 26 August, 1833, sometimes sailing, sometimes rowing, they had reached the waters where Lancaster Sound opens into Baffin Bay. The voyage had taken them just eleven days. The exhausted rowers were lying asleep on a beach when the look-out man called 'Sail-ho!' James Ross leapt up and put his spy glass to his eye. It was a ship. While they prepared to sail, wet powder was burnt to make signals. But the ship did not answer. And, a breeze springing up just then, she was lost to sight to the south-east. Later that morning, another sail was sighted to the north. They set off in desperate pursuit of her. But she, too, bore up under full sail and the distance between her and the boats lengthened every minute. She, too, had not seen them. An hour later, however, the luck turned. The wind fell and the boats closed with the ship. Seeing them at last, she put off her longboat. Ross asked the vessel's name. When it came across the water, the answer was extraordinary.

'The *Isabella* of Hull, once commanded by Captain Ross.'

'I am Captain Ross.'

'No, no, he has been dead two years,' said the mate in charge of the *Isabella*'s boat.

The long ordeal was at last ended – and in an incredible coincidence. Ross and his companions pulled themselves on board his old ship: 'Unshaven since I know not when, dirty, dressed in the rags of wild beasts instead of the tatters of civilization, and starved to the very bone, our gaunt and grim looks, when contrasted with those of the well-dressed and well-fed men around us, made us all feel, I believe for the first time, what we really were, as well as what we seemed to others. Poverty is without half its mark unless it is contrasted with wealth.' In time, all were shaved, washed, fed and clothed. The sick were looked after and by nightfall all were in bed but, 'long accustomed to a cold bed on the hard snow,' says Ross, 'few could sleep amid the comfort of our new accommodation. I was myself compelled to leave the bed which had been kindly assigned me and take my abode in a chair for the night, nor did it fare much better with the rest.'

In England they were received with enthusiasm. When they arrived in Hull, Ross was wearing a pair of sealskin trousers, with the hair outwards. He was called on by the mayor and aldermen in procession while the church bells rang. Going on to London, Ross hurried to Windsor to see King William. He wished to ask His Majesty's gracious permission to name the Magnetic Pole after him! The Admiralty advanced £4,580 so that each member of the crew might have double pay up to the day the *Victory* was abandoned. For Ross, their employer, had no money left. James Ross was promoted to post captain. John Ross, who was not in the navy, was voted £5,000 by Parliament. His had been an extraordinary sojourn in the Arctic. It had lasted during four winters, a record that was not surpassed for generations. It was a triumph of stamina and tenacity. But what had it accomplished?

The *Victory* had hardly budged after she was first gripped by the ice. The exploration by sledge and boat had covered only a small area of the Arctic archipelago. They had not found their way through to the Western sea. Ross, indeed, was certain that no such way existed, at least not south of the seventy-fourth parallel. If it existed at all, it could not be used for commerce or war. His nephew, James, thought differently. From what he had seen of the west coast of the Boothia Peninsula, he believed in the channel, although it would probably be navigable only in weather conditions better than he had experienced. Already, for other reasons, there was some disagreement between uncle and nephew. The nephew insisted that his part in the expedition had been almost independent of his uncle's. The uncle denied it. He and he alone had been in command, he maintained. Whatever the truth of the matter, it seems that John Ross possessed, with all his gift for leadership, a jealous and sensitive nature, quick to resent any slight, real or fancied. But these unimportant outbreaks of bad temper between the two leaders were little heeded by the public at home, dazzled as it was by the miraculous return of men who had long been given up for lost. The people were willing to make allowances for those who had given such inspiring proof of endurance and courage, and who had been tested so hard and had not broken.

At a time when no news from Ross had arrived in Britain, Dr Richardson offered to look for him. However, the government thought it would be a hopeless task. Then, in 1833, Commander George Back led an expedition, partly financed by the Colonial Office, to explore the Great Fish River. One day in 1834 when he was not far from Montreal, news reached Back that Ross had returned safely. Back went on with his mission and, on the way, met Akaitcho, now very old, who was full of gloomy forebodings about an enterprise which must pass through Eskimo territory. Undeterred, Back reached the mouth of the Great Fish River which enters the Polar Sea through a series of lakes and over 83 rapids. Another piece of the jigsaw puzzle had been slotted into place. Back's next journey, two years later, almost ended in disaster when his ship, the *Terror*, was forced on her beam ends in Foxe Channel by an underwater iceberg. In this crisis, he and his crew behaved magnificently. The berg, twenty-four feet across, was sawn through, the ship's two boats were provisioned and worked clear. After fifteen hours of frantic labour, the ice relaxed its grip and the *Terror* was righted – to escape destruction by no more than a hair's breadth in an Atlantic gale!

More successful was the overland journey of Thomas Simpson, a Scotsman aged 28, and Peter Dease, in 1837. These two young officers of the Hudson's Bay Company set out from Fort Chipewyan and reached the Arctic Ocean by way of the Mackenzie River. Making westwards along the coast by boat, they paused at Smith Bay, where Simpson with five others pushed on overland. For the first time, Point Barrow, a long, low gravel spit, was reached from the east – 'I poured forth my grateful orisons to the Father of Light.' In the following spring, Simpson set out along the Coppermine and then eastwards along the Arctic shore as far as Cape Alexander on the Kent Peninsula. In a third journey in 1839, he reached further east in the same direction, but missed Rae Strait which divides King William Island from the mainland. The Strait was under ice at the time and he passed over it. He and Dease returned to their starting-point at Fort Confidence determined that, in another journey, they would complete their survey of the coast to Fury and Hecla Strait, thirty degrees – and many miles – further east. Simpson was on his way to England to persuade the directors of the Company that this new survey should be undertaken when he was murdered by two half-breeds who had become his enemies. If he, Dease and Back had not solved the riddle of the North-west Passage, they had added substantially to man's knowledge of the Arctic. They had helped to reduce the size of the problem.

Franklin Vanishes

'Can't say I have ever been lost but once I sure was puzzled for a couple of weeks.'

Old Prospector in the Arctic

Ten years after the miraculous homecoming of the two Rosses, the British people began once more to breathe the icy, alluring air of Arctic discovery. The country felt rich and confident. The Polar seas were, as one writer said, 'too eminently a theatre of British enterprise and daring to be long deserted'.* Scores of naval officers fretted in the long peace. There was, too, a good deal of unemployment among seamen. Above all, Sir John Barrow was still Secretary of the Admiralty, and still aflame with enthusiasm for the Northwest Passage. So much had been done, he wrote, so little now remained to be done! Only three hundred leagues separated Melville Island, which Parry had reached, from the Bering Strait which had many times been passed. Between them was a broad open sea – broad enough for a ship of war. There was no great danger that ships would be lost. In most Polar voyages, the crews had enjoyed excellent health.

This was rousing stuff. If it brushed aside too much, Sir John could be forgiven. At eighty, after a lifetime devoted to propaganda for the project, he was an old man in a hurry. The Royal Society, to which Sir John addressed a lecture, echoed the call to action. When the First Lord of the Admiralty, Lord Haddington, ventured to wonder what benefit a new voyage would bring, the batteries of scientific value and national prestige opened fire. There was a broadside from the redoubtable Sir John, who spoke of humiliation, defeat and similar inflammatory themes. On the whole, the victors of Trafalgar agreed with him. True, a wind of criticism blew from one quarter.

Dr Richard King had gone searching for Ross in 1833 under the leadership of Captain Back. On that occasion the expedition had journeyed to

*J. J. Shillinglaw, *Narrative of Arctic Discovery*, p. 264.

the mouth of the Great Fish River, which runs into the Arctic Ocean about two hundred miles south of the spot where Ross had spent so many winters. King wrote to Sir John in terms that were downright offensive: Naval expeditions, he said, were so much nonsense, whereas land journeys had surveyed almost the whole northern coast of America. If Sir John were to devote to the advocacy of a land journey one-tenth of the zeal with which he urged a new expedition by sea, he would deserve not a baronetcy but a peerage. 'If you are really in earnest upon this subject . . . search for the truth, and value it when you find it.' Here, then, was a pretty comedy! The arch-prophet of Arctic exploration accused of not knowing what he was talking about! Worse still, the intolerable implication that he had been inspired by nothing other than hankering after a title. 'Smash the impudent fellow!' cried Sir John, and went on with his propaganda for a new attempt to find the Passage by sea until, at last, he was compelled by age to resign his post at the Admiralty. However, he had already succeeded in his main objective. Lord Haddington was now convinced that a case existed for a new naval expedition. The question had still to be decided, however; who was to lead it? Who was to preside over the seaborne party which, as King had written bitingly to Barrow, would inevitably spend the winter 'in acting plays and other Merry Andrew tricks that these officers may make a book out of the sterility around them?'

At this moment, Sir John Franklin put in a claim for the post, for which Captain Fitzjames had already been chosen. Franklin felt that he needed a new opportunity. Since his return in 1827 from his second exploration in Arctic Canada, his career had been varied and, on the whole, disappointing. After a spell of naval service off the coast of Greece, he had spent seven years as a Colonial governor in Australia where his term of office had not been a success. Part of the trouble seems to have been that Franklin had a strong-minded and ambitious wife. He was undoubtedly senior in the Navy to Fitzjames, but that could not be the only criterion. When Lord Haddington reminded him that he was fifty-nine, Franklin was shocked; he was two months short of that birthday. He suffered from cold, Haddington told him. Franklin obtained a certificate of good health from his old exploring comrade, Dr Richardson. Parry chimed in, 'He is a fitter man than any I know. If you don't let him go, he will die of disappointment.' Haddington then surrendered.

Franklin left on 18 May 1845, in a bomb vessel of 370 tons, the *Erebus*, accompanied by Captain Fitzjames as his second-in-command. In a slightly smaller vessel, the *Terror*, was Captain Crozier, who had served under

Parry and James Ross. The ships carried 139 officers and men with provisions for three years. Franklin's original intention was to sail westwards through Lancaster Sound and Barrow Sound, after which he expected to find enough sea-room south of Banks Land to allow him to reach Bering Strait. He shared Sir John Barrow's belief that Banks Land was probably an island of no great size. However, if he found that his way to the west was barred, he would turn north along Wellington Channel looking, as he went, for a break out to the west. His orders from the First Lord were to push along Barrow Strait without wasting any time on exploring openings on either hand. When he reached Cape Walker at the western end of the Strait, he was to keep to the south and west, as far as ice or undiscovered land permitted. If he could make no headway there, he could seek an anchorage in Wellington Channel until spring brought new opportunities.

Three weeks to Stromness in Orkney, four weeks to Disco Bay in Greenland – Franklin had plenty of time on the voyage to catch up with his reading of Arctic literature. He observed that the explorers who had gone before him painted a picture of his task that was somewhat less simple than Sir John Barrow's fervent prose had suggested: 'I am inclined to think,' Franklin wrote to Parry, 'that there exists much land between Woolaston and Banks Lands, which I hope may be separated into islands.' Sobered by what he read in the works of those who had preceded him, Franklin set off from Disco on 13 July, northward along the Greenland coast where, in Melville Bay, just north of the seventy-fourth Parallel, he fell in with a whaler, the *Prince of Wales*. The whaler's log noted that all Franklin's men were well, in good spirits and confident that they would finish the job in good time. It was the last time that the crews of the *Erebus* and *Terror* were seen alive.

By the autumn of the following year, September 1846, nobody had heard anything from Franklin and his men. But then, nobody expected to. Accordingly, there was no particular anxiety but only some irritation when Sir John Ross told the Admiralty that he had promised Franklin to head a search expedition in 1847. To begin with, he would leave provisions and boats at Parry's old anchorage, Winter Harbour on Melville Island. When Parry was consulted he knew nothing of the plan. Richardson had never heard of it. James Ross, nephew of Sir John, with whom Captain Crozier had stayed just before the expedition left, had something even more crushing to say. He had heard the plan mentioned but only as an absurdity proposed to Franklin by Ross! Ross, cantankerous, pushful, with a chip on his shoulder ever since his first quarrel with Sir John Barrow, was suspected to be a disappointed explorer probably looking for a new chance of employment and fame. However, he nagged at the Admiralty until they wrote to four experts on the matter, Parry, James Ross, Colonel Sabine and Richardson. They replied that, while no immediate anxiety need be felt, there would be no harm in preparing an expedition for the following year.

Four months later, Sir John Barrow proposed that two ships should be sent out, one to go westwards through Lancaster Sound, the other eastwards, through Bering Strait. Dr King, who took the gloomiest view of Franklin's chances, pressed for an overland journey to the Polar Sea, a desperate enterprise which called for a leader of exceptional strength of mind and body, requisites which he believed could be found in one man alone, himself. In spite of – or perhaps because of – this claim, the Admiralty picked Richardson for the post. King was furious: he had been the first to show how 'the puzzle of three centuries' could be solved, now he hoped that at last he would be given his due. But the Admiralty would have none of him; the Colonial Office rejected him. The Press gave him space. It was, however, not enough.

In November 1847 the Admiralty announced that it was about to send out three relief expeditions. One would sail at once for Bering Strait; another, under James Ross, would make for Baffin Bay in the early months of 1848, and the third, under Richardson, would travel northwards down the Mackenzie River to the Arctic Ocean, which he expected to reach in August 1848, and then move eastwards along the coast. Thus Richardson would follow the course that he had travelled in Franklin's second expedition.

It was a pretty far-reaching programme. In addition, Lady Franklin was willing to put up £2,000 for a search in Prince Regent Inlet, Jones Sound or Smith Sound, which for one reason or another, her husband might have visited.

Sailing in June 1848, in two ships, the *Enterprise* and the *Investigator*, Sir James Ross took with him two officers, Robert McClure and F. L. McClintock, of whom more would be heard. Finding ice in the middle stretch of Baffin Bay, he went round it, north about, and arrived at the entrance to Lancaster Sound. Sailing further to the west, he fired guns at regular intervals, sent up rockets by night and, every day, dropped a cask containing papers, so that anyone who picked them up would know what he was doing. Among other things, he left messages for Franklin which he hoped would reach him, warning the lost explorer that no whaler had been able to cross Baffin Bay that season. Franklin could not, therefore, hope for help from that quarter. After great difficulties, Ross was able to put into Port Leopold at the meeting-place of Lancaster Sound, Prince Regent Inlet, Barrow Strait and Wellington Channel. That winter he caught some foxes and fastened copper collars round their necks on which the position of the ships and supply dumps were given. Then he let them loose. In the spring, search parties set off westwards along the shore of Somerset Island until they reached a point where the coast turned to the south for fifty miles or more, No sign of life. Parties investigating the east coast of the island came back with the same news. Believing that Franklin must have sailed further to the west, Ross decided to do likewise. Crossing Barrow Strait, his two ships were caught in vast fields of ice, which were moving eastwards at ten miles a day. When, after extraordinary difficulties, the ships got clear, Ross decided that it was time to go home.

Richardson's search by land was equally unsuccessful. Everywhere he went, for eight hundred miles along the coast of the Arctic Sea, he questioned the Eskimos. None of them had seen any ships. Richardson would have liked to have crossed to Wollaston Land, an island, or, as it turned out, a peninsula on the west side of Victoria Island, which he thought Franklin might have passed on a thrust towards the Bering Strait. But the ice imposed a barrier that defeated him. He returned to Canada, leaving the exploration of Wollaston Land to Dr Rae. Rae was unlucky. Ice and a savage winter defeated him, and he pulled back to the Great Bear Lake.

Meanwhile, the third expedition to Bering Strait had suffered from bad luck. After reaching the Strait at the end of an eight months' cruise from England, the commander, Pullen, decided that he could not pass through Bering Strait that year; seven months later, the two ships which made up the flotilla were on the coast of Alaska. From that point, the exploration went on by boat along the Arctic Coast towards the mouth of the Mackenzie River, where the party divided, half returning southwards along the American coast to Mexico, half, under Commander Pullen, going up-river to Fort Good Hope and so to York Factory on the coast of Hudson's Bay.

Ross had no results to report. Richardson's journey had been unfruitful. The Admiralty had now only Pullen to rely on. They sent him orders to return down the Mackenzie to the coast. He set out in July 1850. Next month, after frantic attempts to get through the ice-pack in Franklin Bay, he gave up. The swell – so he told the Admiralty – was enough to overwhelm his boats and, as for the ice, 'I can only compare it to floating rocks which would go through a boat like a sheet of brown paper for, smart as you may be, you cannot always get out of its way.' Pullen returned to England.

Meanwhile, Dr Rae, from his base on Great Bear Lake, probed to the north. Crossing into Victoria Island, a territory larger than Iceland, he went first to the east and then to the west along its coast; after that, he followed the mainland coast to the east and, crossing on to the island once more, he explored many miles of unknown territory until, at last, he had to give up. He had reached the most easterly point of Victoria Island, which he named Pelly Point. By September 1851 he had returned to his base at Fort Confidence on the eastern arm of the Great Bear Lake.

The three searching operations which the Admiralty had set in motion in 1848 had covered an arc of the Arctic about 1,600 miles across. They had settled some outstanding questions of Polar geography. They had come upon no traces of Franklin, his ships, or the 130 men who had sailed in them six years before. At home, in England, the faint-hearts who thought that nothing that Arctic exploration was likely to yield could possibly be worth the danger or the expense of attempting it, were confirmed in their opinion; the old Polar hands multiplied their theories: Dr King said, with no excessive modesty, that this was just what he had foreseen. Lady Franklin alone remained inflexible in her faith that her husband and his comrades should be sought, and might still be found. Every region in the Arctic had been explored, with one unlikely exception which the odious Dr King had pointed to. And the outcome of it all had been negative. The *Erebus* and the *Terror* and all who sailed in them had vanished from the face of the sea. What, in fact, had happened to them?

Although he did not know it, Dr Rae had come nearest to solving the riddle. When he turned back on the east coast of Victoria Island, he was about fifty miles from the place where Franklin's ships had been caught in the ice in September 1846.

The End of Franklin

The great net of investigation which had been thrown over the Arctic by the expeditions of 1848 had left the riddle of Franklin's disappearance unsolved and more mysterious than ever. But it was hardly thinkable that the search should be given up even if the hope of finding any living survivors of Franklin's voyage must now be regarded as faint indeed. It was true that Ross and his men had lived through four Arctic winters. But that expedition had been on a much smaller scale than Franklin's. Moreover it had been able to use the large supply dump left by the *Fury*. At the Admiralty, the defeated strategists prepared new operations which, as before, rejected Dr King's persistent and tiresome propaganda that the most hopeful area of search lay to the north of the Great Fish River (now known as the Back River) which runs into the sea to the west of the Boothia Peninsula.

That river was, in the official view, an obsession with the doctor for no better reason than that he had explored it fifteen years before as a surgeon with Sir George Back's party. The ten grave eminences of the Arctic Council, in which was concentrated the wisdom and experience of Britain's Polar science, would not consider that Franklin, if in an emergency he deserted his ships, was likely to sail or march southwards towards the river. Nobody was more vehement in rejecting King's thesis than the man who led the expedition to that region in which King had served, Sir George Back. It is quite likely that King's ideas which, of course, included a new expedition to be led by himself, would in any case have been rejected by the Council. His bad manners and arrogance had made it almost certain that they would be. The Council listened with much more respect to the ideas put before it by Sir Francis Beaufort, the Admiralty Hydrographer. He thought that, if either the *Terror* or the *Erebus* had been crushed by the ice, the survivors of the disaster would have tried to make their way to the mainland. In that case, some word of them would have been picked up from the Eskimos or some clue would have been found on the coast by the search parties. Nothing of the kind had been reported. So it seemed most likely that Franklin's ships were held in the ice to the west of Melville Island. That being Beaufort's opinion, he suggested that rescue ships should be sent to Bering Strait with orders to sail as near to Melville Island as they could. The plan was accepted and put in hand as quickly as possible.

Two ships, the *Enterprise* and the *Investigator*, which had already proved their worth in the Arctic, were earmarked for the task and dispatched from the Thames in January 1850, the year in which the search for Franklin reached its climax. In addition to the Bering Strait expedition there were five search parties, one financed by Lady Franklin, one by a New York merchant, Henry Grinnell, the others organized by the Admiralty. A winter encampment of Franklin's was found at the entrance to Wellington Channel; three graves of members of his crews were seen on Beechey Island. That was all. And for months there was no news of the two ships that were tackling the problem from the western side.

Captain Richard Collinson in the *Enterprise*, led the flotilla which left for the Bering Strait. Commander Robert McClure was in the *Investigator*. Collinson was an experienced naval officer of forty; McClure aged forty-three, had already served in the Arctic under Sir James Ross. They made their way through the Strait of Magellan to the Pacific. Soon they were parted by a gale, never to meet again until the adventure was all over. McClure made his way northwards round the Alaskan coast where, off Cape Lisburne, he fell in with a naval vessel, the *Herald*, whose captain, Henry Kellett, was at first minded to detain him in the hope that Collinson could catch up with him. But McClure was eager to go on and Kellett finally agreed that he might do so. 'Had you better not wait forty-eight hours?' Kellett signalled as the distance between him and the *Investigator* lengthened. 'Important duty,' McClure replied, 'cannot on my own responsibility.'

He was now entering Beaufort Sea, one of the most forbidding areas in all the seven seas. To the north of the shoreward water lay an icefield of vast extent, composed of ice infinitely older than that of the Eastern Arctic. No vessel could break through it. With no knowledge of the nature of the problem before him, he hoped that he might find a direct route to Melville Island, which was about eleven hundred miles from the point where he sent his farewell signal to Kellett. But very soon it was clear to him that his only hope was to steer a course eastwards, hugging the coast. After rounding Point Barrow, he sighted a settlement of Eskimos and asked for news of Franklin's ships. They had none. When he asked if any land lay to the north, the Eskimos shook their heads. The furthest they had been able to travel in that direction was thirty miles. There they had seen no sign of land. When he reached the mouth of the Mackenzie, McClure steered for Banks Island. But after a promising start, he was forced to turn back in order to avoid being trapped in the ice. He resumed his way along the coast. Off Cape Bathurst, he talked again with Eskimos on the shore. They, too, knew nothing about the region to the north. It was the 'Land of the White Bear' which they regarded with superstitious dread.

When he reached Cape Parry, eighty miles further on, he sighted a bold headland across the channel which lay to the north-east. His charts did not make any mention of this promontory and, thinking that it might mark some opening in the land, he sailed towards it and went ashore. Although he did not realize it then, he had reached the southern part of Banks Island. The headland was a thousand feet high and from its summit, McClure saw open water further north. Forty miles of it! Sailing north-east, he found himself threading a channel, thirty miles wide but narrowing between two shores. To the east, there were glimpses of a mountain range, with peaks that looked like volcanoes. McClure knew that he could be no more than sixty miles from Melville Sound which led into Barrow Strait and – the charts were clear on the point – so to the Atlantic!

There was, at that moment, extraordinary excitement in the *Investigator*. Were they about to solve the problem of three hundred years – the problem, not of Franklin's fate, but of the North-west Passage? McClure put his emotions into language which belonged rather to the high-flown, evangelical convention of the time than to his own natural, ambitious self, a young officer eager for glory. 'Can it be,' he asked, when he wrote about the incident later, 'that so humble a creature as I am will be permitted to perform what has baffled the talented and wise for hundreds of years? But all praise be ascribed to Him who hath conducted us so far in safety. His ways are not our ways . . . ' The answer to McClure's question was, as it turned out, No.

A gale sprang up from the west, driving the ship towards the eastern side of the channel and building up around her a daunting array of ice. It was already September; soon winter would arrive. Making his way slowly but bravely forward, McClure reached a point within thirty miles of Melville Sound. Then he resolved that the moment had come to pause. He might, with luck, return to the mainland but he remembered that, all the way eastwards along the coast, he had spotted no likely harbour. McClure prepared to spend the winter where he was, in the hazards of the icepack, in a narrow channel unexplored and, until his voyage, unsuspected, between two large and desolate islands, almost within sight of the seaway that, when the ice allowed, led inevitably to the Atlantic. To stay there was a difficult decision to take and every day that followed made it seem more doubtful. For the thermometer fell and the ice grew.

The *Investigator*, in the grip of a current stronger than any anchor she could put out, drifted to the south for thirty miles before she came to rest. Then came a wind from the south, driving the vessel and the floes in which she was caught back along the course she had just covered. It seemed for a little that the helpless ship was about to be destroyed under the cliffs, four hundred feet high, of an island that stood in the middle of the strait. But, when every hurried preparation had been made to meet the disaster that seemed imminent, at the last minute fate relented. The ice pack swerved away from the shore and the *Investigator* came peacefully to rest somewhere to the north of the mid-way island.

Three weeks after the ship had been settled in for the winter, McClure with seven chosen companions set out, with sledges, over the ice to find out once and for all if they were really on their way to the North-west Passage. Food was severely rationed: supper consisted of a handful of oatmeal in a pint of water. Snow fell, turning the ice into slush. Progress was slow and wearisome. But after three days' journey to the north, McClure saw the land fall away to the east. He was at the opening of Melville Sound. Miles ahead he caught sight of a peak from the summit of which he might obtain the answer to the question he – and all of them – were asking. Before dawn on 27 October, they climbed it and, from its six-hundred feet summit, looked over an expanse of ice stretching forty or fifty miles ahead of them. To the east was Prince Albert Land; on the other shore, about twelve miles ahead, the coast of Banks Island turned unmistakably to the west. Ahead, for more miles than they could see, lay the ice of Melville Sound. It was a moving moment. McClure and his little party of explorers were looking at the North-west Passage! Or, at any rate, they were looking at a channel which led to Barrow Strait and so to the Atlantic. But could it be navigated? That did not seem at all improbable to men who had reached a point not much more than a hundred miles from Parry's westernmost limit in 1820.

They lit a bonfire and drank a tot of grog. If they had not sailed through the legendary Passage, they had at any rate the evidence before their eyes that it existed. While McClure waited for winter to pass and conditions to return in which sailing would be possible, he sent out three parties to look for the lost Franklin. East, west and south they went, covering an area of several hundred square miles. They found nothing. When open water returned in the summer of 1851, the *Investigator* resumed her cruise northwards through the Strait. But McClure had not finished yet with the power and caprice of the Arctic ice. First, the ship was carried slowly, inexorably eastwards; then it was halted twenty-five miles short of Melville Sound. If only it could reach the pack-ice of the Sound, then there was a chance – a good chance – that it might drift eastwards into Baffin Bay. Why not? That had happened to Sir James Ross years before. But, just then, McClure became aware of an alarming fact. New ice was beginning to form on the water round the ship. He decided to turn tail, and move southwards down the channel he had threaded the year before. After that, he would try to reach Melville Sound by sailing along the western coast of Banks Island.

Favoured by the wind, he covered three hundred miles in three days and, having reached the north-west of Banks Island, thought that he might sail to the north of Melville Island, avoiding Melville Strait altogether. This was certainly an audacious idea, for it meant sailing into seas that had never before been navigated. But the sea was calm – Melville Sound was choked with ice – the gamble seemed to be worth taking. However, the Arctic has its own brand of humour. Without warning, McClure found that the *Investigator* was sailing towards what seemed, at first sight, to be a barrier of ice as unbroken as the Great Wall of China and a hundred feet high. Soon afterwards, for it was too late to alter course, he found himself in a narrow channel of free water hardly wider than a creek, between the ice and the shore. He could not bring the ship about in so narrow a defile. He must press on, looking all the while for a harbour where the ship could spend the coming winter in safety. Progress was slow, for the *Investigator* was so caught in the ice that, finally, explosives had to be used to free her.

For a week they continued on their way towards the north, until, at last, they had rounded the north cape of Banks Island and were ready to sail to the Atlantic. They were in a broad seaway leading to the east and only a few miles south of Melville Island. Once again, when everything seemed to be set fair for an early triumph, the genius of the Polar Sea interposed its veto. Ahead of them, to the east, stretched a vast icefield and now it was too late in the year to think of drifting eastwards with it into Lancaster Sound, the gateway to the Atlantic. McClure made up his mind to settle down for the winter in a large harbour to the north-east of Banks Island, which he called Bay of Mercy. That winter, the crew of the *Investigator* occupied themselves, agreeably enough, by hunting, while their captain, McClure, made an attempt to reach Melville Island in a search for any sign of another of the relief expeditions which had been sent out from England to look for Franklin.

He came upon a note left at Winter Harbour, on Melville Island, by Lieutenant McClintock who, in June of the previous year, had made a journey there by sledge from his ship anchored three hundred miles further east. The note told McClure that he would find no ship at Winter Harbour. By this time, his crew were suffering from the physical and mental effects of their long stay in the Arctic. At all costs he must avoid spending another winter in the ice. After waiting for more than two months, it seemed that the day of departure had arrived. But no! The mercury in the thermometer fell, the ice tightened round the ship. And the *Investigator* was condemned to a fourth winter in the Polar Sea, in the anchorage that McClure had named the Bay of Mercy. But if they all stayed, all would starve. That was certain. Accordingly, McClure divided his crew into three – the main party, numbering thirty men, would stay with him in the ship; a smaller number would make for the Mackenzie River, six hundred miles to the south-west, while the third party would set off for Lancaster Sound, seven hundred miles to the east.

So far as opinion in England was concerned, McClure had now been added to the roll of lost sailors of the Arctic. So, too, had Captain Collinson, originally McClure's commanding officer and now, like him, vanished behind the curtain of fog and ice.

In the meantime, some relics of Franklin's expedition had been found – signs of a camp here, three graves there. Not much, and not encouraging. But although the Admiralty was now ready to give up the search, the formidable Lady Franklin was not. Besides, a new duty had arisen: to look for McClure and Collinson. Accordingly, a flotilla of four ships were sent out in the spring of 1852, under Captain Edward Belcher. His orders were to sail through Lancaster Sound and then divide his forces so that Wellington Channel and Melville Island could simultaneously be investigated.

The latter voyage, led by Captain Henry Kellett in the *Resolute*, was, in effect the search for McClure. It turned out to be the more important of the two. Early in September, when Melville Island was sighted, it was clear that winter was approaching. While Kellett made ready to settle down until warmer weather returned, he sent out reconnaissance parties in different directions. One of these discovered a sandstone boulder near the entrance to Winter Harbour, on which Parry all those years ago had inscribed a memorial of his stay. But more interesting by far to the search party of 1852 were the notes McClure had left there, five months before, telling any reader who chanced to find them what he had done and what he meant to do. He would go home, said McClure, by way of Melville Island. Anyone who read the message might leave food for him at Winter Island. In short, Kellett had stumbled on the fact that McClure meant to spend the winter months in the Bay of Mercy. He might even still be there! The trouble was that Kellett could not complete the journey before the cold season set in. In consequence, he must wait until the spring.

At this time, McClure, two hundred and fifty miles further west, and ignorant of what was going on in the outside world, was completing his plans for the departure of half of his crew. Fifteen men, under a lieutenant, were to travel due south while fifteen, also led by a lieutenant, would travel to the east in the hope of finding rescuers in Lancaster Sound. Each party was given an ample supply of food. They were to depart on their separate, desperate missions on 14 April. Eight days before that, while they were making their last frantic preparations, McClure was walking up and down on the ice outside the ship in company with the first lieutenant. They had a solemn matter to discuss, for the day before a member of the crew had died, and the question before them was, could they cut a grave in the ground while it was still barely frozen, although liable to freeze at any moment? Absorbed in this gloomy question, they did not notice a figure walking towards them from the rough ice at the entrance of the bay. When, at last, they sighted him they noticed that his movements were rapid and energetic. He was probably, they thought, one of the *Investigator*'s crew being pursued by a bear, although from his clothes, he certainly did not resemble any of the men who had been their comrades during their long, solitary voyage. When they were about two hundred yards away from him, he threw up his arms and shrieked some words which they could not understand. McClure and his lieutenants stopped, and allowed the stranger to come on. They saw his face was as black as ebony. He called: 'I am Lieutenant Pym, of the *Resolute*. Captain Kellett is in her at Dealy Island' (a hundred and sixty miles to the east). McClure and the lieutenant rushed forward and grasped his hand. In an instant, the scene on the ship was transformed. The invalids leapt from their hammocks. The artificers dropped their tools. The deck was crowded with wildly excited men. Pym had been twenty-eight days on his journey which, when the sledge broke, he had insisted on finishing with only two companions.

The day after Pym's arrival at the ship, McClure left to meet Captain Kellett at Dealy Island, which he did twelve days later. He meant to make arrangements to send his sick men back to England. He had no intention of going there himself. He had seen the North-west Passage and he was determined, if he could, to sail his ship through it! At the worst, he would wait through another winter and then go eastwards on foot to a place on the coast of North Somerset where he knew that ample supplies existed. From there, with luck, he would pick up a whaler that would take him home or, failing that, he would wait for a new relief expedition to come. He drafted a letter to the Admiralty announcing that, among other things, he had discovered 'the accurate knowledge of that Passage between the Atlantic and Pacific Oceans, which for so many hundred years has baffled maritime Europe.' He would sail through the channel he had found. Captain Kellett, however, took a different view. He saw the ravages of scurvy among the sick men from the *Investigator* and ordered a medical inspection of all the crew. The doctors found that all but two of them showed symptoms of the disease. With bitterness in his heart, McClure was forced to abandon his plan. The stores in the *Investigator* were put ashore, in the hope that they would be useful to the lost Captain Collinson should he pass that way. The colours were nailed to the ship's masthead. Then she was abandoned.

By the time McClure returned to England at the end of September, the public was informed that he had found the North-west Passage. He was promoted to Captain and given a knighthood. There was, however, another question. Should he be given the reward which Parliament had earmarked for the discoverer of the Passage? The bodies of four white men had been found near the mouth of the Great Fish River (the Back River) four years earlier. They must have belonged to Franklin's expedition. In that case, they must have completed the circle of sea communication between Barrow Strait and the open waters along the mainland coast which overland explorers had found. Should not their families be given the prizes? Lady Franklin, whose opinion in these matters was heard with deep respect, said she thought that her husband had found another, and more navigable, channel than McClure's, but that McClure was the first who had made his individual way from one ocean to the other. This, she said, might not be the object which had 'engaged the attention of the civilized world for centuries' but it was a distinction of which any man might be proud. After this nicely balanced verdict, Parliament voted McClure £10,000. So the riddle of the centuries had at last been solved – or had it? For, after all, the first explorers had gone out to find a commercially viable route. Apparently it did not exist. Later, they had searched for a navigable passage. And, so far, nobody had navigated it!

The first real clue to the fate of Franklin came in a report to the Admiralty by Dr John Rae who was, like so many servants of the Hudson's Bay Company, an Orkney man and, like Franklin's old friend, Sir John Richardson, was a surgeon trained in Edinburgh. He had been in the service of the Company since 1833. When Richardson led an overland expedition to look for Franklin, Rae went with him. In 1851, now aged 38, he set off again on a sledge journey which took him from Great Bear Lake 1,100 miles along the coast of the Wollaston Peninsula. Immediately afterwards, he made a survey by boat of the south and east coasts of Victoria Island. After that, turning south, Rae and two companions journeyed up the Coppermine River. After eight months, Rae had travelled 5,380 miles. This vigorous explorer was leading an expedition for the Hudson's Bay Company on a survey of the western coast of Boothia when he came on the traces of Franklin. At Pelly Bay in 1854, Rae fell in with an Eskimo who repeated to him a story he had heard. According to it, four years before, white men had been seen by Eskimos making their way to the south over the ice off King William Island. It appeared that their ships had been crushed in the ice. Now, with food running short, they were hoping to find game on the Canadian mainland. Later on, these Eskimos came on the bodies of thirty-five of the men. They also found a telescope, a gun and ammunition. But the white men had found no game and it was apparent to the Eskimos that they had tried to stave off death by cannibalism. The Eskimo who told this grim story to Dr Rae was able to produce some evidence to support it, table goods which had been found at the white men's camp including a small silver plate inscribed 'Sir John Franklin, K.C.H.' Rae went at once to York Factory on Hudson's Bay and sent his news to the Secretary of the Admiralty. It reached London soon after the return of the McClure expedition.

Next year, 1855, the Admiralty, by this time fully occupied with managing the naval part of the Crimean War, asked the Hudson's Bay Company to send an expedition to the mouth of the Back River in the hope of coming on more clues to Franklin's fate. There, in Eskimo huts, between Lake Franklin and the estuary, the search party found tent poles, oars, tools, etc. which the Eskimos said came from a boat belonging to white men who had starved to death some years before. On Montreal Island in the estuary itself, other relics were found, including a stick on which somebody had carved the name 'Terror'.

In the meantime, there had broken out a controversy in England about who should receive the £10,000 which the Admiralty, five years before, had undertaken to pay to the man bringing the first reliable information about Franklin's fate. James Anderson, a servant of the Hudson's Bay Company, who had led the latest search, had a strong claim. Dr Rae, with the support of the Company, put in a bid and became impatient when the Admiralty proposed to wait until Mr Anderson's party returned. He pointed to a letter the Admiralty had written to the Company in 1854 in which Rae was said to have settled the question of Franklin's fate. After consulting his lawyers, Rae had decided to wait until Anderson returned. But now, when the result of Anderson's journey was known and the question would shortly be adjudicated, a shoal of new claimants appeared. Among them was, naturally, Dr King. He had a good case and a genius for spoiling it. He had insisted from the beginning that Franklin would try to make his way to the Back River. And now it seemed that Franklin – or the survivors of his expedition – had done just that. He accused Dr Rae of 'culpable negligence' for failing to go to the river as soon as he heard the story the Eskimo told. 'Respectfully but firmly', Dr King reminded their lordships of the Board of Admiralty that he had been proved right in a 'remarkable manner' both about the end of the Franklin Expedition and about the North-west Passage. While other Arctic explorers had been showered with honours and emoluments, he alone was unrewarded. In short, Dr King wanted a slice of the £10,000.

A weightier champion now entered the lists. Lady Franklin objected to Dr Rae's claim being admitted. In a letter to the Admiralty, she pointed out that the fate of most of her husband's crews was still unexplained. His two vessels had not been found and the journals which were said to be in the hands of the Eskimos had not been recovered. How, then, could it be said that the fate of the expedition had been discovered? Lady Franklin was, above all, anxious lest the Admiralty should look upon what had been found as an excuse for not searching for more. As a widow with an acute emotional interest in the question, Lady Franklin was inclined to attach less importance to the new anxieties in the Crimea than the Admiralty was compelled to do. While the Admiralty awarded £10,000 to Dr Rae and his team in final settlement, Lady Franklin prepared a new expedition on her own initiative and, partly, at her own expense. She raised funds by an appeal to the public which had some response, especially from old Arctic hands. She bought a pleasure steamer, the *Fox*, for £2,000 and chose Captain Francis L. McClintock to command it. The *Fox* sailed in July 1857, supplied in generous measure by the Admiralty. It spent April of the following year drifting in the ice pack in Baffin Bay. When, at last, the ship could free herself, she was in much the same spot as she had been in the previous summer. Next season, McClintock sailed through Lancaster Sound to Barrow Strait until he was stopped by ice. Then he turned southwards along Prince Regent Inlet with the intention of threading the narrow channel, Bellot Strait, which separates Somerset Island from the Boothia Peninsula. But after waiting in vain for the ice in the strait to clear, McClintock returned eastwards and put up for the winter outside the Strait.

Later, he made a long overland journey to the south, on foot, accompanied by sledges drawn by dogs. At the end of it, he fell in with Eskimos who possessed some articles that had belonged to a party of white men who had died of starvation. One Eskimo recalled that a three-masted ship had been crushed in the ice, west of King William Island, although her crew came safely to land. After that McClintock carried out searches to the south. Eskimos said that they had seen two ships, one of which had sunk and the other been driven ashore. The crews had left with their boats in the direction of the Back River. McClintock's search party now divided into two; one, under his leadership, made its way down the east coast of King William Island, while the other, led by Lieutenant Hobson, examined the western shore. McClintock's group came on silver articles of English manufacture which Eskimos said they had taken from a wreck on the west shore of the island. An old woman reported that the white men had gone to the south and had died, one by one, on the way. Following these clues, McClintock scoured the desolate lands round the Back River estuary. Approaching Cape Herschel he came upon a skeleton lying on its face in a gravel ridge near a beach. It had once been a young man, slightly built and above the average height. He was wearing his neckerchief in a loose bowknot and was probably, therefore, a steward. His blue jacket had slashed sleeves and braided edging; near him, a clothes brush and a pocket comb were found. It seemed that he had fallen down and died – of cold, exhaustion, or starvation? – as he walked. A little further on, McClintock learned that one of his officers, Lieutenant Hobson, had been there before him.

Under a cairn was a note which reported that, during Hobson's search of the western shore of the island, he had chanced upon a metal box under a cairn containing a message dated May 1846, from Lieutenant Gore, leader of a party of eight from the *Erebus* and the *Terror*. It recorded that the ships had wintered at Beechey Island and that all were well. But there was also a later, and very different, entry. In this, Captains Crozier and Fitzjames reported the two ships had been deserted five leagues from the spot where the message was left, after having been held fast in the ice for nineteen months. Franklin had died in June 1847. The total loss of life had been twenty-four. At the time this message had been left, 25 April 1848, 105 men under Crozier's command were on their way to the Back River. And that was all.

When McClintock went to the place where Hobson had come upon the message, he found, fifty miles from Victory Point, a small boat mounted on a sledge. Two skeletons were in it, a vast amount of clothing, books, *Christian Melodies* and other devotional works, also *The Vicar of Wakefield*, guns and so forth. There was some tea and forty pounds of chocolate; tobacco and an empty pemmican tin, marked 'E', which might have stood for *Erebus*. Twenty-six pieces of plate were found in the boat. McClintock was puzzled that any food at all had been left. Also, why had so much clothing and equipment been taken so far before being abandoned? He decided that two men had been left at the boat and that the main party had gone on, meaning to come back for them. In that case, both parties had overestimated their strength. One question is even more puzzling. The *Erebus* and *Terror* were provisioned for three years when they left England in May 1845. The survivors of their crews, 105 men in all, abandoned the ships in April 1848 and, it seems, died soon after. They might have been on short rations. But why did they die of starvation? However, McClintock had found what had happened to Franklin and his men and where it happened. After that, he lost no time in returning to the *Fox*, and in it, to England.

McClintock brought back not only the secret of Franklin's fate, but also a conviction of how the North-west Passage could be navigated. He thought that if Sir John Franklin had sailed to the east of King William Land and not to the west, he would probably have not been beset in the heavy ice which comes down from the north-west. But Franklin had not known there was a channel to the east of King William Land. His charts showed it as a peninsula off the American continent. Since he sailed, it had been discovered – for Rae had found it – that a channel to the east existed. 'Perhaps,' wrote McClintock, 'some future voyager, profiting by the experience so fearfully acquired by the Franklin expedition, and the observations of Rae, Collinson and myself, may succeed in carrying his ship through from sea to sea; at least he will be enabled to direct all his efforts in the true and only direction.' But almost half a century passed before anybody acted on the clue McClintock had given.

Of the final stages in Franklin's disastrous voyage, something is known and more can be deduced. Finding his way to the west along Barrow Strait blocked by ice, Franklin had turned north through Wellington Channel as far as the 77th parallel. There, it seems, he was again obstructed by ice, for he spent the winter of 1845–6 at Beechey Island. Next spring, he found a large opening to the south (Peel Sound) and sailed down it until his ships were caught by the ice on 12 September. They were about thirty miles north-west of King William Island. When the spring of 1847 came, Lieutenant Gore led a party to that island where his record was found eleven years later under a cairn. On his return to the ships he found that Franklin had died. Next year (1848) with sickness rife and food running short, the ships were abandoned and the 105 survivors went by foot towards the Back River. Progress was painfully slow – no more than five miles a day to begin with and less than that as the days passed. Men fell as they trudged. Baggage was dropped by men who could carry it no further. By the time they reached the mainland they were reduced to thirty or forty men. And soon there were none ...

In England, the last to lose heart was Lady Franklin. For her, the rescue and, later, the fate of her husband became an obsession, which everyone respected. When a monument to Franklin was to be erected in Westminster Abbey, she hoped to write the epitaph. But the words which came did not satisfy her and Tennyson finished the task. By the time the monument was unveiled, Lady Franklin was dead and Dean Stanley added a footnote explaining that it was 'Erected by his widow who, after long waiting and sending many in search of him, herself departed to seek and to find him in the realm of light.' It was July 1875 and Lady Franklin had died at the age of eighty-three.

The Conquest

'No tragedy of the Polar ice has so stirred mankind as that of Franklin and his crew, stirred them not simply to sorrow but also to stubborn resumption of the struggle.'

Roald Amundsen, *The North-west Passage*

At midnight on 16 June 1903, there was a violent and persistent rainstorm in the city of Oslo, then called Christiania, patriotism and pedantry having not yet done their transforming work on the city's name. The rain beat furiously at the window frames and streamed endlessly along the gutters. The few who were forced to be about went on their way as quickly as possible, looking as disgruntled as the weather suggested. Seven young men, however, who moved as swiftly as the others under the deluge wore an air of high purpose and suppressed excitement. They were making their way through the streets to a wharf on the harbour and, for good reason, the rain was very much to their liking. A few hours earlier, their leader, a young seaman with an imperious nose, high cheekbones and a sweeping blond moustache, had confided to them the threat which at the last minute had loomed over their enterprise.

The threat was legal and financial. The seven young men were threatened with a writ of attachment by a creditor who had supplied them with goods and, with the obstinacy which sometimes marks his kind, insisted on being paid in cash. He was, it seemed, not the sort of man to be argued out of his resolve by eloquent pleas about the scientific importance of the enterprise which, were he too exacting, he would be frustrating, its patriotic interest, its significance for the international prestige of Norway which was, at that very time, preparing to cast off the last remnants of its union with Sweden. To all such arguments this Norwegian merchant remained impervious. He wanted his money. If it was not forthcoming within twenty-four hours, the bailiff would nail a writ to the mast of the yacht *Gjöa* in Christiania harbour and Roald Amundsen would be arrested for fraud. When Amundsen told his dismal story to his six companions, he did not need to add that the money *could* not be forthcoming in the time. They knew it already.

There they were then – seven adventurous young Norwegians – Amundsen, the leader, with a mate's ticket and experience in both the Polar seas; First Lieutenant Godfred Hansen, born in Copenhagen, second in command; Anton Lund, first mate on the voyage, an experienced harpoonist; Pedar Ristvedt, first engineer; Helmer Hansen, second mate; Gustav Wiik, a meteorologist who was going to ship as second engineer; and Adolf Lindstrom, cook and zoologist. Seven men with a ship and an idea. The *Gjöa* was admittedly not an imposing vessel – a single-masted yacht built thirty-one years before in the Hardanger Fjord. Forty-seven tons, seventy-two feet from stem to stern, and of shallow draught, with a fifteen horse-power engine. But Amundsen, her owner, had made a trial in her to the Arctic and had found her satisfactory. She was provisioned – mostly on credit – for a voyage of five years. Five years? Amundsen and his companions were going to take her through the North-west Passage or die in the attempt, as Franklin and his company had died. This was the dream that had haunted Amundsen since, as a boy, he had been stirred by the story of Franklin's tragedy. He trained for it, schemed for it, saved for it. Five years before, he had bought all the available literature on the Passage from an old gentleman in Grimsby. And now, at the last minute, it seemed that his ambition was going to be baulked. Or was it?

Amundsen had a plan which he put before his comrades. It was bold and heedless of the niceties of the law. They greeted it with acclamation. And so, in the pitch-black midnight and in the downpour, they made their way to the yacht at its moorings, where they were welcomed by the barking of six Eskimo dogs, tied up on the deck of the yacht and looking wretched in the rain. Without any waste of time, the adventurers cast off the hawsers and set out southwards down the fjord. Then the carefree flight from the law had begun. The yacht was loaded almost to the water's edge, the deck piled high with boxes they could not cram into the hold. The Norwegian expedition to the North-west Passage had begun. The bailiffs would have to swim.

By eleven o'clock next morning, the rain had ceased and they were off Færder lighthouse in the mouth of the fjord, under full sail, close to the wind. They were as happy as young men should be who have just cast off legal embarrassments and a tedious financial burden and are launched on a high adventure. Two months later they caught sight of Cape York on the west coast of Greenland, which seemed to be only two hours' sailing away, although, in fact, it was forty miles distant. On that day they met their first iceberg. 'One of those wonders only to be seen in the never-to-be-forgotten realms of ice, [which] make us long to return and feel again their enchantment.' Turning to the west the *Gjöa* paused so that the hunters could go ashore after a little bird like the most delicious fieldfare. After surveying the Greenland coast on a magnificent morning – glacier after glacier glistening to the north, as far as the eye could see – they cast anchor so that, by careful observation, they could decide where the Magnetic Pole was situated.

Before leaving Europe, Amundsen had decided that his expedition must have a serious scientific purpose, if he was to get any financial backing for it. He wrote to Kew, to the Oslo Observatory and, finally, he sought an interview with the director of the German Marine Observatory in Hamburg, a benevolent bachelor named Professor Dr Geheimrat Georg von Neumayer. 'Young man,' said Neumayer, after listening patiently, 'you have something more on your mind. What is it?'

'To be the first to conquer the North-west Passage.'

'Ah, there is still more.'

'To fix the true location of the North Magnetic Pole.'

Neumayer rose and embraced the Norwegian: '*That*,' he said, 'is the great adventure!' Amundsen might think that exploration was more important than science, but he was resolved to give his scientific backers full value for their support.

On the old route of the North-west seekers, the ship's company of the *Gjöa* entered Lancaster Sound with the sun in their eyes. They were to be faced, as Ross had been a century before, by an unbroken mass of ice stretching across their path from shore to shore. But it turned out to be only one of the illusionist tricks of the Arctic caused by the sun shining on a sea on which a myriad small pieces of ice were floating. Amundsen bore to south along Peel Sound. Here the sea was uncharted. They were too near the Magnetic Pole for the compass to be of any use. They were forced to rely on the stars and soundings. Soundings and caution! For on one side of the yacht the water might be unbelievably deep while, on the other, jagged rocks were visible just below the surface. They had plenty of excitement – fire in the engine room a few feet from their tanks of petroleum; a gale that blew too strongly for engine and anchor; once they ran aground on a hidden reef and were saved only by sacrificing all their deck cargo and by driving the ship over the rocks, a risky operation.

The worst blow of all came when, one day, the rudder refused to work. Impact with a reef had lifted the pintles onto the mounting. But luck was with them. Another and more violent impact brought the rudder back into its proper place. It was one of the rare occasions during that voyage when those taciturn Norwegians gave way to noisy jubilation. On the great problems of navigation, fortune smiled. At a point where, thirty years earlier, an English expedition had met a barrier of ice they could not pass, Amundsen felt the ship heave beneath his feet. She was moving in a swell. They way to the South was open! Opposite Bellot Strait, that narrow channel between North Somerset and Boothia, McClintock had waited two years to get through. Amundsen found it ice-free. It seemed that the Polar Sea was opening its gate to the explorers. But now it was time to find winter quarters so that the delicate instruments provided by the German scientists could be set up on land and used. One day, while they were making their way through the uncharted waters of Rae Strait, between Boothia and King William Land, Hansen sang out cheerfully from the crow's nest, 'I see the finest little harbour in the world!' Amundsen climbed beside him. He saw a small harbour, sheltered from all the winds. This would be their base. They named it Gjöahaven and dropped anchor in four fathoms of water.

By the time October had begun, the yacht was covered over with sail-cloth and they were ready for winter. It was high time, for the seawater, driven by the north-east gale, began to freeze at once, covering the *Gjöa* with ice. The snow and the sea, mixed together, turned into a kind of soup. It was the first stage in the formation of ice. Then the hunters went out, patient and clever and well-armed, although not as patient as the Eskimos. Herd after herd, the reindeer came down from the north and tested the ice to see if it would bear them to the mainland, forty miles away. Meanwhile, the scientists were busy with their magnetic observations, pitied by their companions as they worked in a temperature forty below zero and a biting snow. When Christmas came, the scene was grand and tranquil with a wonderful aurora borealis and, by that time, they had learnt to make snow huts, Eskimo-fashion, and had discovered that Eskimo winter clothes were better than European and that an igloo was warmer than a tent. With the fur next to the skin, there was more room for the air to circulate.

By that time they had met the local Eskimos and the first approach was cautious on both sides. At the critical moment Amundsen told his army to throw down their weapons. The Eskimo did likewise and a friendship, wary at first, and later warm and confident, grew up between these amiable savages and their alarming visitors. It was seventy-two years since white men had come to these parts under the command of Sir James Clark Ross. But the Eskimos had passed down the story of that extraordinary event from father to son. Now, just when that earlier visit was passing into legend and before it took wing into the realms of mythology, the white strangers had returned! The Eskimos asked Amundsen if their tribe could settle about his camp. Very soon, fifty Eskimo huts, housing two hundred people, were established at Gjöahaven and their inhabitants were beginning to learn western skills, like the use of the ski. For their part, the Norwegians were comfortable enough and had enough to do to keep them from being bored.

On one point, Amundsen's orders were emphatic. They were living, seven white men among two hundred Eskimos, who might be amiable but were certainly unpredictable. The seven were safe so long as the Eskimos believed in their godlike superiority. They could be ruthless, cruel, unjust – all that was expected of gods. To one weakness, however, they must not succumb. They must not tamper with the Eskimo women, for that would prove that they were only human after all. The ship's company of the *Gjöa* recognized the wisdom of the edict and, readily or reluctantly, obeyed it. This was not always easy for although most of the Eskimo women were not to the taste of Europeans, most of them being bandy-legged – one or two were attractive by any standard. There was, for example, a woman called Magito, whom they met in the vicinity of the Magnetic Pole. She was a lively, flirtatious little thing of twenty, who inflamed more than one Norwegian heart. To make matters worse, her husband, as Amundsen remarks in disgust, would have sold her for a rusty nail.

By March, the Norwegians saw the first ptarmigan of the year, and one of their Eskimo friends caught twelve cod through a hole in the ice. Spring was coming to King William Land. Amundsen, who had brooded over the narratives of the earlier explorers, had decided that the vital factor was to avoid the stream of ice coming down McClintock Channel from the Beaufort sea. It was this ice which, advancing from the north-west, in a tremendous, terrifying, lethal procession, destroyed Franklin's ships and piled up a rampart fifty feet high along the north coast of Canada. It could not reach, like the Greenland ice, the warm water of the Atlantic. It remained imprisoned in the Arctic archipelago, choking the outlets and crushing intruding ships. It was the ultimate secret of the Arctic.

On 1 March 1904, Amundsen, with three companions, began the first of his overland journeys by dog, northwards towards the Magnetic Pole. The weather – 63.5 degrees below zero, Fahrenheit – seemed tolerable to those hardened Arctic sojourners. Putting their Eskimo lore to use, they built a snow hut and crawled into it to eat their evening meal, cooked over a Primus stove. After a few days, however, even Amundsen was forced to acknowledge that a temperature of 79 degrees below zero was too cold for travel. The party – four in number – made their way back to the *Gjøa*. The next reconnaissance came a fortnight later when the weather had moderated to a mere 40 degrees below. However, the weather turned cold again, too cold for their Eskimo guide. Once more they went back to the ship. On 6 April Amundsen, with Lieutenant Hansen and Ristvedt, set out again in the comparative warmth of 22 degrees below zero. After crossing the James Ross Strait over awkward ice to the mainland of Boothia, with attendant Eskimos, they went northwards along the west coast of that vast peninsula, passing the Magnetic Pole on the way. Ristvedt saw to it that their menu was the best the Arctic could provide – reindeer meat, fish and reindeer tripe, the whole garnished with blubber chopped up in squares. Ristvedt's favourite dish was seal meat fried in oil, a taste that Amundsen did not share. Seventy miles north of the Magnetic Pole, they turned back. The coast of Boothia had been flat and featureless, although a few peaks could be seen, far in the interior. And Amundsen had to lie up for a day or two and rest his foot, painful as a result of over-tight lacing on the ankle. Two of their dogs they lost; they had gone out after bear and never came back.

When the party reached the yacht once more on 7 May, they found her buried in snow half-way up her mast; the ice in the harbour was twelve feet thick. Such was early spring in the Arctic. But the three men they had left behind were on excellent form. They had even put on weight thanks to their success in shooting ptarmigan. In the first week of June, the Eskimos returned for seal-fishing. They brought blubber to the ship, exchanging it for wood and iron. As summer advanced, the diet grew more varied: trout from the lake on which the ice was breaking up; small, fresh cod, and reindeer meat which became their favourite breakfast dish. The Eskimos were partial to very rotten entrails from which the dogs reared away in horror. Men do not survive in the Arctic through the centuries by being over-nice in their eating. On the whole, then, that summer of 1904 beyond the Arctic Circle was happy, active and well-fed. When cold nights, snow showers and the flights of birds moving southwards heralded the return of winter, the seven Scandinavians were well-equipped to meet it. After a cold summer when there had not been enough open water for navigation, they could only hope for better luck with the return of spring. The North-west Passage had still to be conquered.

At the end of December, they were visited by an Eskimo who, in reasonably good English, presented himself as Mr Atangala. He had just travelled with a party of white men from Chesterfield Inlet on Hudson's Bay to the Coppermine River – a matter of eight hundred miles as the crow flies. There he had picked up the news of a ship at King William Land and thought that he might do some business with its captain. Amundsen decided to use him to take letters to ships which, it seemed, were lying off Cape Fullerton at the entrance of Roe's Welcome, on the north-west corner of Hudson's Bay. Atangala set off on his journey of 500 miles or more with the letters of seven homesick Scandinavians strapped to his back. They did not see him again for 174 days. By that time winter had passed.

Lieutenant Hansen and Ristvedt, with food for fifty days, had made a long journey by sledge which took them north-west over Victoria Strait and then northwards along the coast of Victoria Island which, in celebration of Norway's new-born independence, they named King Haakon VII Coast. At the 72nd parallel, they turned south again and reached Gjöahaven on 25 June. In a little less than three months, they had covered something like 500 miles. A month earlier, Atangala had returned with a small tin box on his sledge, well-soldered against snow and ice. The men on the *Gjöa* learned that war had broken out between Russia and Japan. They also learned, which was more to the point, where the whalers would be found on the north-west coast. Best of all, however, Atangala brought with him a present of five huskies from Major Moodie of the Royal Canadian Mounted Police.

As the summer of 1905 wore on, Amundsen decided that the time had come to move on. The scientific equipment which, for nineteen months, had been registering their magnetic recordings, was dismantled and packed. The Eskimos received priceless gifts like empty tins and odd pieces of wood. A spare sledge was given to a family with a crippled son whom for years his parents had dragged about on a sealskin. The young man, who was reputed to be a sorcerer, gave Amundsen his magic brow-band of deerskin in gratitude. When leaving the German Marine Observatory in Hamburg, Amundsen had promised Professor Neumayer to leave a photograph of him as near the Magnetic Pole as possible. This promise was duly performed at a time when no inquisitive Eskimo was about. As June drew towards its end, the weather grew warm, snow cleared from the land, and channels began to open through the ice. Every augury promised a year as favourable for sailing as 1903 had been. At the end of July a freshwater pond near the boat was used as a swimming pool. The Eskimos looked on in amazement but did not try to imitate the white men, who were undoubtedly mad. One Eskimo, whom they had planned to take home with them, suffered an emotional crisis at the last minute: he was afraid that the white men would kill him. When Amundsen argued that, on the contrary, the Kabluna were angels of benevolence, the Eskimo pointed to alarming pictures of the Boer War which he had found in illustrated magazines in the ship's cabin. After this, another Eskimo volunteered for the post as honorary white man and was ceremonially scrubbed down and dusted with insecticide. By this time the harbour was free of ice and the ice in Rae Strait had become the blue colour which indicated that soon it would melt. On 13 August the *Gjöa* set sail to the west. The wind was in the north-east, breaking up the ice.

Amundsen was launched on – as he said – the most fascinating of all the problems of exploration before humanity, the discovery of the North-west Passage. The weather was bad – thick fog and a contrary, changeable wind. Ten fathoms and a dry bottom, the leadsman reported. At Booth Point they came to a halt, faced by great masses of ice drifting towards them. When the fog cleared, they saw islands to the west, with clear water beyond. In Victoria Strait there were ice-floes across the way from shore to shore but the ice was loose enough for them to get through. Picking his way through one archipelago after another, guided by a man posted in the crow's nest to give warning of any reefs beneath the surface of the water, Amundsen made a devious course round King William Island. The channel swiftly changed from deep to shallow, from seventeen fathoms to five. The leadsman and the look-out sounded and shouted, watched and signalled in wild, sustained activity, hour after hour without sleep. At the helm, Amundsen, his heart pounding with excitement, translated into quick changes of course the information sent him by the others. A man stood ready to drop the anchor if the water became too shallow. After nudging their way through a chaos of sharp, low-lying rocks, at last they left the islands behind. And on 17 August, they cast anchor on the west side of Cape Colbourne by the south of Victoria Land. From now onwards they would be entering waters which ships coming from the west had traversed. *They had sailed through the unexplored section of the North-west Passage.*

But they still had to complete their task. There was always the chance that the Arctic had one last trump up its sleeve. For Amundsen, the long-continuing nervous strain was intense. For days he could neither eat nor sleep. 'Day after day,' he said, 'for three weeks, the longest three weeks of my life, we crept along, sounding our depth with the lead, trying here, there and everywhere to nose into a channel that would carry us clear through to the known waters to the coast. Food stuck in my throat when I tried to swallow. Every nerve was strained to the limit . . . We must succeed.'

And then, suddenly, it was over.

'Vessel in sight, sir!' Lieutenant Hansen threw upon the door of the cabin and shouted the message.

Amundsen wept as he threw on his clothes.

The distant outlines of a black two-masted whaler to the west. The Norwegian flag was pulled to the masthead of the *Gjöa*. The other ship showed the Stars and Stripes. It was the end of years of hope and toil. The North-west Passage had been conquered.

The vessel they met was the *Charles Hepson* of San Francisco which had sailed through Bering Strait. Where it had floated, Amundsen's ship could float. The date was 26 August 1905. Instantly, the strain was over. Amundsen's appetite returned with violence. Carcasses of caribou were hanging from the shrouds. Knife in hand, he swarmed up the rigging, cut off sliver after sliver of the raw meat and ate like an animal. He was sick at once and at once ate again. This time he kept the meat down. Those who saw him at that time guessed his age at anything between fifty-nine and seventy-five. He was thirty-three.

Meanwhile, the ice was thickening and soon it was clear that the *Gjöa* would have to spend another winter in the Arctic. Amundsen's chief desire at that moment was to reach a telegraph office to tell the world of their feat. The nearest telegraph was on American territory five hundred miles to the south, beyond mountains that rose as high as 9,000 feet. As it happened, one of the whaler skippers, an Englishman, Captain William Mogg of the *Bonanza*, whose vessel had been wrecked, was anxious to return to San Francisco overland, so that he could fit out another vessel and be back in the Arctic by spring. Amundsen was by no means eager to take Mogg with him as he was a fat little man who could not run with the sledges; nor had he any experience whatever of overland travel in the North. But Mogg had money and Amundsen was in the same state that he had been in when he left Christiania – penniless.

With an Eskimo and his wife, two sledges and twelve dogs, the pair set off, making twenty-five to thirty miles a day through heavy snow, over the mountain range and down the Porcupine River to the Yukon. It was hard going, although Amundsen was a fine skier. Food, however, was quite inadequate, for Mogg had rejected pemmican as food unfit even for dogs. They would travel on beans. But Mogg, who sat in the sledge all day, insisted that the others should travel without food from breakfast to dinner. He was in a hurry to reach San Francisco. As the financier and commander of the expedition, his will would prevail. That he made clear. Amundsen said nothing until they had reached the half-way mark between one road-house and the next on their way down the Yukon River. There the Norwegian stopped the sledge and announced to Mogg that he was returning to the roadhouse they had left. The dogs, the sledges and the supplies were Mogg's property and would, of course, be left with him. Mogg was appalled at such high-handed and heartless conduct. He could not walk, could not manage a dog team etc. 'That,' said Amundsen, 'is your affair. I will not go one foot further until you feed me properly.' Captain Mogg could not surrender quickly enough. They reached Eagle City and the northernmost American Army post, Fort Egbert, on 5 December. The temperature was sixty degrees below zero.

From this place, Amundsen sent the telegram which told the world that the North-west Passage had, after four centuries, been conquered. And Captain Mogg? What happened to poor plump Mogg? Amundsen ran into him at Barrow Point, the most northern point of the Alaska coast, in the summer of 1906. There, Mogg was serving as ice pilot on an American revenue cutter. What was said between them, the imperious Norwegian and the portly little Englishman? Amundsen does not tell. But, in the circumstances, he could afford to be generous. After two months Amundsen set out again for the North. The *Gjöa* bore south-west along the Alaskan coast and, after passing through Bering Strait, at last reached San Francisco where Amundsen left her as a souvenir of his momentous voyage, the first navigation of the North-west Passage.

After so many ardours and tragedies over so many years, Amundsen's final victorious attempt made the task seem almost too easy. He was, undeniably, lucky with the weather. The first summer, in which he could, perhaps, have completed the task, if it had not been necessary to spend so many months on the scientific work which was ostensibly the purpose of his voyage, was followed by a second and severer summer. Then, miraculously, came a third summer as favourable as the first. Where Franklin's men had died from starvation, Amundsen found game and fish in plenty. But it was not, by any means, entirely a matter of luck. The *Gjöa* was the best informed and the most carefully planned of all the voyages to conquer the Passage. The ship was the right size; its crew of seven were a well picked, trained and experienced élite of explorers. They were, too, as they needed to be, a hardy, well-adjusted group. Even so, they suffered one casualty, Gustav Wiik, the meteorologist, who died after the Passage was conquered of a sudden illness which seems, according to Amundsen's description, to have been an attack of appendicitis. Unhappily, there was no room on the *Gjöa* for a surgeon.

The ship's supplies might have been unpaid for, but they were ample. And Amundsen had not wasted his time over the Arctic books he bought from the old gentleman in Grimsby. In one of them he had read Sir Leopold McClintock's opinion that the channel to the west would probably be found by an explorer who followed a route further to the south than anyone had tried before. Amundsen had been convinced by that prediction.

The obvious route had seemed to be due west from the North end of Somerset Island. There the channel seemed to stretch to the west, wide and open, tempting to ambitious seamen, But, one after another, explorers who had taken that path, had failed. Amundsen had sailed south for four hundred miles to the farthest south point of King William Island before he turned the *Gjöa*'s bow to the west. The North-west Passage had proved to be a much more tortuous, serpentine, narrow and unlikely route than anyone might have guessed from looking at the map, if indeed there had been a reliable map to look at!

The voyage completed, one task remained: to pay for it. Amundsen was now condemned to the treadmill which oppressed the spirits of so many explorers of that era – lecture tours. In the end he was able to go back to Norway with enough to pay all his creditors, including the obstinate individual who had been the cause of the midnight flight from Christiania in June 1903.

The Sense of Glory

And so it ended. The enterprise that had begun four centuries earlier and had been pursued, generation after generation, with such extraordinary persistence, through so many hardships, dangers, losses and disillusionments. And by such a strange assortment of seekers! The adventurers, some of them no better than they should be, fitting an expedition to the Arctic in between two piracies. The men who stayed at home, dreaming over their charts, the surface of which was one-third empty, one-third imaginary and one-third more or less correct. The capitalists in their City offices, gambling on the hope of a vast new trade. And then interruption – more than once in the story – when 'accursed war, with its licensed cruelty and empty pageantry, led away and distracted the national mind' and, for a time, the seamen had other things to do than grope through unknown seas to a phantom goal. When war passed and the sailors were faced, after Trafalgar for instance with what, to them, seemed the grey prospect of peace and idleness, the search was taken up again, this time by a generation of battle-hardened captains, men of a stern evangelical stamp attuned to the desolate theatre of their self-imposed ordeals, 'that mysterious thing, the North. A part of the globe which had no care for human life, which was not built to man's scale, a remnant of the Ice Age which long ago had withered the world . . .'*

The Rosses, Parry, Franklin, Richardson, McClure – how much they have in common, how manifestly they belong to the same human type, the product of race, training and religion; how well suited the cast is to the central, the intensest, the most tragic act in the drama! Not that one nation has a monopoly of the chief rôles. There are French, English, Scots, Welsh in the story. The magnet of the North attracts men of every race. When Charles Francis Hall read that Franklin's expedition was lost, he threw up his business in Cincinnati, heartlessly abandoned his family and put all his money into a search of the Arctic for the *Erebus* and the *Terror*. Later on, he

*John Buchan, *Sick Heart River*.

aimed at the North Pole – and was lost with all his companions in mysterious circumstances. By that time, Hall was too deeply infected with the bacillus of the Arctic to recover. He was enslaved by the Franklin story as the boy Amundsen was, later on.

No doubt it was galling for the British who had done most and suffered most in the cause when a Norwegian crew snatched the final laurel from them. But there was some poetic fitness in an ordering of things which decreed that the saga which began when Eric the Red found Greenland ended when another man of his race took the *Gjöa* to Nome nine centuries later.

The enterprise began in cockleshells of fifteen or twenty tons. Then 'crazy craft gave way to floating palaces of from 300 to 500 tons' as an enthusiastic writer said in 1862.* Sails, which had been supplemented by oars, came to be aided by steam and, later, by oil-driven engines. There was a real technical advance, although it will be noted that the yacht Amundsen sailed in was not much bigger (forty-seven tons) than the cockleshells of the first attempts. But as the years passed, science had brought other advantages: food could be preserved; the doctors were able to deal with scurvy; navigation was an exacter science; and bit by bit, painfully, over the centuries, men had accumulated lore about the Arctic and its ways. The later explorers had a vastly easier task than their predecessors: 'The longer our experience has been in the navigation of the Icy Seas,' said Parry, 'and the more intimate our acquaintance with all its difficulties and all its precariousness, the higher have our admiration and respect been raised for those who went before us.'†

They were, let it be acknowledged, a special breed of men, and not only the sailors among them. For although the sea voyages claim most of the dramas, the passions, of the story, it was the land journeys that did more than anything else to put together the key pieces of the great riddle. Hearne, Mackenzie and after them, Franklin and Richardson, Back, Dease and Simpson – they went down the great north-flowing rivers of Canada; they reached the hostile seaward plains where 'away beyond are the Barrens and rivers of no name and then the Polar Sea and the country where only the white bear and the musk-ox live. And at the end a great solitude.' In doing so, these reckless navigators in their little canoes, with only the thickness of a birchbark between them and death in the rapids or death from a storm at sea, marked out the sea route for the ships.

*John Brown, *The North-west Passage.*
†*Journal of the Third Journey for the Discovery of a North-west Passage.*

By the time their journeys were ended, they had mapped the Canadian Arctic coast from Point Barrow where Bering Strait begins to Victoria Headland where the Great Fish River runs into the sea. And they were able to report that, in the right season, with luck, ships could make their way 1,800 miles along that coastwise route. By the time they had finished their surveys and the sailors had probed the coves and inlets of the archipelago further north, only a small segment of the journey had still to fall into place, the intricate and infinitely deceptive system of straits and bays east of King William Island. Had Simpson been given permission by the Hudson's Bay Company to make another journey he would probably have completed the picture of the Arctic coast. But the task had to wait on other men.

But what had they accomplished, the men in the ships and their comrades in the canoes and the sledges? What had they really done? They had found a North-west Passage which was not at all the Passage which the original explorers had sought. It could not be said to reach Cathay; commercially speaking, it reached nowhere. It was a circuitous way between the frozen sea and the granite shore. That it was useless was something that had dawned on men long before the Suez Canal was opened or the Panama Canal was cut. What then? Was that all? By no means. The search for the Passage gave a fortuitous but powerful impetus to the opening-up of the Canadian North, land of the muskeg and the permafrost, the pingos and the esters,* land of ten thousand lakes which is today the world's richest known reserve of minerals. The explorer, the trapper and the prospector march ahead of the colonist.

Things have changed in the North since Franklin passed there. In Yellowknife, near where he all but died of starvation, is a community possessing 1,400 motor cars. The Great Slave Lake, where his Indians fished, sends fish to market every year worth a million and a half dollars. But make no mistake, the wilds are not far away. Whole tribes of Indians and Eskimos have been wiped out by starvation. And when an aeroplane crashes, its occupants may turn cannibal through famine as yellow men and white men, too, have done before them. The North is turning warmer: that has been the process for half a century. How long will it continue?

And what was the ultimate force behind the men who sought the North-west Passage? Greed we have heard of, but as we have seen, as a motive it was soon exhausted. Mammon was the first deserter on the voyage of discovery. What then? Strategic importance. National prestige. Scientific

*Pingos are conical ice-covered hills, rising to about 150 feet, and are most numerous near the Mackenzie Delta. Esters are ridges of sand or gravel, left by former glaciers.

curiosity. Geographical information, useful to navigators. One after another, the reasons for the exploration are put forward, solemnly or passionately. Yet, at the end, we are not convinced that the propagandists have disclosed their true motive. Was there not something else which they have not had the boldness to acknowledge – or, perhaps, the percipience to recognize in their own hearts? Should we not see the North-west story as a continuation into the nineteenth century, and even the twentieth, of the childlike wonder of the sixteenth? While the grave arguments fade, curiosity persists. It is the basic reality, the poetry, almost the mysticism behind the long search. A problem has been set and must be solved, as Everest soars and must be climbed. The solution, when it is found, may have no interest for science. It may 'prove' nothing. But who can tell until the voyage, or the climb, is completed.

Nor is the spirit of enquiry limited by what it expects to find. If these journeys into the ice, repeated with such insistence through the changing states of the human mind between 1500 and 1905 prove anything, it is the durability of the emotional strain in man's ambitions. Behind the scientist's curiosity lurks something harder and more primitive, something that can make myths, found systems of thought and people the empty seas. What should we call this primeval force below – or above – reason? 'At certain moments,' says Herbert Read, 'the individual is carried beyond his rational self, on to another ethical plane, where his actions are judged by new standards. The impulse which moves him to irrational action I have called the sense of glory.' The quest for the North-west Passage is so extraordinary a phenomenon of the human spirit that, it seems, only the sense of glory can account for it: man was for the last time in history 'face to face with something commensurate to his capacity for wonder'.

Notes on Sources

CHAPTER I

Golden Cathay must Wait

Frobisher's three voyages, which opened a new and more determined English attack on the problem of the North-west Passage, should be studied in

Vilhjalmur STEFANSSON, *The Three Voyages of Martin Frobisher*, London, Argonaut Press, 1938. This is a critical edition of the early narratives and gives a short biography of Frobisher, whose career is often shrouded in obscurity for reasons which are not hard to guess.

Individual, and contemporary, narratives of the voyages are found in HAKLUYT's *Navigations*:

Christopher HALL, *The First Voyages of M. Martin Frobisher.*

George BEST, *A True Discourse of the late Voyages.*

Unfortunately no satisfactory biography of Frobisher exists. Probably the best is

William McFEE, *The Life of Sir Martin Frobisher*, London, John Lane, The Bodley Head, 1928.

There is also a brief section relating to the explorer in

Thomas FULLER, *The Worthies of England*, London, Bivington, 1811.

The political and financial complications of the voyages are dealt with in

Conyers READ, *Sir Francis Walsingham*, Oxford, Clarendon Press, 1925.

William M. SCOTT, *Constitution and Finance of Joint Stock Companies* (3 vols), Cambridge University Press, 1910–12.

Various references to Frobisher's activities are to be found in the Calendar of State Papers (Domestic) Elizabeth.

CHAPTER 2

The Hope Continually Increaseth

For this chapter the authorities consulted have already been mentioned in the notes to Chapter 1. In addition there is the *Dictionary of National Biography* entry for Michael Lok. The inventory of Frobisher's 'Admiral' (flagship) the *Aid*, is in the Public Records Office, London among the State Papers (Domestic) Elizabeth. John White's paintings of the Eskimos are to be found among the prints in the British Museum.

The Greenland icecap is described in the *Encyclopedia Britannica*, article 'Greenland'.

CHAPTER 3

The Land of Desolation

The Voyages and Works of John Davis, the Navigator, (ed. A. H. Markham) London, Hakluyt Society, 1880.

The First Voyage of Master John Davis, written by John JAMES.

The Second Voyage attempted by Master John Davis, written by Henry MORGAN.

The Third Voyage Northwestward made by John Davis, written by John JAMES. In Richard HAKLUYT, *The Principal Navigations*, vol. III.

The Voyage of Captain John Davis to the Eastern India written by himself.

The Second Voyage of John Davis with Sir Edward Michelborne.

In *Purchas, His Pilgrims*, vols. III, IV, V and VI, Glasgow, Maclehose, 1905–1907.

The account of Lok the elder's meeting with Juan de Fuca is found in *Purchas His Pilgrims*, vol. XIV, p. 415.

John DAVIS, *The Seaman's Secrets*, London, Thomas Dawson, 1595.

John DAVIS, *The World's Hydrographical Description*, London, Thomas Dawson, 1595.

Donald B. CHIDSEY, *Sir Humphrey Gilbert*, London, Hamish Hamilton, 1932.

For Gilbert see also Richard HAKLUYT, *The Principal Navigations*, vols. III, VII and VIII.

Sir Humphrey GILBERT, *A discourse of a Discovery for a new Passage to Cataia* (ed. G. Gascoigne), London, H. Middleton for R. Jhones, 1576.

The Voyages and Colonising Enterprises of Sir Humphrey Gilbert, with introduction by D. B. Quinn, (2 vols.) London, Hakluyt Society, 1940.

George Weymouth, see *Purchas, His Pilgrims*, vol. XIV.

Thomas Cavendish, see *Dictionary of National Biography* and HAKLUYT, vols VIII, XI.

CHAPTER 4

The River of the Steep Cliffs

Most of the sources on Hudson have been conveniently assembled and edited in *Henry Hudson*. Original documents in which his career is recorded, with introduction by G. M. Asher, London, Hakluyt Society, 1860.

Ivar I. BARDSEN (Bardarson), *Sailing Directions of H. Hudson*, Albany, Joll Munsell, 1869.

Henry C. MURPHY, *Henry Hudson in Holland*, The Hague, Linschoten Vereenigen, 1909.

Llewelyn POWYS, *Henry Hudson*, London, John Lane, 1939.

Divers Journeys and Northern Discourse of Henry Hudson, written partly by J. Playse and partly by Henry Hudson.

A Second Voyage . . . The third Voyage. A larger discourse of the same voyage, written by A. Prickett. See *Purchas, His Pilgrims*, vols. XIII, XIV.

Sir Hugh WILLOUGHBY, *The New Navigation and Discovery of the Kingdom of Muscovia, enterprised by Sir Hugh Willoughby and performed by Richard Chancellor*, Richard HAKLUYT, *Principal Navigations*, vols. II, III, XII.

For William Barentz, see J. H. CAMPE, *Polar Scenes*, London, John Harris, 1822.

Articles on Hudson, Willoughby and Chancellor in *Dictionary of National Biography*.

CHAPTER 5

'Wickedness Sleepeth Not'

To the authorities given for the previous chapter should be added

Cecil H. L. EWEN, *The North West Passage*, Light on the murder of Henry Hudson, London, Privately printed, 1938.

Articles on Sir Dudley Digges, Sir John Wolstenholme and Sir Thomas Smith are in the *Dictionary of National Biography*. The opinions of Digges on commerce will be found in

The Defence of Trade, London, William Stansby for John Barnes, 1615.

Digges also wrote a pamphlet on the North-east Passage – *Of the Circumference of the Earth*, London, W. W. for J. Barnes, 1612.

CHAPTER 6

A Swelling Sea out of the West

The account of the Baffin – Bylot voyage of 1615, T. RUNDALL (ed.), *Narratives of Voyages towards the North-west*, London, Hakluyt Society, 1849.

This also contains what is known of

The Voyages of William Baffin, 1612–22 (ed. Clement R. Markham), London, Hakluyt Society, 1881.

Of Bylot, the little that is known will be found in RUNDALL's *Narratives*.

The lives of these three sailors are in the *Dictionary of National Biography*.

CHAPTER 7

North-West Foxe

In their different styles, Luke Foxe and Thomas James tell their own stories of their voyages to Hudson's Bay.

Luke FOXE, *North-west Foxe* or *Foxe from the North-west Passage*, London, B. Alsop and T. Fawcet, 1634.

Thomas JAMES *The Strange and Dangerous Voyage of Captain Thomas James in his intended Discovery of the North-west Passage*, London, J. Liggatt for J. Partridge, 1633.

An abridged version is in Rundall's *Narratives*, Hakluyt Society.

The Voyages of Foxe and James are printed together along with other narratives of voyages (2 vols.) London, Hakluyt Society, 1894.

CHAPTER 8

A Winter in the Forest

The sole source for the extraordinary ordeal of James and his crew in the Bay is his own account.

The nature of scurvy, the treatment of it and early ideas about the disease may be studied in

J. J. KEEVIL, *Medicine and the Navy* (4 vols.) Edinburgh and London, Livingstone, 1957–63.

Sir Richard HAWKINS, *Observations in his Voyage into the South Sea, 1893* (*Purchas, His Pilgrims*, vol. XVIII, p. 75).

Hawkins says: 'It is wont to help and increase the misery of man; it possesseth all those of which it taketh hold, with a loathsome slothfulness, that even to eat they would be content to change with sleep and rest . . . Were it not for the moving of the sea by the force of winds, tides and currents, it would corrupt all the world.' The best prevention? 'To keep clean the ship, to besprinkle her with vinegar, or to burn tar.' In twenty years, reported Sir Richard, ten thousand English had died of the scurvy. Ahead of his time, he recommended sour oranges and lemons as a remedy and a patent medicine he called Dr Stevens Water.

CHAPTER 9

Mr Gooseberry and M. Radisson

For the travels of Champlain, see

Samuel DE CHAMPLAIN, *Les Voyages du Sieur de Champlain*, 1613; *Voyages et découvertes faites en la Nouvelle France*, 1619; *Les Voyages de Sr. de Champlain*, 1620; *Les voyages de la Nouvelle France Occidentale*, 1632. All published in Paris, Collet.

Champlain's works have been translated and annoted by Canadian scholars under the general editorship of the Champlain Society. Toronto, H. P. Biggar, 1922–26.

E. E. Rich. *The History of the Hudson's Bay Company*, Toronto, Champlain Society, 1958.

E. E. Rich, *Hudson's Bay Company* (3 vols.), New York, Macmillan, 1961.

CHAPTER IO

Seventeen Rivers from Churchill

The Dobbs – Middleton controversy:

Christopher Middleton, *A Vindication of the Conduct of Captain C. Middleton*, London, Printed by Author's appointment, 1743.

Arthur Dobbs, *An account of the countries adjoining to Hudson's Bay . . . with an abstract of Captain Middleton's Journal and observations upon his behaviour*, London, J. Robinson, 1744.

C. Middleton, *A Reply to the Remarks of A. Dobbs*, London, G. Brett, 1744.

Desmond J. Clarke, *Arthur Dobbs Esquire*, London, Bodley Head, 1957.

See also biographies in *Dictionary of National Biography*.

James Knight: see article in *Dictionary of National Biography* and reference in *History of Hudson's Bay Company*.

P. Lauridsen, *Russian Exploration, Vitus Bering*, trans. J. E. Olson, Chicago, S. C. Griggs, 1899.

Constantine John Phipps, *A Voyage towards the North Pole*, London, Nourse, 1774.

Richard Pickersgill, *A concise account of Voyages for the discovery of a North West Passage*, By a sea officer, London, 1782.

William Coats, *The Geography of Hudson's Bay* (ed. John Barrow), London, The Hakluyt Society, 1852.

Sir John Barrow, *Voyages of Discovery and Research within the Arctic Regions*, London, John Murray, 1846.

Daines Barrington, *The Probability of Reaching the North Pole*, London, Heydinger, 1775.

The Possibility of approaching the North Pole asserted, London, Allman, 1818.

John Byron, *A Journal of a Voyage round the World in His Majesty's ship, The Dolphin, commanded by the Hon. Commodore Byron*, London, 1767.

Samuel Hearne, *A Journey from Prince of Wales's Fort in Hudson's Bay to the Northern Ocean in 1769–1772*, London, Strahan and Cadell, 1795.

Sir Alexander MACKENZIE, *Voyages from Montreal through the continent of North America to the Frozen and Pacific Oceans*, London, Cadell and Davies, 1801.

James Cook: James COOK and J. KING, *A Voyage to the Pacific Ocean*, 1784.

The Journals of Captain James Cook (ed. J. C. Beaglehole), London, Hakluyt Society, 1955.

Also E. E. RICH, *History of the Hudson's Bay Company*.

A general narrative of the middle period of Arctic exploration is to be found in

Glyndwr WILLIAMS, *The British Search for the North-west Passage in the 18th century*, London, Longmans, 1962.

This book admirably tells the story of what was done between the earlier voyages and the enthusiastic burst of exploration which followed the end of the Napoleonic war.

CHAPTER 11

At the End of the Bay

William SCORESBY, *An Account of the Arctic Regions*, London, Religious Tract Society, 1849.

R. E. SCORESBY-JACKSON, *Life of William Scoresby*, London, 1861.

Frederick. W. BEECHEY, *A Voyage of Discovery towards the North Pole . . . under the command of Captain D. Buchan, R.N.*, London, Richard Bentley, 1843.

John Ross, *A Voyage of Discovery . . . in H.M. Ships Isabella and Alexander* (2 vols.), London, John Murray, 1819.

Sir E. SABINE, *Remarks on the account of the late Voyage of Discovery . . . published by Captain J. Ross*, London, J. Booth, 1819.

John Ross, *An Explanation of Captain Sabine's Remarks*, London, John Murray, 1819.

Dictionary of National Biography articles on Banks, Barrow, John Ross, Beechey and Sabine.

CHAPTER 12

'The Threshold Passed'

W. H. BISHOP, *The Voyages and Expeditions of Captains Ross, Parry and Franklin*, London, Dean and Munday, 1834.

Ann PARRY, *Parry of the Arctic*, London, Chatto and Windus, 1963.

Sir W. E. PARRY, *Journal of a Voyage for the Discovery of a North-west Passage. 1819-20*, London, John Murray, 1821-4.

Alexander FISHER, *Narrative of a Journey to the Arctic Regions*, 1821.

CHAPTER 13

To the Hyperborean Sea

Sir George BACK, *Narrative of the Arctic Land Expedition to the mouth of the Great Fish River*, London, John Murray, 1836.

Sir George BACK, *Narrative of an Expedition in H.M.S. Terror*, London, John Murray, 1838.

Sir John FRANKLIN, *Narrative of a Journey to the Shores of the Polar Sea. 1814, 1820, 1821 and 1822*, London, John Murray, 1823.

Sir John FRANKLIN, *Narrative of a Second Expedition . . . 1825, 1826 and 1827*, London, John Murray, 1828.

JOHN MACILRAITH, *Life of Sir John Richardson*, London, 1868.

CHAPTER 14

'Dieu, que nous sommes maigres!'

For the grim story of this expedition of Franklin's, so costly in suffering and life, the explorer's own account mentioned in the notes on the previous chapter, is the authority. It should be read in conjunction with BACK's narrative.

CHAPTER 15

Good-bye to the Search

Sir William Edward PARRY, *Journal of a Second Voyage for the Discovery of a North-west Passage . . . performed in the years 1821–23 in H.M. ships the Fury and Hecla*, London, John Murray, 1824–25.

Sir W. E. PARRY, *Journal of a Third Voyage*, London, John Murray, 1826.

G. F. LYON, *The Private Journal of Captain G. F. Lyon during the recent voyage of Discovery under Captain Parry*, London, 1824.

CHAPTER 16

Interviews with the Savages

H. D. TRAILL, *The Life of Sir John Franklin, R.N.*, 1896.

Bernard O'REILLY, *Greenland, the Adjacent Seas and the North-West Passage to the Pacific Ocean*, 1818.

George F. LYON, *A Brief Narrative of an Unsuccessful Attempt to reach Repulse Bay*, 1825.

CHAPTER 17

A Glimpse of the Goal

R. HUISH, *The Last Voyage of Captain Sir J. Ross*, London, 1835.

Sir John ROSS, *Narrative of a Second Voyage in search of a North-west Passage . . . during the years 1829–1833*, London, C. Hodgson, 1824.

Sir John ROSS, *Observations on a work entitled 'Voyages of Discovery and Research'*, London, 1846. Ross's reply to Barrow.

Narrative of the Second voyage of Captain Ross, London. 1834.

Alexander SIMPSON, *The life and travels of T. Simpson*, London, 1895.

For Sir Felix Booth and Thomas Simpson see *Dictionary of National Biography* articles.

CHAPTER 18

Franklin Vanishes

J. J. SHILLINGLAW. *Narrative of Arctic Discovery . . . with details of the measures adopted by the Government for the Relief of the Expedition under Sir J. Franklin*, London, 1850.

John RAE, *Correspondence with the Hudson's Bay Company*, Hudson's Bay Record Society, vol. 16, London, 1953.

John RAE, *Narrative of the Expedition . . . in 1846 and 1847*, London, 1850.

Richard KING, *Narrative of a Journey . . . under command of Captain Back* (2 vols), London, 1836.

Richard KING, *Polar Expeditions and Polar Land Journeys*, (*Letter to Sir J. Barrow*), London, 1895.

CHAPTER 19

The End of Franklin

Frances J. WOODWARD, *Portrait of Jane. A Life of Lady Franklin*, London, Hodder and Stoughton, 1957.

W. H. GILDER, *Schwatka's Search . . . in quest of the Franklin records*, 1881.

Richard KING, *The Franklin Expedition from first to last*, London, 1835.

Sir F. L. McCLINTOCK, *The Voyage of the Fox* (fifth edition), London, John Murray, 1881.

R. MACCORMICK, *Narrative of a boat expedition*, 1854.

John RAE, M.D., *The melancholy fate of Sir John Franklin*, 1884.

Leslie H. NEATBY, *The Search for Franklin*, London, Barker, 1970.

Leslie H. NEATBY, *In Quest of the North-West Passage*, London, Constable, 1958.

The Search for Franklin. A narrative of the American expedition under Lieut. Schwatka, London, T. Nelson & Sons, 1882.

Sir Robert J. Le M. MACCLURE, *The Discovery of the North-west Passage by H.M.S. Investigator* (ed. S. Osborn), London, 1856.

Sir John RICHARDSON, *Arctic Searching Expedition*, London, 1851.

CHAPTER 20

The Conquest

For the story of Amundsen's life and voyages:

Gerald BOWMAN, *With Amundsen to the North Pole*, London, Frederick Muller, 1963.

Roald Engebregt AMUNDSEN, *My Life as an Explorer*, London, Heinemann, 1917.

Roald Engebregt AMUNDSEN, *The North-West Passage, being the record of a voyage of exploration by the ship 'Gjöa' 1903–1907*, (2 vols.), London, Constable, 1908.

Odd ARNESEN, *Roald Amundsen som han var*, Oslo, 1929.

Sven HØIDAL, *Roald Amundsen. Verdens største polarforsker*, Oslo, 1947.

Bellamy PARTRIDGE, *Amundsen*, London, Robert Hale, 1953.

CHAPTER 21

The Sense of Glory

John BUCHAN, *Sick Heart River*, London, Hodder and Stoughton, 1941.

John BROWN, *The North-west Passage and the plans for the search for Sir John Franklin* (second edition), London, Stanford, 1860.

Bibliography

A general historical introduction to the Search for a North-west Passage will be found in:

Nellis M. CROUSE, *In Quest of a Western Ocean*, London, J. M. Dent and Co., 1928.

A thorough, modern account of the early explorations of the North American continent is:

Samuel Eliot MORISON, *The European Discovery of America: The Northern Voyages*, Oxford University Press, 1971.

This book carries the story of American exploration down to the founding of the Second Virginian Settlement, 1587. It pays special attention to the navigational controversies aroused by some of the early voyages.

It need not be added there is also a large amount of first-hand material in the marvellous collection made by:

Richard HAKLUYT, *The Principal Navigations* (12 vols.) Glasgow, Maclehose, 1903–5. And

Samuel PURCHAS, *Purchas, His Pilgrims* (20 vols.) Glasgow, Maclehose, 1905–7. (References throughout these notes are to the Maclehose edition.)

With these preliminary surveys, the reader may go on to a more detailed study of the voyages.

For the early, mainly Scandinavian, interest in Greenland and the territories lying to the west of it an abundant literature exists. It begins with the Latin chronicle of

ADAM OF BREMEN, *Gesta Hammaburgensis Ecclesiae*. History of the Archbishops of Hamburg-Bremen, trans. Francis J. Tschan, New York, Columbia University Press, 1959. The first book to mention the discovery of Vinland.

Another early book of expectional interest is

The King's Mirror – Speculum Regale, trans. Laurence Marcellus Larson, New York, American Scandinavian Foundation, 1917.

Fridtjof NANSEN, *In Northern Mists* (2 vols.), London, Heinemann, 1911. This discusses in a dispassionate way the fate of the Viking settlement in Greenland and the reason for its extinction.

Gwyn JONES, *A History of the Vikings*, Oxford University Press, 1968. Gives a compact account of the Greenland settlement.

Johannes BRONSTED, *The Vikings*, London, Penguin, 1962. Succinct on the motives of the Viking voyages.

Vilhjalmur STEFANSSON. *The Three Voyages of Martin Frobisher*, London, Argonaut Press, 1938. In the early part valuable on the Viking voyages.

James A. WILLIAMSON, *The Cabot Voyages and British Discovery under Henry VII*, London, Hakluyt Society, 1962. Provides a comprehensive guide to the main sources. An earlier book by the same author is *The Voyages of the Cabots and the English Discovery of America*.

The notes after Chapter VI of Samuel Eliot MORISON's *The European Discovery of America: The Northern Voyages* Oxford University Press, 1971, furnish the acutest criticism of the various theories relating to Cabot's voyages and of the highly coloured account by Sebastian Cabot.

An early English prophet of western discovery is

Sir George PECKHAM, *A True Report of the Late discoveries*. London, John Hinde, 1582.

For the topography, climate and natural history of Arctic Canada, and the characteristics of the Eskimos, a large number of authorities are available:

Edward CARPENTER, Frederick VARLEY, Robert FLAHERTY, *Eskimo*, University of Toronto Press, Toronto, 1959.

Kaj Birkett SMITH, *The Eskimos*, trans. from the Danish by W. E. Calvert, London, Methuen, 1936.

Moira DUNBAR and Keith GREENAWAY, *Arctic Canada from the Air*, Ottawa, Canada Defence Research Board, 1956.

C. F. HALL, *Life with the Esquimaux* (2 vols.) London, 1864. Discovery of Frobisher relics.

For the French explorations in Canada, the leading authorities include

Charles de la RONCIÈRE, *Jacques Cartier*, Paris, 1931.

James Phinney BAXTER, *Memoir of Jacques Cartier*, New York, Dodd, Mead and Co., 1906.

Samuel CHAMPLAIN, *Traitté de la marine et du devoir d'un bon marin*, Champlain Society.

Jacques CARTIER, *A Short and Brief Narration*, trans. John Florio, Hakluyt, Glasgow, Maclehose, 1903–5. Cartier's account of his second voyage.

H. P. BIGGAR (ed.), *Voyages of Jacques Cartier*.

H. P. BIGGAR (ed.), *Collection of Documents relating to Jacques Cartier and the Sieur de Roberval*, Ottawa, Public Archives of Canada, Publications 11 and 14, 1924 and 1930.

Morris BISHOP, *Champlain*, London, Macdonald, 1949.

A fuller account of the voyages of Giovanni Verrazzano and Luis Vacques de Ayllon along the American coast will be found in MORISON, *The European Discovery* etc.

This is the Arctic, Canadian Department of Northern Affairs, Ottawa, Queen's Printer, 1964.

The Arctic Year, Peter Freuchen and Peter Salomonsen, New York, G. P.

Putnam's Sons, 1958, and London, Jonathan Cape Ltd, 1959.

Arctic World, John Euller, London and New York, Abelard-Schuman Ltd, 1958.

A Soldier's Guide to the North, Canadian Directorate of Military Training, Ottawa, Queen's Printer, 1955.

The Unbelievable Land, Canadian Department of Northern Affairs, Ottawa, Queen's Printer, 1964.

Le Grand Voyage du Pays des Hurons, Fr. Gabriel Sagard-Theodat, Paris, Chez Denys Morcai, 1632.

True Relation or News from Virginia, Captain John Smith, London, John Teyppa, 1608.

For the Colony in Virginia Britannia, William Strachey, London, Walter Burra, 1612.

Richard Hakluyt and the English Voyages, George Bruner Parke, New York, American Geographical Society, 1928.

Index

Index

283

287

THE ULTRA SECRET

F. W. Winterbotham

'The greatest British Intelligence coup of the Second
World War has never been told till now'
Daily Mail

For thirty-five years the expert team of cryptanalysts
who worked at Bletchley Park have kept the secret of
how, with the help of a Polish defector, British
Intelligence obtained a precise copy of the highly
secret and complex German coding machine known
as Enigma, and then broke the coding system to
intercept all top-grade German military signals.
Group-Captain Winterbotham was the man in charge
of security and communication of this information.
Now he is free to tell the story of that amazing coup
and what it uncovered.

'A story as bizarre as anything in spy fiction ... the
book adds a new dimension to the history of World
War II'
New York Times

'Military historians, like the general reader, will be
astonished by this book ... Group-Captain
Winterbotham cannot be too highly commended'
The Listener

'Superbly told'
Daily Express

THE LIVES OF THE GREAT COMPOSERS VOLUME ONE

Harold C. Schonberg

Harold Schonberg traces the lives and influences of the great composers and their music with a lively and imaginative tread. Volume One begins with the early masters Bach, Handel and Mozart and covers a host of important figures including Haydn, Beethoven, Chopin, Mendelssohn and Verdi and finishes at the end of the nineteenth century with Brahms and Wolf.

'A delight to the eye, an encouragement to sustained enjoyable reading . . . the like of which we have not had for some time. It is both witty and amusing'
Punch

'It is extremely readable; it is well founded in scholarship and well written'
The Times Literary Supplement

THE LIVES OF THE GREAT COMPOSERS
VOLUME TWO

Harold C. Schonberg

Harold Schonberg traces the lives and influences of composers and their music in the nineteenth and early twentieth century. Volume Two begins with the lively waltzes and polkas of Strauss and Offenbach and covers a host of major figures including Rimsky-Korsakov, Tchaikovsky, Grieg, Mahler, Stravinsky, and Shostakovich, finishing in the 1940's with Schoenberg.

'Panoramic, wittily detailed ... an important addition to the reference and handbook library of music ... equally pleasing to read from end to end, to dip into casually, or to consult in pursuit of that specific kernel that is so much part of the music-lover's experience'
The New York Times Book Review

'Recommended as a wisely planned general history to be read from cover to cover ... a valuable guide to the study of selected composers in greater depth'
The Gramophone

ALEXANDER THE GREAT

Robin Lane Fox

Even after 2,000 years no career has been so disputed or spectacular as that of Alexander the Great. In June 323 B.C. when he died in Babylon aged thirty-two, his empire comprised more than two million square miles. He had conquered Greece, Egypt and the Persian Empire in Asia and fought his way east to the foothills of the Himalayas and the deserts of the Punjab. He founded eighteen new cities and was remembered in legend from Iceland to China. He was an explorer, a romantic and a lover of Homer, of wine and music, of women and boys. A Colossus among men, Alexander of Macedon could well justify his claim of descent from Zeus himself.

'An achievement of Alexandrian proportions ... Mr Lane Fox has a marvellous eye for detail'
New Statesman

'I do not know which to admire most, his vast erudition, his exact scholarship or his imaginative grasp of so remote and complicated a period and such a complex personality'
Sunday Times

'A magnificent, compelling epic ... he discovers the most extraordinary king and general of antiquity, the last Homeric hero. He has honoured him splendidly'
Sunday Telegraph